Chandogya Upanishad

With Devanagari Script, Translation and Notes

Translated from original Sanskrity by
Jayaram V

Publised by
Pure Life Vision LLC
New Albany, Ohio

Chandogya Upanishad

Copyright © 2013 by Jayaram V. All rights reserved.
Publised and Distributed Worldwide by Pure Life Vision LLC., USA.
First edition 2013

This book is copyrighted under International and Pan American conventions. Printed in the USA. All rights reserved. No part of this publication may be reproduced stored in a retrieval system, or transmitted in any form or by any means, electronic, mecanical, photocopying, recording, scanning or otherwise, without the prior written permission of the publiser or the author. Requests to the publiser for permission or for bulk purcase of the book should be made online at http://www.PureLifeVision.com.

Limit of Liability/Disclaimer of Warranty: While the publiser and the author have used their best efforts in preparing this book, they make no representation or warranties with respect to the accuracy or completeness of the contents of this book and specifically disclaim any implied warranties of merchantability or fitness for particular purpose. No warranty may be created or extended by sales representatives or written sales materials. The advice and strategies contained herein may not be suitable for your situation. You should consult with a professional where appropriate. Neither the publiser nor author shall be liable for any loss of profit or any other commercial damages, including but not limited to special, incidental, consequential or other damages.

Pure Life Vision books and products are available through bookstores and online websites. For Enquiries,please visit http://www.PureLifeVision.com.

Cover illustration The Descent of Cosmic Prana © Jayaram V

Publiser Cataloging-in-Publication Data

V, Jayaram, (Vemulapalli)
Chandogya Upanishad
    p. cm
    Includes bibliographical references
    ISBN- 13: 978-1-935760-08-5
    ISBN -10: 1-935760-084
    1. Upanishads. 2. Upanishads. English. 3. Upanishads.-- Commentaries. I. Title.

BL1124.7.C532. V15 2013
294.5/9218 — dc22   2013905115

Printed in the United States of America
10 9 8 7 6 5 4 3 2 1
First Edition

To all those who helped me, fed me, taught me, influenced me and shaped my life in their own perfect and imperfect ways.

About the Author

Jayaram V is an author of 12 books on Hinduism, Spirituality and Self-help. He is the founder president of Hinduwebsite.com. He has been writing regularly for the last several years on Indian religions, spiritual subjects, yoga, self-help, current affairs and information technology. He holds a Masters degree in Botany, a Diploma in Journalism, and a Bachelor of Science in Information Technology.

His recent works include The Bhagavadgita Complete Translation, Brahman, Introduction to Hinduism, The Awakened Life, Chandogya Upanishad, and Selected Upanishads. He is currently working on a book on the philosophy and teachings of the Upanishads and a translation and commentary on the Yogasutras.

Jayaram is an Indian American born and raised in India. He worked in India, Nigeria and USA in both public and private sectors in various positions before he turned to writing fulltime. He writes regularly for Hinduwebsite.com and other websites, apart from managing a hectic schedule to publish several books on Hinduism, Buddhism, Yoga and related subjects.

ALSO BY JAYARAM V

1. Think Success: A Collection of Writings on Success and Achievement through Positive Thinking, Volume I
2. Think Success: A Collection of Writings on Success and Achievement through Positive Thinking, Volume II
3. Think Success: A Collection of Writings on Success and Achievement through Positive Thinking, Combined Volume
4. The Awakened Life: A Collection of Writings on Spiritual Life
5. Brahman
6. The Bhagavadgita Complete Translation
7. The Bhagavadgita Simple Translation
8. Essays on the Bhagavadgita
9. Introduction to Hinduism
10. Selected Upanishads
11. Brihadaranyaka Upanishad

FORTHCOMING

1. The Secret Knowledge - Essays on the Upanishads
2. The Yogasutras – Translation and Commentary
3. Perspectives on Hinduism
4. Selected Thoughts and Quotations

Chandogya Upanishad

With Devanagari Script, Translation and Notes

Jayaram V

Editor & Translator

Contents

Author's Note 17
Introduction 19

Chapter 1 29
Aum as the Essence of the Udgita 29
Sense Organs as the Udgita 31
Breath and Other Deities as the Udgita 34
Aum as the Immortal Sound 37
Udgita as the Sun and the Sound in Breath 39
Symbolism of Rik and Saman in Creation 40
Symbolism of Rik and Saman in the Body 42
A Discussion on the Udgita 44
Space as the Udgita 47
The Legend of Usati Cakrayana 48
The Deities of Sacrifice 50
The Udgita of Dogs 52
The Secret Knowledge of Sounds in Samans 53

Chapter 2 55
Meditation on the Whole Saman 55
The Fivefold Saman With Regard to Worlds 56
The Fivefold Saman With Regard to Rain 57
The Fivefold Saman With Regard to Water 57
The Fivefold Saman With Regard to Seasons 58
The Fivefold Saman With Regard to Animals 58
The Fivefold Saman With Regard to Breaths 58
The Sevenfold Saman With Regard to Speech 59
The Sevenfold Saman With Regard to the Sun 60
The Sevenfold Saman With Regard to Itself 62
The Saman Hidden in the Senses 63
The Rathantara Saman in the Fire 64
The Vamadeva Saman in the Coitus 64
The Brhat Saman in the sun 65

The Vairupya Saman in the Clouds 65
The Vairaja Saman in the Seasons 66
The Sakavari Saman in the Clouds 66
The Revati Saman in the Beings 67
The Yajnayajniya Saman in the Limbs.. 67
The Rajana Saman in the Deities 68
The Saman Woven in All... 68
Different Ways of Singing the Saman... 69
The Threefold Nature of Merit, Worlds and Aum........................ 71
How To Perform Soma Sacrifices Correctly 72

Chapter 3 76

The Sun as the Honey of Gods - Rigveda.................................... 76
The Sun as the Honey of Gods - Yajurveda 77
The Sun as the Honey of Gods - Samaveda 77
The Sun as the Honey of Gods - Atharvaveda 78
The Sun as the Honey of Gods - The Vedas................................ 78
The Vasus as the Nectar 79
The Rudras as the Nectar 80
The Adityas as the Nectar 81
The Maruts as the Nectar 81
The Sadhyas as the Nectar 82
The Secret Teaching of Brahma 83
The Greatness of Gayatri 84
The Five Openings of the Heart 86
Sandilya Vidya Regarding Brahman and Self 88
Brahman as the Imperishable Chest 89
Daily Sacrifices Compared to Phases of Life 91
The Life of a Person as a Sacrifice 92
Twofold Meditation Upon Brahman 94
Separation of Worlds from the Cosmic Egg 96

Chapter 4 98

The Fame Of Raikva, the One With The Cart 98
Janasruti and Raikva - The offering of Gifts 99

Air and Breath, the Absorbers 101
The Legend of Satyakama Jabala 103
The One Foot of Brahman 104
The Second Foot of Brahman 105
The Third Foot of Brahman 106
The Fourth Foot of Brahman 107
The Importance of a Teacher 108
Upakosala Receiving the Knowledge of Fires 108
The Forms of Garhapatya Fire 110
The Forms of Anvaharya Fire 110
The Forms of Ahvaniya Fire 111
The Purifying Knowledge of the Self 111
The Divine Path to the World of Brahman 112
The Role of the Brahman Priest in a Sacrifice 113
The Methods of Rectifying a Sacrifice 115

Chapter 5 117

The Superiority of Breath to the Body 117
A Mantha Rite to Attain Greatness 120
The Paths by Which Souls Travel upon Death 122
The Heaven as Sacrificial Fire 124
The Rains as Sacrificial Fire 124
The Earth as Sacrificial Fire 124
Man As Sacrifical Fire 125
Woman as Sacrificial Fire 125
Water the Fifth Libation 126
The Two Paths to Liberation 126
Vaisvanara, the Eater of Food 129
Incomplete Worship of Brahman as Gods 130
Incomplete Worship of Brahman as the Sun 131
Incomplete Worship of Brahman as Breath 132
Incomplete Worship of Brahman as Space 133
Incomplete Worship of Brahman as Water 133
Incomplete Worship of Brahman as the Support 134
Worshipping Brahman as the Self 134

Making an Offering of Food to Prana 135
　　Making an Offering of Food to Vyana 136
　　Making an Offering of Food to Apana 136
　　Worshipping Brahman with the Offering of 137
　　Making an Offering of Food to Udana 137
　　The Importance of Correct Knowledge 138

Chapter 6 140
　　Uddalaka Aruni's Teaching to Svetaketu 140
　　How Creation Manifested 141
　　Threefold Origin of Beings 142
　　The Triple Qualities of Creation 143
　　Threefold Nature of Food, Water and Fire 145
　　The Subtle Aspects of Food, Water and Fire 145
　　The Connection Between Food and Memory 146
　　The Being as the Source of All Beings 147
　　The Self as the Essence of All Beings 149
　　The Self as the Subtle Essence 150
　　The Self as the Root of All Beings 151
　　An Example of Seed in Reference to the Self 152
　　An Example of Salt in Reference to the Self 153
　　The Importance of a Teacher in Liberation 154
　　Awareness in the Final Moments Of Death 155
　　The Self as the Truth 156

Chapter 7 157
　　Meditation upon the Names of Brahman 157
　　Speech as Brahman 158
　　The Mind as Brahman 159
　　Intention as Brahman 160
　　The Discerning Mind as Brahman 161
　　Meditation as Brahman 162
　　Learned knowledge as Brahman 163
　　Strength as Brahman 164
　　Food as Brahman 165

Water as Brahman 166
Fire As Brahman 166
Memory as Brahman 168
Hope as Brahman 168
Breath as Brahman 169
Truth and Speech 170
Understanding and Truth 170
Thinking and Knowing 170
Faith and Thought 171
Steadfast Service and Faith 171
Action and Steadfast Service 171
Happiness and Actions 171
The Infinite as Happiness 172
The Difference Between Finite and Infinite 172
The Ego and the Self 173
The Self as the Source of All 174

Chapter 8 176

The Body as the City of Brahman 176
The Desires of a Self-Realized Person 177
True Desires and False Desires 179
The Self as the Bridge and the Boundary of the Worlds 180
Brahmacharya as a Sacrifice 181
Prajapati's Instruction Regarding True Self 184
The Demonic View of the Body as the Self 185
Indra's Quest for the True Knowledge of Self 187
The Self that Wanders in Dreams 188
The Self in Sleep 189
The Self as the Knower and Enjoyer 190
Reaching the World of Brahman Overcoming the Obstacles 192
A Prayer of the Soul to Prajapati 192
Instruction Regarding Instruction 192

A Note on Cover Page Illustration 194
Bibliography 195

Author's Note

The Chandogya Upanishad is unlike any other Upanishad you may know. It occupies a singular place in the history of Vedic literature and the development of Hinduism. Historically, it is one of the oldest, and, in terms of number of verses, the largest. It is also difficult to translate, as it contains verses dealing with an ancient ritual and ceremonial imagery that defy our understanding. Fortunately, the Upanishad is not a mere extension of metrical knowledge, as its title implies. It contains verses explaining the relationship between the individual Self and the highest Self and their essential nature. An understanding of both is necessary for our spiritual development, and this Upanishad facilitates our progress in that direction. Janasruti, Raikva, Uddalaka Aruni, Svetaketu, Narada, Sanatkumara, Prajapti, Indra and Vairocana are the important teachers we find in the Upanishad.

At first, I was hesitant to translate this Upanishad, as I felt it would delay my other book assignments. The same was true with the Brihadaranyaka Upanishad also. Both were voluminous and the idea of translating them was daunting. But then, I picked courage and went ahead. Eventually, I translated both. I am glad I did it, because it put me in the short list of a few individuals who translated 16 major Upanishads, including these two. I am happy, when I am gone, I would be leaving behind a major work for the posterity. If they cannot appreciate it, they can at least do a comparative study and learn from its faults.

I made this translation as simple and comprehensible as possible and useful to both scholars and lay practitioners of Hinduism alike. I added explanatory notes, wherever necessary, to explain the hidden meaning and symbolism of difficult verses, words and phrases. To the extent possible, I adhered to the original line of thought and way of expression, even if it meant some interruption and compromise with the flow and style.

The Chandogya and Brihadaranyaka Upanishads are like the two eyes or two wheels of the Vedanta. Without studying them, it is difficult to gain insight into the Vedic philosophy and its mindset. Both cover a wide range of topics and provide a rare glimpse, to a keen observer, into the origins of Hinduism and the development of its ritual and spiritual thought. It is a privilege for me to have an opportunity to study them and more so to translate them. Undoubtedly, they have the potential to open our minds to the ageless wisdom of the ancient seers and sages who once breathed and lived in the sacred land of the Vedas. With these works now behind me, I can plan to translate the Yogasutras and the Brahmasutras.

Jayaram V

Introduction

Technically speaking, the Chandogya Upanishad is a Brahmana because it forms part of the Chandogya Brahmana of the Samaveda. Out of the ten chapters of the Brahmana, the first two form part of the Brahmana, containing the knowledge of sacrifices and methods of worship, while the last eight constitute the Chandogya Upanishad. Historically, it is one of the most ancient Upanishads, which played a significant role in the emergence of the Vedanta Philosophy. It is believed that the Upanishad might be a collection of several independent texts that were brought together in its current form to signify the ritual and spiritual significance of Saman chants. It is evident from the verses that the composers of the Upanishad, had specialized knowledge of Vedic rituals and excelled in the practice of singing the Samans. Hence they interpreted the knowledge of Brahman and Atman through the eyes of a Udgatri priest, who specialized in the knowledge of Samaveda and was grounded in Vedic ritualism. The Upanishad begins with the declaration that one should meditate upon Aum as the High Chant (Udgita). Now one may wonder what a High Chant (Udgita) means. Literally speaking, Udgita means an uplifting chant or a song of praise. It is meant to lift up the spirit of the sacrificer and elevate the sacrifice to the heights of heaven. Traditionally, Udgita means chanting of the Samans or the hymns of the Samaveda. Symbolically, chanting of Aum is considered equal to Udgita or the singing of Samans.

The Chandogya Upanishad was studied and commented upon by several scholars in the past. Notable among them are the translation and commentary by Shankaracharya, the translation into Persian forming part of the translation of 50 Upanishads by Dara Shikoh, the eldest son of Shahjahan, the Mughal Emperor, the translation by Rajendralal Mitra forming part of the Bibliotheca Indica, and the translation into French by Anquetil Duperron, which was further translated into English and other European languages.

With 629 verses arranged into eight chapters and 154 sections, in terms of sheer size, the Upanishad is the largest among the principal Upanishads, and in significance, comparable only to the Brihadaranyaka Upanishad. Of the eight chapters, the first one contains the highest number of verses and the lowest number of sections; and the seventh chapter has the lowest number of verses and highest number of sections. Both Chandogya and Brihadaranyaka Upanishads have common themes. Their antiquity is gauzed from the references made about them in texts such as the Brahmasutras, which are very ancient. The Upanishad is also famous for the great saying (mahavakya), "Tatvamasi," meaning, "You are That." An overview of the Upanishad in the form of a table showing the number of verses, sections and chapters can be seen below.

Chapters	Sections	Verses*	Theme
Chapter 1	13	104	Parts of Saman
Chapter 2	24	82	Whole Saman
Chapter 3	19	95	Brahman, Parts and Whole
Chapter 4	17	78	Breath
Chapter 5	24	88	Worshipping Brahman
Chapter 6	16	69	The Individual Self
Chapter 7	26	51	Names of Brahman
Chapter 8	15	62	Knowing Brahman
Total	154	629	

*Note: The number includes the invocations also

The following is a discussion on the important themes of the Upanishad.

The symbolism of the Udgita

We have already discussed the literal and traditional meaning of the Udgita. The first chapter begins with the declaration that one should meditate upon Aum as the High Chant because the High Chant begins with the utterance of Aum. Aum is the essence of the Udgita and Udgita is the essence of Saman. The support of the hymns of the Rigveda is speech and the support of the Samans of the Samaveda is breath. Both are interrelated, like a couple in union, because priests sing the hymns of the Rigveda as Samans. Aum is not only a High Chant but also a syllable of compliance, because priests utter Aum while giving their compliance. With the help of Aum only the triple Vedas are studied and practiced. The priests use Aum in their chanting, singing and recitation. Those priests are more successful who perform sacrifices knowing the importance of Aum.

Based upon the syllables Ut, Gi and Ta present in the word Udgita, the High Chant is compared to various aspects of creation, namely, the heaven, the sky and the earth, the sun, the air and the fire, the Samaveda, the Yajurveda, and the Rigveda respectively. This analogy is also based upon certain similarities and the three main functions of Udgita, namely its exalted status as the high above, its ability to absorb and carry forward the offerings made and its ability to support the sacrifice. The Comparison with breath and the sun is also based upon the analogy that the purpose of Udgita is ensuring protection and purity of the Sacrifice which are also ensured by the breath in the body and the sun in the worlds. Both keep darkness and impurities away and ensure the continuity of the sacrifice in the body and the sacrifice in the world.

The Superiority of Breath

The theme is similar to the one found in the Brihadaranyaka Upanishad. The High Chant (Udgita) is a protector and purifier of Sacrifice. Every organ is the body is vulnerable to demonic activity as they are susceptible to selfishness, greed and egoism. But breath has no such agenda. Breath remains the same always. It does not depend upon an external motivation to perform its actions. Whether we are asleep or awake, hungry or well-fed, we continue to breath until we depart from here. This superiority of breath is illustrated in a story in which gods tried to find a resting ground in the body where, as in case of Udgita, they could find protection and remain free from the influence of evil. They tried to use the speech, various sense organs and the mind to see whether any of them would give them protection in the body from the evil forces. They found that in the body none of the organs were able to manifest the purifying and protective power of the Udgita, except breath. Only with the help of the breath in the mouth, they were able to vanquish the demons and keep the body pure and divine. Therefore, the Upanishad declares that breath is a purifier and a protector. As the purifier and protector of the body, it is similar to the Udgita, which is also a purifier and protector of the sacrifices we perform.

The Symbolism of Samans

The Chandogya Upanishad is difficult to understand because it presents cryptic symbolism of Samans. The hymns of the Samaveda are called Samans. They are considered special in Vedic sacrifices because they have to be sung according to specific meters and intonations to ensure the efficacy of the sacrifices. Since a lot depends upon proper singing, the singers of Samans, known as the Prastotris, Udgatris and Pratihartris, are required to possess specialized knowledge, including the knowledge of the musical notes and specific meters, grammar, pronunciation and the various types of divinities associated with them. They have to know the intricate details of certain special syllables, known as the stobhas, which are added to the hymns to facilitate correct rhyming and singing. They also need to know the support of the Samans and their parts.

The support for the Samans is the Rigveda, because most of the Samans are derived from the Rigveda only. The first two chapters of the Chandogya Upanishad deal with the symbolism of the Samans. The first chapter explains the symbolism of the constituent parts of the Saman while the second chapter deals with the symbolism of the Samans as a whole. The parts of a Saman are compared to breath, to speech and to food in the body, while they are compared to the earth, the air, the water, the fire, the sky, the sun and the heaven in creation. Saman is an important aspect of Vedic sacrifice and the sacrifice itself is compared in the Vedas to creation and existence. Creation, preservation and dissolution are different aspects of sacrifice only. Day and night is a sacrifice. The working of the sun, the moon and the worlds are sacrifices in themselves. The body itself is a sacrificial pit, just as the earth is, in which the food we eat is an offering to the deities in the body. The seers of the Chandogya Upanishad explored this analogy using the Saman as the basis. Since sacrifice is central to creation and existence, they tried to see whether they could draw comparison between the part of Saman with the aspects of creation; and in that we have to say they succeeded greatly. The Bhagavadgita recognizes the significance of Samans. Lord Krishna states that among the Vedas, He is the Samaveda. This is because the Samans uplift a sacrifice and make it divine and auspicious.

Three Branches of Duty

The second chapter (2.23) ends with a declaration on the threefold nature of duty (dharma). Sacrifice, study and charity. The three constitute the first duty of those who follow the path of the householders. Those who take up the duties of a householder as part of their asrama-dharma have to perform sacrifices to nourish the gods and fulfill their own wishes. They have to study the Vedas to prepare themselves for their liberation. Most importantly, they have to practice charity to overcome the impurities of greed and selfishness.

Austerity (tapas) is the second duty. It is defined as practicing meditation, self-restraint, fasting and self-discipline to purify the mind and body and generate spiritual energy. This is meant for those who retire from worldly life and live in secluded places as ascetics to prepare themselves for the next phase of their lives, namely Sanyasa. These people have completed their lives as householders or decided to skip it altogether in their quest for liberation. Brahmacharya is the third prescribed duty. It is meant for those who pursue the study of the Vedas as students under a knowledgeable teacher, while practicing celibacy.

These three classes of humans do not attain liberation, but a place in the world of ancestors and a good birth in their next lives. You may consider them more or less as karma yogis. There is however, a fourth class of humans not mentioned directly but inferred. They are those who renounce their worldly lives completely and take to Sanyasa to focus their lives entirely upon achieving liberation. They stabilize their minds in Brahman. They alone are entitled to achieve liberation and enter the immortal world of Brahman.

Man and His Life as a Sacrifice.

In the third chapter of the Upanishad (3.16) we find reference to a human being as a sacrifice performed on three different occasions during his lifetime, just as the priests perform daily sacrifices three times each day in the morning, afternoon and evening respectively. The first twenty four years of his life is compared to the morning sacrifice, during which the Gayatra Saman is chanted and the morning extraction of Soma juice is offered to the Vasus. 24 years is specified because the Gayatri meter has 24 syllables. The breaths in the body are compared to the Vasus. The next 44 years are compared to the midday offering, during which oblations are made to Rudras. Rudras are mentioned because during this period, as adults, people cause a lot of pain and suffering to others and make them cry through their actions. The number 44 is based upon the Tristubh meter which is used during the midday offering and which has 44 syllables. The next 48 years are compared to the evening libation, during which offerings are made to the Adityas. The number 48 is specified because the evening libation is offered with Jagati meter which has 48 syllables.

The next section (3.17) compares the actions of human beings with certain rites. Actions which lead to bodily discomfort such as hunger, thirst, and abstinence are compared to the initiatory rites. Actions where one eats. drinks and enjoys pleasures are compared to the Upasada ceremonies in which worshippers are allowed to drink limited quantities of food and experience some relief from the pain they experience during the initiatory rites. Experiences such as laughing, eating and sexual intercourse are compared to Stuta and Sastra hymns which are usually recited with dance and music.

Finally, virtues like austerity, charity, straightforwardness, non-injury and truthfulness are compared to the sacrificial fee earned by the sacrificer, which in this case is the person who is performing the sacrifice of his life. The end result of this sacrifice is attaining liberation and seeing the light of Brahman, high above.

Rebirth and Liberation

The Upanishad (5.9-10) mentions two paths available to the souls who depart from here, the path of the gods and the path of the ancestors. One leads to liberation and immortality and the other to rebirth. The first is called the path of gods (devayana) and the second is called the path of ancestors (pitrayana). The path of gods is available to those who practice austerities in deep forests with great faith, renouncing their desires and fixing their minds upon Brahman. Upon their death, they go to the region of light through the air, from the region of light to the day, from the day to the bright fortnight, from the bright fortnight to the six months during which the sun travels northwards. From there they go to the year, then to the sun, then to the moon, then to the lightning. There they meet a mind-born son of Brahma who leads them to the world of Brahman.

The other path is available to those who live in communities, who practice sacrifices to realize their desires and who indulge in good actions such as charity. Upon their death they go to the region of smoke. From there they go to the region of night. From night to the darker fortnight; from the darker fortnight to the six months during which the sun travels southwards. They do not reach the year, but go to the world of ancestors, and from there to the moon through space. There they become food to the gods, that is, the gods exhaust their karmic fruits or their casual bodies. After exhausting their karmas, they return to the earth through mist and rain. From the earth, they enter into plants. Through plants they become food to whoever eats them. Through the food, they enter into semen, through semen into the wombs of their mothers and then into the fetuses. Their rebirth depends upon their past lives. Good actions lead to good life and bad actions lead to birth in impure wombs. Now those who do not qualify for either of these paths (5.10.8), they become insects, worms etc. They live and die repeatedly in these lower life forms. For this reason, even though the souls are numerous, the world is said to be never full.

The Chandogya Upanishad envisages life as sacred and divine. The body is equally divine, a microcosm of the highest deity, the Cosmic Self. Duty is an essential part of liberation. The divinities in the body need to be nourished through food, breath, knowledge, intelligence, duty, singing, chanting and sacrificial ceremonies. Communication with the heavenly gods through the Udgita is as important as performing one's duties upon earth and keeping the mind and body pure and well nourished. At the same time one must know the source of all and the goal of all. Through the Self only Brahman is realized and for that one must have a correct knowledge of Brahman. One must also know that the Self alone is Brahman. When the realization dawns in the mind that "I am indeed Brahman," one becomes free from the cycle of births and deaths.

Translation

Chapter 1

Section 1

Aum as the Essence of the Udgita

1. aum ity etad aksaram udgitam upasita, aum iti hrd gayati tasyopa vyakhyanam.

1. Aum, this is that syllable one should meditate upon as the Udgita, the uplifting chant. Aum, with this one sings loudly (the Saman). Of that (syllable) this the explanation.

Notes: Udgita meant the high chant or the uplifting chant. It is uplifting because it enhances the power of the chant and enables the sounds arising from it to reach the gods in the heaven and invite them to the place of sacrifice. In every Saman, there is a hidden deity who provides it with the manifesting power. The source of this power is Brahman in the form of speech and the breath hidden in it. The power and the mobility of the mantra are augmented greatly when it is joined by the power of Aum or Brahman in word form. Aum multiplies the upward mobility of the sounds and the manifesting power of the mantra. Hence it is Udgita.

2. esam bhutanam prithivi rasah prithivya apo rasah; apam osadhayo rasa osadhinam puruso rasah purusasya vag raso vaca rigrasa ricah sama rasah samna udgitho rasah.

2. The essence of all beings is the earth, the essence of the earth is water, the essence of water the plants, the essence of plants man, the essence of man speech, the essence of speech the Rigveda, the essence of the Rigveda the Saman (chant), the essence of the Saman the Udgita (which is Aum).

Notes: Rasa actually means sap. It is loosely translated as essence. All beings possess elemental bodies derived from the elements of the earth in the form of food. Hence the earth is the essence of the beings. Living beings and sacrifices are connected to the earth through a chain of causes and effects, the culmination of which is Aum, the Udgita. The idea implied is the power to chant the Samans comes from the earth through food and water. Rigveda is described here as the source of the Samaveda or Samans because Rigveda is the source of many hymns of the Samaveda, and for that matters, many hymns of the other three Vedas.

3. sa esa rasanam rasatamah paramah parardhyo'stamo yad udgitah.

3. That Udgita (Aum) is the essence of all essences, the Supreme, deserving the highest place, the eighth.

Notes: Essence also means source. A cause is always hidden in its effect, like the DNA of a father or mother. Aum as Brahman is the source of speech and all the singing and chanting in the Vedas. Hence, it is rightly the essence of all things (parama rasatma) manifested. The number eight means the eighth position starting from the earth described before.

4. katama katama rk katamat katamat sama katamah katama udgita iti vimristam bhavati.

4. What then is (essence of) the Rik? What is (the essence of) the Saman? What is the (essence of) the Udgita? "This is (now) critiqued.

Notes: Having said that the essence of all things is Aum, the teacher is examining these aspects and their essences.

5. vagevarkpranah samomityetadaksaramudgitah; tadva etanmithunam yadvakca pranascarkca sama ca.

5. The speech is Rik, the breath is Saman, the syllable (Aum) is Udgita. Now these are couples in union, speech and breath, and Rik and Saman.

Notes: As per tradition it is believed that the efficacy of Rigveda hymns depend upon chanting and correct pronunciation. Hence, speech is the basis of Rigvedic hymns. The efficacy of Samans depend upon singing and for singing breath is very important. Hence breath is identified with Saman. The efficacy of both these further enhanced when they are joined with Aum.

6. tad etan mithunam aum ity etasminn aksare samsrijyate; yada vai mithunau samagaccata, apayato vai tav anyonyasya kamam.

6. And that couple is joined together in the syllable Aum. When a couples is joined in sexual union, they fulfill each other's desire.

7. apayita ha vai kamanam bhavati ya etad evam vidvan aksaram udgitam upaste.

7. Thus, he who knowing this, meditates on the syllable (Aum), the Udgita, becomes indeed a fulfiller of desires.

8. tad va etad anujnaksaram yaddhi kimcanujanaty aum ityeva tadahaiso eva samriddhiryadanujna samardhayita ha vai kamanam bhavati ya etadevam vidvanaksaramudgitamupaste.

8. That (syllable) is a syllable of compliance, for whenever we comply with anything, we say Aum. Now compliance is gratification. He who knowing this meditates on the syllable (Aum), the Udgita, becomes indeed a gratifier of desires.

Notes: Anuja means the eldest. The words of elders are respected and followed. Aum is used not only to chant mantras but also express consent or agreement.

9. teneyam trayi vidya vartate aum ity asravayaty aum iti samsaty aum ity udgayaty etasyaivaksara asyapacityai mahimna rasena.

9. By this (Aum) only, the threefold knowledge is practiced. Saying Aum (the Adharvayu priest) gives an order; saying Aum (the Hotri priest) recites; saying Aum the (Udgatri priest) sings. They do so in honor of that syllable, because of its greatness and essence.

Notes: The threefold knowledge is the knowledge contained in the triple Vedas, practiced by the three classes of priests mentioned here. Although the Vedas are presently four, originally they were only three Vedas. Atharvaveda is a later day addition.

10. tenobhau kuruto yascaitad evam veda yasca na veda; nana tu vidya cavidya ca yadeva vidyaya karoti sraddhayopanisada tadeva viryavattaram bhavatiti khalv etasyaivaksarasyopavyakhyanam bhavati.

10. Now, both perform sacrifices using this (Aum), he who knows and he who does not. However, knowledge and ignorance are different. The sacrifice, which a man performs with knowledge, faith, and the secret teaching of the Upanishad, is more powerful. This is the full account of the syllable Aum.

Section 2

Sense Organs as the Udgita

1. devasura ha vai yatra samyetire ubhaye prajapatyas tadd ha deva udgitam ajahrur anenainan abhibhavisyama iti.

1. When both the gods and demons, born of Prajapati, fought with each other, the gods took away the Udgita thinking they would vanquish the demons with it.

Notes: This and the following verses are meant to imply how evil can penetrate into our lives and influence our spiritual and sacrificial actions. The demons took away the high chant means it became polluted with the impurities of selfish desires and evil intentions. You can perform sacrifices with both good and bad intentions. When the organs in the body are used for selfish purposes, they become instruments of evil. So is the case with knowledge, our perceptions and our bodily functions. Life is a battle between good and evil. Every action of our can be pierced with evil. Every aspect of our minds and bodies has the potential to be good or bad. What you do with them is where your discretion (vivekam or buddhi) plays an important role.

2. te ha nasikyam pranam udgitam upasam cakrire tam hasurah papmana vividhuh tasmat tenobhayam jighrati surabhi ca durgandhi ca papmana hy esa viddhah.

2. *They meditated upon the Udgita as the breath in the nose. The demons pierced it with evil. Therefore, what is smelt with the nose is either good smelling or bad smelling for the breath has been pierced by evil.*

3. atha ha vacam udgitam upasam cakrire tam hasurah papmana vividhuh tasmatt ayobhayam vadati satyam canritam ca papmana hy esa viddha.

3. Then they meditated upon the Udgita as speech. The demons pierced it with evil. Therefore, what is spoken is either true or false, for speech is pierced by evil.

4. atha ha caksur udgitam upasam cakrire taddhasurah papmana vividhuh tasmat tenobhayam pasyati darsaniyam ca darsaniyam ca papmana hy etad viddham.

4. Then they meditated upon the Udgita as the eye. The demons pierced it with evil. Therefore, what is seen is either pleasant or unpleasant for the eye is pierced by evil.

5. atha ha srotram udgitam upasam cakrire taddhasurah papmana vividhuh tasmat tenobhayam srinoti sravaniyam casravaniyam ca, papmana hy etad viddham.

5. Then they meditated upon the Udgita as the ear. The demons pierced it with evil. Therefore, what is heard is either pleasant to hear or unpleasant to hear for the ear is pierced by evil.

6.atha ha mana udgitam upasam cakrire taddhasurah papmana vividhuh tasmat tenobhayam samkalpate samkalpaniyam ca casamkalpaniyam ca papmana hy etad viddham.

6. Then they meditated upon the Udgita as the mind. The demons pierced it with evil. Therefore, what is willed or resolved is either lawful or unlawful for the mind is pierced by evil.

7. atha ha ya evayam mukhyah pranastam udgitam upasam cakrire tamhasura ritva vidadhvamsur yathasmanam akhanam ritva vidhvamseta.

7. Then they meditated upon the Udgita as the breath in the mouth. When the Asuras tried to attack it, they were smashed (into smithereens) just as a piece of clay is smashed (upon hitting a hard object).

Notes: A similar theme is found in the Brihadaranyaka Upanishad also. The High Chant (Udgita) is a purifier and protector of sacrifices. When it is sung, the vibrations drive away evil from the area of sacrifice and keep it fit for the arrival of the gods. Now, which part of the body can perform a similar task and keep the body, which is also a pit of sacrifice, pure and free from evil. This was the problem which the gods tried to resolve, testing each organs. In their attempts, they found that every part in the body was vulnerable to demonic influence, except the breath in the mouth. Hence, they identified it as the Udgita of the sacrifice in the body. Indeed, we know that with the help of breath we can calm our minds and bodies and regain our balance and composure. Hence, in the practice of yoga, we use breath control (Pranayama) to control our thoughts and emotions and experience peace and stability. Desire guides and motivates every organ in the body. You see, hear, feel, touch, and taste things out of desires. You eat and drink out of hunger and thirst. They are desire-ridden actions. But when it comes to breath, you breath involuntarily, whether you have desire to breath or not. In other words, your breath is not guided by desires or selfish motives. You breath when you are asleep or awake, when you are conscious or unconscious and when you are hungry or not. Hence, your breath stands apart in comparison to the other parts in the body.

8. evam yathasmanam akhanam ritva vidhvamsata evam haiva sa vidhvamsate ya evam vidi papam kamayate yascainama bhidasati sa eso'smakhanah.

8. Thus, just as (a clump of earth) is destroyed upon hitting a solid stone, so will he be scattered who wishes evil to one who knows this, or who hurts him; for he is a solid stone.

9. naivaitena surabhi na durgandhi vijanaty apahata papma hy esa tena yadasnati yat pibati tenetaran pranan avati etam u evantato'vitt votkramati vyadadaty evantata iti.

9. With this (breath in the mouth), one cannot know good smell from the bad smell for it is free from evil. Indeed, whatever we eat and drink with it, supports the other vital breaths. In the end, not finding that breath, one departs. Hence, in the end one opens the mouth.

10. tam hangira udgitam upasam cakra etam u evangirasam manyante anganam yad rasah.

10. Angiras meditated upon this breath as the Udgita, and people hold it to be Angiras, for it is the sap of the limbs.

11. tena tam ha brihaspatir udgitam upasam cakra etam u eva brihaspatim manyante vagghi brihati tasya esa patih.

11. Brihaspati meditated upon this as the Udgita and people hold it to be Brihaspati, for speech is brihati, and this is the lord of speech;

12. tena tam hayasya udgitam upasam cakra etam u evayasyam manyanta asyadyat ayate.

12. *Ayasya meditated upon this as the Udgita and people hold it to be Ayasya, because this comes from the mouth (Asya).*

13. tena tamha bako dalbhyo vidamcakara sa ha naimisiyanam udgata babhuva sa ha smaibhyah kaman agayati.

13. Balka Dalbhya knew it. He officiated as the Udgatri priest for the people of Naimisa; and by singing, he obtained fulfillment of their desires.

Notes: Naimisa is a forest where seers and sages used to live with their households and students. Balka Dalbhya is mentioned in the Mahabharata. He is a historic figure who is mentioned in other Upanishads also.

14. agata ha vai kamanam bhavati ya etad evam vidvan aksaram udgitam upasta ity adhyatmam.

14. He who knows this, and meditates upon the Udgita as the syllable (whose source is the breath in the mouth), he obtains all wishes by singing. This is with regard to (singing the High Chant within) oneself.

Notes: The breath in the mouth plays an important role in the singing of the High Chant. He who breaths with this knowledge is accomplishing the same merit as the singer of a Saman because like an Udgatri priest, he is also performing a sacrifice within himself.

Section 3

Breath and Other Deities as the Udgita

1. athadhidaivatam ya evasau tapati tam udgitam upasitodyan va esa prajabhya udgayati; udyams tamo bhayam apahanty apahanta ha vai bhayasya tamaso bhavati ya evam veda.

1. Now (Udgita) in reference to the gods. Upon Him, who shines brightly, one should meditate as the Udgita. While He rises, he sings aloud (Udgayati) for the beings. He takes away darkness and fear. He, who knows this, verily, takes away fear and darkness.

Notes: The one who shines brightly above is the sun. Like the Udgita, He is the protector of the worlds. He drives away evil and darkness from our minds and bodies as the source of heat (tapas) and from the world as the source of light. With his radiant energy, he keeps the worlds pure and resplendent. Hence as the purifier and protector, the Sun is the High Chant among the deities of creation. Those who know this meditate upon the sun and become free from fear and inner darkness.

2. samana u evayam casau, cosno'yam usno'sau svara iti-mam acaksate svara iti pratyasvara ity amum tasmad va etam imam amum codgitham upasita.

2. *This (the breath in the mouth) and that (the sun) are the same. This is hot and that is hot. This they call svara (sound), and that they call pratyasvara (echo). Therefore, let a man meditate upon this (breath) and that (sun) as the Udgita.*

Notes: The breath in the body keeps the body warm, pure and alive. The sun above keeps the worlds warm, bright and alive. The High Chant protects the sacrifice and keeps it warm, aglow and alive. Thus they are both similar to the High Chant in their function.

3. atha khalu vyanam evodgitham upasita yadvai praniti sa prano yad apaniti so'apanah. atha yah pranapanayoh samdhih sa vyano yo vyanah sa vak, tasmad apranan ananapanan vacam abhivyaharati.

3. Then let a man meditate upon the Udgita as the diffused breath (vyana) indeed. When we breathe in, it is in-breath (prana), when we breathe down it is down-breath (apana). The junction of the in breath and down breath is diffused breath (vyana). This vyana is speech. Therefore, one speaks, without in breath or down breath.

4. ya vak sa rk tasmad apranann anapanann ricam abhivyaharati ya rk tat sama tasmad apranan ananapanan sama gayati yatsama sa udgitas tasmad apranann anapanann udgayati.

4. Speech is Rik, and therefore one utters a Rik without in breath or down breath. Rik is Saman, and therefore one utters a Saman without in breath or down breath. Saman is Udgita, and therefore one sings the Udgita, without in breath or down breath.

Notes: The hymns of Rigveda are known as Riks, of Samaveda as Saman and of Yajurveda as Yajus. The Riks are sacrificial chants. The Samans are chants in the form of songs and the Yajus are chants in the form of formulas. There are five different types of breath. We will hear about them frequently in almost all the major Upanishads. Their proper functioning and unobstructed movement is vital to one's physical and spiritual wellbeing.

5. ato yany anyani viryavanti karmani yathagner manthanam ajeh saranam dridhasya dhanusa ayamanam apranann anapanams tani karoty; etasya hetor vyanam evodgithamupasita.

5. Therefore, other actions also which require strength, such as igniting fire by churning, running a race, stringing a strong bow, are performed without in breath or down breath. Therefore, let a man meditate upon the diffused breath (vyana) as the Udgita.

6. atha khaludgitaksarany upasitodgitha iti prana evotpranena hy uttisthati vag gir vaco ha gira ity acaksate annam tham anne hidam sarvamsthitam.

6. Now, one should meditate upon the syllables of the Udgita (ut, gi, tha). Ut is breath (prana), for by breath one rises (uttisthati). Gi is speech, for speeches are called girah. Food is tha, for by food all is stabilized.

Notes: This is a meditation upon the syllables of the Udgita. Udgita shares upward motion with breath represented here by 'Ut' (pronounced as Ud), which is used as a prefix to nouns and verbs to denote upward motion or northward motion. The syllable 'Gi' represents the speech in the Udgita. Speech is also known as gira, meaning speech, words, language or invocation.

7. dyaur evod antariksam gih prithivi tham aditya evot vayur gir agnis tham samaveda evot yajurvedo gir rigvedas tham; dugdhe-asmai vagdoham yo vaco doho nnavan annado bhavati ya etany evam vidvan udgitaksarany upasta, udgita iti.

7. Ut is heaven, gi the sky, tha the earth. Ut is the sun, gi the air, tha the fire. Ut is the Samaveda, gi the Yajurveda, tha the Rigveda. Whoever thus knowing meditates upon those syllables of the Udgita, to him speech yields the milk, which is the milk of speech itself and he becomes Rik in food and an eater of food.

Notes: This analogy is also based upon certain similarities. and the three main functions of Udgita, namely its exalted status as the high above, its ability to absorb and carry forward the offerings made and its ability to support the sacrifice. Ut is heaven because it is high above and in the northward direction, a reference to the world of Brahman. According to Shankara, the sky is gi because it swallows regions or directions. Ta is the earth because it is the stana, the place, where beings live. Ut is the sun because it is high above. Gi is air because it swallows fire and other things. Ta is fire because it supports the sacrifice. Ut is Samaveda because the Samans rise upwards in the direction of heaven. Gi is Yajurveda because the Yajus swallow the enemies and evil omens. Ta is Rigveda because the Samans are derived mostly from the Rigveda. The knower of this symbolism extracts the milk of the speech because of his specialized knowledge and mastery of the sacrifices.

8. atha khalv asih samriddhir upasarananity upasita yena samna stosyan syat tat samopadhavet.

8. Now, on how the wishes are fulfilled. One (the Udgatri) should take refuge in that which can fulfill the desire (upasarana) and quickly reflect upon the Saman with which one is going to praise.

Notes: The meaning of this is, one should not sing the High Chant mechanically, because a sacrifice is both a verbal and mental process. The singing should be accompanied or even preceded by thinking and visualization.

9. yasyam rici tam ricam yad arseyam tam risim yam devatam abhistosyan syat tam devatam upadhavet.

9. One should meditate upon that Rik, upon which the Saman is based; one should meditate upon the seer (rsi) by whom it was originally seen and upon the deity to whom he was going to offer the prayer.

Notes: How to invoke the deities during a sacrifice and obtain their favors is explained. Upasaranams are the objects of worship where you rest your mind during the invocations.

10. yena ccandasa stosyan syat tac canda upadhaved yena stomena stosyamanah syat tam stomam upadhavet.

10. One should meditate upon the meter in which one is going to praise; one should meditate upon the tune with which one is going to sing for himself.

Notes: One should focus upon the rhythm and the particular meter in which the High Chant should be sung.

11. yam disam abhistosyan syat tam disam upadhavet.

11. One should meditate upon the quarter of the space, in that direction in which one is going to praise.

12. atmanam antata upasritya stuvita kamam dhyayann aprama-tto'bhyaso ha yad asmai sa kamah samridhyeta, yat kamah stuviteti, yat kamah stuviteti.

12. Lastly, returning to oneself and looking into oneself, one should sing the hymn of praise carefully, concentrating upon one's desire, avoiding all mistakes in pronouncing it. Quickly will the desire be then fulfilled for him, for which he offered his hymn of praise, yes, for which he offered his hymn of praise.

Section 4

Aum as the Immortal Sound

1. aum ity etad aksaram udgitam upasitom iti hy udgayati tasyopavyakhyanam.

1. Aum, one should meditate upon these syllables as the Udgita because one always sings (the hymns) beginning with Aum. Of this, this is the account.

Notes: Aum takes you closer to Brahman. It purifies and uplifts the chants as well as the souls. Therefore it is called High Chant or the uplifting chant, Udgita.

2. deva vai mrityor bibhyatas trayim vidyam pravisams te candobhir accadayan yad ebhir accadayams tac candasam candastvam.

2. The gods, being afraid of death, took shelter in the triple Vedas. They covered themselves with the meters. Because they covered themselves with these meters, therefore the meters are called Chandas.

Notes: Ca means that which covers are envelops. The hymns are composed according to specific meters knows as candas. The hymns, and the deities to which they belong, are thus technically hidden or enveloped in the meters.

3. tan u tatra mrityur yatha matsyam udake paripasyed evam paryapasyad rici samni yajusi, te nu viditvordhva ricah samno yajusah svaram eva pravisan.

3. Then Death watched the deities hidden in the Rik, Saman and Yajus, just as one might see fish in the water. When gods saw this, they ascended out of the Rik, Saman and Yajus and entered into the sound (svara) itself.

Notes: When hymns are sung or chanted, the power of the deities hidden in them ascend into the sounds arising from the speech of the chanters. The hymns are thus brought to life by chanting. This is the meaning.

4. yada va ricam apnoty aum ity evatisvaraty evam samaivam yajur esa u svaro yad etad aksaram etad amritam abhayam tat pravisya deva amrita abhaya abhavan.

4. Verily, when one learns the Riks, one utters Aum loudly, so also with Saman and so also with Yajus. This sound is that syllable which is immortal and fearless. Since the gods took shelter in it, they also became immortal, and fearless.

Notes: Aksara means both syllable and imperishable. Hence we may also translate this verse as this sound is that which is imperishable, immortal and fearless.

5. sa ya etad evam vidvan aksaram pranauty etad evaksaram svaram amritam abhayam pravisati, tat pravisya yad amrita devas tad amrito bhavati.

5. Knowing this, he who, thus, loudly worships this syllable enters into that imperishable, immortal and fearless sound. Upon entering it, he becomes immortal just as the gods became immortal.

Notes: The Vedas by themselves do not offer any protection from death or decay. The protection comes from the sound uttered during their chanting or singing. The gods in the body therefore hid themselves in the sounds rather than in the verses. For this very reason, the hymns of the Vedas are not chanted silently, as in case of other prayers, but loudly so that they can be effective. The singing or chanting should also be done according to specific meters or rhythm (chandas). The protecting power of the Vedic hymns increases further when they are chanted beginning with Aum, as suggested here. Then their chanting not only protects the sacrifice but also helps them to achieve liberation.

Section 5

Udgita as the Sun and the Sound in Breath

1. atha khalu ya udgitah sa pranavo yah pranavah sa udgita ityasau va aditya udgita esa pranava aum iti hy esa svarann eti.

1. Now, truly Udgita is pranava and pranava is Udgita. The Udgita is the sun up there and it is also the pranava because it keeps chanting Aum.

Notes: Pranava is the sound of Aum. We have already heard that Aum is Udgita. Therefore it logically follows that Pranava is Udgita. It is called Pranava in reference to the chants of Rigveda and Udgita in reference to the Samans of the Samaveda. Their purpose is the same. To elevate the chanting or the singing and make the sacrifice effective. The comparison of both with the sun is already explained in the previous section.

2. etam u evaham abhyagasisam tasman mama tvam eko'siti ha kausitakih putram uvaca rasmims tvam paryavartayad bahavo vai te bhavisyantity adhidaivatam.

2. "To Him I sang my praise. Therefore you are my only one (son)," thus said Kausitaki to his son. "You must worship his effulgent rays, so that you will have many sons." This is (Aum) with regard to the gods.

Notes: Kausitaki worshipped the Sun as Aum, instead of the rays. Since the sun was one and alone, he obtained only one son. He advised his son to worship the rays, so that he would have many sons like the rays of the sun. The sun symbolizes Brahman. The rays symbolize the divinities or the gods and beings in the heaven and the mid-region. This is worshipping of Aum as one and many (adhidaivam).

3. athadhyatmam ya evayam mukhyah pranas tam udgitam upasitom iti hy esa svaranneti.

3. Now with reference to the body. One should meditate upon the breath in the mouth as the Udgita for it keeps chanting the Udgita (Aum).

Notes: Aum is the sound arising from the breath in the mouth in the form of speech. This is manifestation of Aum in the body (adhyatma).

4. etam u evaham abhyagasisam, tasman mama tvam eko'siti ha kausitakih putram uvaca pranams tvam bhumanam abhigayatad bahavo vai me bhavisyantiti.

4. *"To Him I sang my praises. Therefore you are my only one (son),"* thus said Kausitaki to his son." *"You must worship this breath as manifold so that you will have many sons."*

Notes: Kausitaki sang the praises of only the breath in the mouth. Since it was one and alone, he obtained only one son. He advised his son to worship the various forms of breath so that he would have more sons. This is worshipping of Aum with reference to one's own body (adhibhautika).

5. atha khalu ya udgitah sa pranavo yah pranavah sa udgita iti hotrisadanadd haivapi durudgitam anusamaharatity anusamaharatiti.

5. *Now, truly, the Udgita is Pranava (Aum) and Pranava is the Udgita. The Hotri priest, who knows thus, cancels any mistakes in singing the Udgita; yes, he does cancel it.*

Notes: Aum is a purifier. It not only uplifts and liberates but also expiates and neutralizes any mistakes committed in the performance of rituals.

Section 6
Symbolism of Rik and Saman in Creation

1. iyam eva rg agnih sama tad etad etasyam ricy adhyu'dham sama tasmad ricy adhyudham sama giyata iyam eva sagnir amas tat sama.

1. *This (earth) is Rik, and the fire is Saman. This Saman rests upon that Rik. Therefore, the Saman is sung as resting upon the Rik. This (earth) is sa and fire is ama, and that makes up Saman.*

Notes: The earth is Rik because it is the support for the Samans. Most of the Samans of the Samaveda are derived from the hymns of the Rigveda. Hence it is rightly the support, and as the support it is comparable to the earth, which supports all. Now, the Saman is compared to fire, because like fire it rises upwards and like fire it purifies and protects the sacrifice. Just as the Samans rest upon the Rigveda, fire rests upon the earth. This is true even in case of sacrificial fire. The sacrifice itself is performed upon the earth and the Samans are sung by the priests sitting upon it. Thus, for the whole activity in a sacrifice, the earth provides the support for the sacrificial fire while the Rigveda provides the support for the Samans. In the body, the source of the Saman is speech (fire), for which the body (earth) is the support.

2. antaricsam eva rg vayuh sama tad etad etasyam ricy adhyudham sama tasmad ricy adhyudham sama giyate antaricsam eva sa vayur amas tat sama.

2. *The mid-region is the Rik and the air is Saman. This Saman rests upon that Rik. Therefore, the Saman is sung as resting upon Rik. The sky is sa and the air is ama and that makes up Saman.*

3. dyaur eva rg adityah sama tad etad etasyam ricy adhyudham sama tasmad ricy adhyudham sama giyate dyaur eva sadityo'mas tat sama.

3. The heaven is Rik and the sun is Saman. This Saman rests upon that Rik. Therefore, the Saman is sung as resting upon Rik. The heaven is sa and the sun is ama, and that makes Sama.

4. naksatrany eva rk candramah sama tad etad etasyam ricy adhyudham sama tasmad ricy adhyudham sama giyate naksatrany eva sa candrama amas tat sama.

4. The constellation of stars is Rik and the moon is Saman. This Saman rests up on that Rik (stars). Therefore, the Saman is sung as resting upon Rik. The constellation of starts is sa and the moon is ama and that makes up Sama.

5. atha yad etad adityasya suklam bhah saiva rg atha yan nilam parah krisnam tat sama tad etad etasyam ricy adhyudham sama tasmad ricy adhyudham sama giyate.

5. Now, that white light in the sun is Rik and that which is blue and very black is Saman. This Saman rests upon that Rik. Therefore, the Saman is sung as resting upon the Rik.

Notes: Blue and black are the colors of the sky arising from the presence or absence of the sun. They also represent the colors of the day and night. These modifications of the sky depend upon the sun. Hence it is considered the support.

6. atha yad evaitad adityasya suklam bhah saiva satha yan nilam parah krisnam tad amas tat samatha ya eso'ntar aditye hiranmayah puruso drisyate hiranyasmasrur hiranyakesa apranakhat sarva eva suvarnah.

6. Now that white light in the sun is Sa and that which is blue and very dark is ama. That makes up Sama. Now that golden person, who is seen within the sun, with golden beard and golden hair, golden altogether to the very tips of his nails...

Notes: The light in the sun, the day, which is blue and the night, which is dark make up Saman, one complete song. The whole day is one Saman, one song of God or Nature. The source of this daily song (Saman) is the deity in the sun, who is golden hued with golden beard and hair. With his singing, he performs a daily sacrifice to keep the beings alive. It may be noted that the seers of Chandogya Upanishad saw the Saman in every aspect of creation. They found in it a great means to harmonize our lives with the rest of creation and ensure its order and regularity. A sacrifice was not a mere ritual act to fulfill one's desires, but a divine effort modeled by God, which can be reenacted upon earth with right knowledge by human beings to manifest their desires and fulfill their obligations.

7. tasya yatha kapyasam pundaricam evam aksini tasyoditi nama; sa esa sarvebhyah papmabhya udita udeti ha vai sarvebhyah papmabhyo ya evam veda.

7. His eyes are (lotus-red) like the seat of a monkey. His name is Ut for he has transcended all evils. Truly, he who knows him thus rises above all evils.

Notes: The sun is the highest object seen during the day by the naked eye. Hence he is called ut, meaning high. The sun also symbolizes light and his very presence removes darkness, which is symbolically compared to evil. He who lights up the sun in one's own consciousness through self-realization also dispels the darkness of impurities and evil tendencies.

8. tasya rk ca sama ca gesnau tasmad udgitah tasmat tvevodgataitasya hi gata sa esa ye camusmat paranco lokas tesam ceste deva kamanam cety adhidaivatam

8. Of Him, Rik and Saman are joints; therefore, He is the Udgita. Therefore, he who sings for Him (Ut) is called Udgathri. He is lord of the worlds beyond that (sun), and the wishes of the gods. This is about the Udgita in reference to the gods.

Notes: What is common between the sun and the high chant is that both occupy an exalted position high above (ut). The sun has elements of light and the colors of the sky. They are compared to Rik and Saman both of which make up the Udgita. These symbols do not have to be taken literally. They are meant to convey a vision of the world in which sacrifice was the sum total of all hidden causes and manifestations. The worlds and beings emerged out of a sacrifice and they are sustained in this world by sacrifice. Because of this, it is possible to superimpose the model of sacrifice and its constituent parts on every aspect of creation, from sun high above to the breath in the body. A high chant is produced by a combination of verses from the Rigveda and Samaveda. The rhythm of creation manifests in the worlds, starting from the earth, acting as the support, and ending with the sun high above in the sky representing the Saman, with the mid-region (antariksam) and the god's heaven (dyauh) occupying the space in between. The high chant travelling all the way towards the immortal world in the heaven dispels evil and manifests auspiciousness for the worshippers. So does the sun in creation. He rises high above and dispels darkness of the sky.

Section 7

Symbolism of Rik and Saman in the Body

1. athadhyatmam vag eva rk pranah sama tad etad etasyam ricy adhyudham sama tasmad ricy adhyudham sama giyate; vag eva sa prano'mas tatsama.

1. Now with reference to the body. Speech is Rik and breath is the Saman. This Saman rests upon that Rik. Hence, Saman is sung as resting upon Rik. Speech is sa and breath is ama, and that makes up Sama.

2. caksur eva rg atma sama tad etad etasyam ricy adhyudhamsama tasmad ricy adhyudham sama giyate caksur eva sa'tma'mas tat sama.

2. The eye is Rik and the Self is the Saman. This Saman rests upon that Rik. Hence, Saman is sung as resting upon Rik. The eye is sa and Self is ama, and that makes up Saman.

Notes: The Self is described in many verses as the person in the eye. Therefore, the eye, which is compared here to Rik, is the support for the person, who is compared to the Saman

3. Srotram eva rn manah sama tad etad etasyam ricy adhyudham sama tasmad ricy adhyudham sama giyate srotrameva sa mano'mastatsama.

3. The ear is Rik and mind is the Saman. This Saman rests upon that Rik. Hence, Saman is sung as resting upon Rik. The ear is sa and mind is ama, and that makes up Saman.

4. atha yad etad aksnah suklam bhah saiva rg atha yan nilam parah krisnam tad sama tad etad etasyam ricy adhyudham sama tasmat ricy adhyudham sama giyate atha yad evaitad aksnah suklam bhah saiva satha yan nilam parah krisnam tad amas tatsama.

4. Now, that white light in the Eye is Rik and that which is blue and very black is Saman. This Saman rests upon that Rik. Therefore, Saman is sung as resting upon Rik. That white light in the eye is sa and that which is blue and very black is ama; and that makes up Saman.

5. atha ya eso'ntaraksini puruso drisyate saiva rk tat sama tad uktham tad yajuh tad brahma tasyaitasya tad eva rupam yad amusya rupam yav amusya gesnau tau gesnau yan nama tan nama.

5. Now, that person who is seen in the eye is Rik, Saman is the recitation, and Yajus is the prayer. The form of that person (in the eye) is the same, as the form of the other person (in the sun), the joints of the one (Rik and Saman) are the joints of the other, the name of the one (ut) is the name of the other.

Notes: The hymn of the Rigveda, Samaveda and Yajurveda are known as Riks (chants), Samans (songs) and Yajus (formulas) respectively. The person in the eye is the inner Self or the embodied Self. The person in the sun is Brahman, the being of golden color with a golden beard.

6. sa esa ye caitasmad arvanco lokas tesam ceste manusya kamanam ceti tadya ime vinayam gayanty etam te gayanti tasmat te dhanasanayah.

6. He is lord of the worlds beneath this one (the self in the eye), and the desires of all people. Therefore, those who sing using the vina, sing of him, and thereby obtain their wealth.

Notes: All desires arise from the Self, who is the ultimate enjoyer in the body. Since He is present in all, he is the source of the desires of all people. The gods oblige our requests and supplications for their fulfillment because they serve Him only.

7. atha ya etadevam vidvansama gayatyubhau sa gayati so'amunaiva sa esa camusmatparanco lokastamscapnoti devakamamsca.

7. Now, knowing this, he who sings a Saman sings for both. Through the former, he obtains the worlds beyond that (sun), and the desires of the gods.

Notes: Now the worshipper sings for both the deity in the body (adhyatma) and for the person in the sun (adhidaiva). One is the inner Lord and one is the over Lord. Those who realize them transcend all.

8. athanenaiva ye caitasmad arvanco lokas tams capnoti manusya kamams ca tasmad u haivam vid udgata bruyat.

8. Through This (Self in the eye), he obtains the worlds that are under That (person in the sun), and the desires of humans. Therefore, an Udgatri priest who knows this should say this (to the sacrificer).

9. kam te kamam agayanity esa hyeva kamaganasyeste ya evam vidvan sama gayati sama gayati.

9. "What desire may I obtain for you through my singing?" Knowing thus, he who sings a Saman becomes capable of fulfilling desires through his singing, yes, by singing the Saman.

Section 8
A Discussion on the Udgita

1. trayo hodgithe kusala babhuvuh silakah salavatyas caikitayano dalbhyah pravahano jaivalir iti te hocur udgithe vai kusalah smo hantodgithe katham vadama iti.

1. There were three, well versed in the Udgita, Silaka the son of Salavat, Caikitayana of the Dalbha clan, and Pravahana son of Jaivali.

They said, "We are well versed in the Udgita. Let us have a discussion on the Udgita."

Notes: These are historical persons. Pravahana Jaivali is mentioned in the Brhadaranyaka Upanishad. He was a Kshatriya who taught to Gautama the knowledge of the paths along which the souls travelled after departing from the mortal world.

2. tatheti ha samupavivisuh sa ha pravahano jaivalir uvaca bhagavantav agre vadatam brahmanayor vadator vacam srosyamiti.

2. "So be it," they said and sat down. Then Pravahana Jaivali, said: "Godmen, you speak first. I want to listen to the words of you two Brahmanas as you debate.

Notes: Pravahana Jaivali was a Kshatriya. Therefore, he took the lead and initiated the debate by choosing to listen rather than speak first.

3. sa ha silakah salavatyas caikitayanam dalbhyam uvaca hanta tva priccaniti; pricceti hovaca.

3. Then Silaka son of Salavat said to Caikitayana of Dalbha clan: "I want to ask you a question." "Ask," he said.

4. ka samno gatir iti svara iti hovaca; svarasya ka gatir iti prana iti hovaca; pranasya ka gatir ity annam iti hovaca annasya ka gatir ity apa iti hovaca.

4. "What is the direction in which Saman moves?" "Voice, (svara)," he replied. "What is direction in which voice moves?" Breath," he replied. What is the direction in which breath moves?" "Food," he replied. "What is the direction in which food moves?" "Water," he replied.

Notes: This verse describes in what gatih or direction does something move or lead to. According to Caikitanya, Saman, (which is actually a reference to the Udighta,) moved in the direction of the voice because without voice one could not sing the Saman. Then, he said that the voice itself moved in the direction of the breath in the mouth because that was where speech was produced. Then, he suggested that breath moved in the body in the direction of food because it gathered food and carried it to various deities in the body. If the body was deprived of food, breath would stop moving. Speech and voice would become weak. Food moved in the direction of water, because when one ate food one needed water both for praying and for eating. Where there was water, there was food. Where there was rain, there was food. If the body was deprived of water, it stopped making food (energy). If it stopped making food, it stopped breathing. When it stopped breathing, the body could not nourish the deities (organs) in the body and they would depart with breath. Without breath, Saman, the song, could not move to its destined goal. Thus, Caikitanya argued that in the body, food and water were vital for singing the Saman effectively.

5. apam ka gatir ity asau loka iti hovacamusya lokasya ka gatir iti na svargam lokam atinayed iti hovaca svargam vayam lokam samabhisamsthapayamah svarga samstavam hi sameti.

5. "What is the direction in which water moves?" "That world (heaven)," he replied. "And what is the direction in which that world moves?" He said, "No one should think of taking the Saman beyond that world. We firmly establish the Saman in the heaven for it is extolled as heaven itself."

Notes: The heaven exists above the sky and above the region of water bearing clouds (ambhas). There is nothing beyond the heaven. Hence the goals of Saman is heaven. It is the ultimate and the highest. Therefore, one should not think of using the Saman to go beyond the immortal heaven, because there is nothing beyond that. This was the interpretation of Dalbhya; but it was incorrect, because according to his interpretation the Saman was not moving upwards in the right direction but in some unknown direction.

6. tam ha silakah salavatyas caikitayanam dalbhyam uvaca pratisthitam vai kila te dalbhya, sama yas tv etarhi bruyan murdha te vipatisyatiti murdha te vipated iti.

6. Then Silaka, son of Salavat said to Caikitayana of Dalbha clan, "O Dalbhya, your Saman is not established (in the heaven). If any one were to say, "Calamity shall fall upon your head calamity will indeed fall upon your head."

Notes: Vipatti means calamity or danger. The verse implies that Caikitanya's singing was ineffective, because he was unaware of the ultimate goal or destination of his Saman. If the Saman had to be effective, it had to reach the highest heaven. It appears Caikitanya had no idea to whom to address the Saman or to whom to offer it. Hence, Silaka said his Saman was not properly established in the highest goal.

7. hantaham etad bhagavato vedaniti viddhiti hovacamusya lokasya ka gatir ity ayam loka iti hovacasya lokasya ka gatir iti na pratistham lokam iti nayediti hovaca pratistham vayam lokam samabhisamsthapayamah pratistha-samstavam hi sameti.

7. He said, "Well then, godman, let me know it from you." "Know it," he said. "What is the direction in which that world (heaven) moves?" "This world," he replied. "And what is the direction in which this world moves" He replied, "None should take (the Saman) far beyond this world, which is the support. We establish the Saman in this world which is the support, for the Saman is extolled as the support."

8. tam ha pravahano jaivalir uvachantavadvai kila te salavatya sama yastvetarhi bruyan murdha te vipatisyatiti murdha te vipatediti hantaham etad bhagavato vedaniti viddhiti hovaca.

8. Then Pravahana, son of Jaivali said to him: "Your Saman, O son of Salavat, has an end. And if any one were to say, calamity shall fall on your head, surely calamity indeed will fall upon your head." "Well then, godman let me know this from you." "Know it," he said.

Section 9

Space as the Udgita

1. asya lokasya ka gatir ity akasa iti hovaca sarvani ha va imani bhutany akasa deva samutpadyanta akasam pratyastam yanty akaso hy evaibhyo jyayan akasah parayanam.

1 "What is the direction in which this world moves?" "Space"," he replied. For all these beings manifest from space, and disappear into space (in the end). Space is greater than them and spaceward they finally travel.

2. sa esa paro variyan udgitah sa eso'nantah, paro-variyo hasya bhavati paro-variyaso ha lokan jayati ya etad evam vidvan parovariyam sam udgitam upaste.

2. This, indeed, is the Udgita, the highest and the best. This is without an end. He becomes the highest and the best and attains the highest and the best, who, knowing thus, meditates upon the highest and the best Udgita.

3. tam haitam atidhanva saunaka udara sandilyayo-ktvovaca yavatta enam prajayam udgitam vedisyante parovariyo haibhyas tavad asmimlloke jivanam bhavisyati.

3. Having followed this, Atidhanvan Saunaka said this to Udara Sandilya,"As long as your descendents know this (space) as the Udgita, so long will their lives will be better and the highest."

4. tathamusmimlloke loka iti sa ya etad evam vidvan upaste parovariya eva hasyasmiml loke jivanam bhavati tatha musmiml loke loka iti loke loka iti.

4. "And so also will they be in the other world. He who knows (the Udgita) thus (as space) and thus meditates upon it, his life will become the best and the highest in this world as well as in the other world, yes indeed in the other world also."

Section 10
The Legend of Usati Cakrayana

1. Mataci hatesu kurusv atikya saha jayayosastir ha cakrayana ibhya-grame pradranaka uvasa.

1. *When the land of the Kurus was devastated by hailstorms (or locusts), Usasti Cakrayana lived in utter poverty in the village of an elephant owner (ibhaya) with his virgin wife.*

Notes: Usati Cakrayana's wife was still a virgin because either she was still young and not reached puberty or he was still learning the Vedas and practicing celibacy (brahmacarya).

2. sa hebhyam kulmasan khadantam bibhikse tam hovaca neto'nye vidyante yac ca ye ma ima upanihita iti.

2. *Seeing the elephant owner eating beans, he begged him (for food). He (the elephant owner) said, "I have none, except these that are served to me."*

3. etesam me dehiti hovaca tan asmai pradadau hantanupanam ity, uccistam vai me pitam syad iti hovaca.

3. *He (Usasti) said: "Give them to me." He (the elephant owner) gave them to him and said, "Have some water also." He (Usasti) said, "That would be like drinking leftover water."*

Notes: Leftover food is considered unclean in Hindu tradition. Those who offer unclean food to others incur sin. Even the food that is not eaten but merely tasted becomes unfit for an offering to a deity or guest. It is more so in case of a brahmana like Usati who was well versed in the Vedas. The elephant owner therefore hesitated to give what he was eating to Usati. However, there are exceptions to this practice which are specified in the law books. When there is famine, when food is scarce and people are starving, one may offer leftover food to a person to save his or her life. The previous verse already suggested that the land was devastated by locusts and there was scarcity of food. So Usati was justified in asking for food and the elephant owner was justified in giving it to him.

4. na svid ete'apy uccista iti na va ajivisyam iman akhadann iti hovaca kamo ma udakapanam iti.

4. *"Are not the beans also leftovers?" "Truly," he replied; "I would not be able to live, if I have not eaten them, but I can get drinking water whenever I want."*

Notes: Actually, this part of the story is not necessary for the purpose the discussion that follows. However it seem, it was included to show the kind of austere life Usati Cakrayana led and his knowledge of propriety.

5. sa ha khaditvatisesan jayaya ajahara sagra eva subhiksa babhuva tan pratigrihya nidadhau.

5. The beans that remained after he ate, he took them and gave to his wife. She had already eaten. So, she took them and kept them.

6. sa ha pratah samjihana uvaca yad batannasya labhemahi labhemahi dhanamatram rajasau yaksyate, sa ma sarvair artvijyair vriniteti.

6. The next day morning, he woke up and said to her, "If only I could get some food, I might (go out and) make some money. The king here is about to perform a sacrifice and he might as well ask me to perform all the priestly duties.

7. tam jayovaca hanta pata ima eva kulmasa iti tankhad-itvamum yajnam vitatameyaya.

7. His wife said to him, "My husband, here are those beans." Having eaten them, he went to the sacrifice which had already begun.

8. tatrodgatrin astave stosyamanan upopavivesa, sa ha prastotaram uvaca.

8. He went and sat among the chorus group near the Udgatri priests when they were about to sing the hymns of praise. He said to the head of the introductory priests.

9. prastotar ya devata prastavam anvayatta tam ced avidvan prasto-syasi murdha te vipatisyatiti.

9. "O Prastotri, without knowing him, if you sing the introductory hymn to the deity to which it belongs your head shall fall off."

Notes: Prastotri was the priest who sang the introductory hymn of praise. Prastava means the beginning song, or initial Saman sung in a sacrifice. It also means beginning, commencement, introduction, suggestion, proposal or premise in a conversation, debate or discussion. Usati wanted to know to which deity the introductory Saman should be addressed

10. evam evodgataram uvacodgatar ya devatodgitham anvay-atta tam ced avidvan udgasyasi murdha te vipatisyatiti.

10. In the same manner, he said to the Udgatri priest, "O Udgatri, without knowing him if you sing the Udgita to the deity to which it belongs, your head shall fall off."

11. evam eva pratihartaram uvaca pratihartar ya devata pratiharam anvayatta tam ced avidvan pratiharisyasi, murdha te vipatisyatiti: te ha samaratas tusnim asamcakrire.

11. In the same manner, he said to the Pratihartri priest: "O Pratihartri, without knowing him if you sing the hymn of protection to the deity to which it belongs, your head shall fall off." They stopped, and sat down in silence.

Notes: Each hymn belongs to a deity who is the moving force of that hymn. Priests who sing them are supposed to know them. Usasti Cakrayana was testing the priests whether they knew what they were singing and for whom they were singing.

Section 11

The Deities of Sacrifice

1. atha hainam yajamana uvaca, bhagavantam va aham vividisanity usastir asmi cakrayana iti hovaca.

1. Then the host of the sacrifice said to him, "I would like to know who you are, Sir." "I am Usasti Cakrayana," he said.

Notes: Yajamana is the owner or the chief patron of the sacrifice who bears the costs of the sacrifice and provides for the fees and gifts due to the priests.

2. sa hovaca bhagavantam va aham ebhih sarvair artvijyaih paryaisisam bhagavato va aham avitty-anyan avrisi.

2. He said, "I truly searched for you, godman, everywhere to perform all these sacrificial duties, and only when I could not find you, I chose the others."

3. bhagavams tv eva me sarvair artvijyair iti tathety atha tarhy eta eva samatisristah stuvatam yavat tv ebhyo dhanam dadyas tavan mama dadya iti tatheti ha yajamana uvaca.

3. "But now, godman, (since you are here) please perform all the priestly duties." "Very well, I accept," he said, "but let the same priests sing the hymns of praise with my permission,. As much wealth as you (agree to) give them that much you should give me also." The host of the sacrifice said, "I accept."

4. atha hainam prastotopasasada prastotar ya devata prastavam anvayatta tam ced avidvan prastosyasi, murdha te vipatisyatiti, ma bhagavan avocat katama sa devateti.

4. Then the priest who was to sing the introductory hymn approached him, saying: "You said to me, 'O Prastotr, if you sang the introductory praise without knowing the deity for which it was meant, your head would fall off,' what then is that deity?"

5. prana iti hovaca sarvani ha va imani bhutani pranam evabhisamvisanti pranam abhyujjihate saisa devata prastavam anvayatta tam ced avidvan prastosyo murdha te vyapatisyat tathoktasya mayeti.

5. He said this, "Breath. Truly, all these beings merge into breath alone (at the time of death), and arise from breath only (at the time of birth). The beginning of the sacrifice (prastava) is connected with this deity. If, without knowing that deity, you sang the hymns, your head would have fallen off, had I said so."

6. atha hainam udgatopasasadodgatar ya devatodgitham anvayatta, tam ced avidvan udgasyasi, murdha te vipatisyatiti: ma bhagavan avocat katama sa devateti.

6. Then the priest who was to sing Udgita approached him, saying: "You said to me, 'O Udgatri, if you chanted the hymns without knowing the deity for which it was meant, your head would fall off,' what then is that deity?"

7. aditya iti hovaca sarvani ha va imani bhutany adityam uccaih santam gayanti; saisa devatodgitam anvayatta tam ced avidvan udagasyah murdha te vyapatisyat tathoktasya mayeti.

7. He said, "The sun. Truly all these beings praise the sun when he is high. This is the deity connected to the Udgita. If, without knowing that deity, you sang the hymns, your head would have fallen off, had I said so."

8. atha hainam pratihartopasasada pratihartar ya devata pratiharam anvayatta tam ced avidvan pratiharisyasi murdha te vipatisyatiti ma bhagavan avocat katama sa devateti.

8. Then the priest who was to sing the hymns of protection approached him, saying: "You said to me, 'O Pratihartri, if you chanted the hymns of protection without knowing the deity for which it was meant, your head would fall off,' what then is that deity?"

9. annamiti hovaca sarvani ha va imani bhutany annam eva pratiharamanani jivanti saisa devata pratiharam anvayatta tam ced avidvan pratyaharisyah, murdha te vyapatisyat tathoktasya mayeti, tathoktasya mayeti.

9. He said, "Food. Truly, all these beings live by food alone. This is the deity connected to the hymn of protection. If, without knowing that deity, you had chanted the hymns, your head would have fallen off, had I said so."

Notes: Three deities are mentioned in this section, breath, the sun and food. They are invoked during the different phases of the sacrifice, since they are the ultimate recipients of the offerings made. Breath protects the sacrifice in the beginning, the sun protects the sacrifice in the middle and food protects the sacrifice in the last. The three are inherently interconnected and vital to our existence. Food is the support for the gross body, breath for the subtle body, and the sun for both.

Section 12

The Udgita of Dogs

1. athatah sauva udgitas tadd ha bako dalbhyo glavo va maitreyah svadhyayam udvavraja.

1. Now follows the Udgita of the dogs. Baka Dalbhya, or, as he was also called, Glava Maitreya, set forth for the self-study of the Vedas.

2. tasmai sva svetah pradur babhuva: tam anye svana upasametyocur annam no bhagavan agayatv asanayama va iti.

2. A white dog appeared before him; and other dogs, gathering round that dog, said to him, "O godman, please get us food by singing, we are truly hungry."

3. tanhovacehaiva ma pratar upasamiyateti tadd ha bako dalbhyo glavo va maitreyah pratipalayam cakara.

3. He said to them, "Come to me tomorrow morning." Vaka Dalbhya, or Glava Maitreya as he was also called, waited for their return.

4. te ha yathaivedam bahispavamanena stosyamanah samrabdhah sarpantity evam asasripus te ha samupavisya him cakruh.

4. The dogs came on, holding together, each dog keeping the tail of the preceding dog in his mouth, just as the priests move in line, holding the back of one another, when they are about to chant the bahispavamana hymns of praise. Then they sat down together and uttered the syllable, "him."

5. Aum adama aum pibama aum devo varunah prajapatih savitannam ihaharat annapate annam ihahara, ahara aum iti.

5. *Aum, let us eat! Aum, let us drink! Aum, may the gods Varuna, Prajapati, Savitri bring us food! O, Lord of food, bring here food, yes bring it here, Aum!"*

Notes: It is not clear why this section was interjected into the Upanishad and what did the dogs symbolize. Obviously they are compared to priests who were hungry for food. It may be a satire against empty ritualism and the vanity of priests who performed sacrifices for worldly ends or it may be a direct criticism of (proud?) Dalbhya himself by his critics who might have been displeased by his lack of knowledge. It may be possible that the inclusion of this section is not an accident. We have indications that certain Samans were sung in specific meters resembling the sound of animals. Probably, the dogs mentioned in this verse might not be actual dogs, but a group of Udgatri priests who specialized in the art singing Samans resembling the barks of dogs. They might have been hungry for some reason and sought the help of Balka Dalbhya to obtain food for them by singing. Going by the previous section, in which Usati Cakrayana had to beg for food and eat even leftovers, it is possible that this might have happened during a famine or pestilence.

Section 13

The Secret Knowledge of Sounds in Samans

1. ayam vava loko haukarah vayur haikaras candrama athakarah atmeha karo'gnirikarah.

1. This world is of the form of the syllable HAU; the air is of the form of the syllable HAI, the moon is of the form of the syllable ATHA, the self is of the form of the syllable IHA, and fire is of the form of the syllable I.

Notes: According to Shankara, these comparisons are based on the stobhas used in the singing of Samans. Stobha is a musical term, known to those who are conversant with Classical Indian music. In the context of the Samaveda, Stobha means the additional or special syllables or letters, not in the original hymns, which are used to facilitate the correct singing of the Samans. A stobha may be a single letter (varna stobha), a word (pada stobha) or an entire sentence (vakya Stobha). Thus, HAU is the stobha used in the singing of Rathantara Saman. Hai is the Stobha used in the singing of Vamadeva Saman. The moon is Atha because it is not self-sufficient but depends (sthitha) upon food or the offerings of Soma sacrifices. The Syllable IHA should be mediated upon as Self because iha means this, which is a reference to oneself. The syllable 'I' represents Fire because all Samans connected with fire end in the vowel 'i'.

2. aditya ukaro nihava ekaro visve deva auhoyikarah prajapatirhimkarah pranah svaro'nnam ya vagvirat.

2. The sun is of the form of the (high) syllable U, the invocation nihava is of the form of the (invocative) syllable E, the Visvadevas (gods of commonality) are of the form of the syllable AU-Ho-YI, Prajapati is of the form of the (indistinct) syllable HIM, breath (being the source) is SVARA (voice), food is (the moving syllable) YA and speech is (the deity) VIRAT.

Notes: Shankara interpreted that the sun is syllable 'U' because in the invocation to the sun, the stobah 'u' is used. 'U' denotes the position of the sunlight in the sky. Invocation is comparable to the syllable 'e' because when calling someone, we use the word 'ehi' meaning come. The Visvadevas are compared to Au-Ho-Yi because these syllable are found in the stobha addressed to them. The syllable Him is described as Prajapati because both are indistinct. Breath is SVARA, because the breath in the mouth is the source of voice or speech. Food is YA because the offering of food moves in the body as well as in the world to reach various deities. Speech (Vac) is VIRAT because the stobha related to speech is found in the Vairaja Saman.

3. aniruktas trayodasah stobhah samcaro humkarah.

3. The indefinable (Brahman) is of the form of the indeterminate thirteenth stobha, the syllable HUM.

Notes: The thirteenth stobah is indeterminate because we cannot say exactly what it is. So is the case with Brahman, who is indefinable and indescribable. Hence Brahman is compared to the thirteenth stobha 'HUM.'

4. dugdhe'asmai vag doham yo vaco doho'nnavan annado bhavati ya etam evam samnam upanisadam vedopanisadam vedeti.

4. Speech milks the milk of speech for him who knows the secret knowledge of the Samans. He becomes Rik in food, an enjoyer of food, yes he who knows this secret knowledge of the Vedas.

Notes: The singing of Samans requires special knowledge, knowledge of the Vedas, knowledge of the musical notes and specific meters, knowledge of the symbolism hidden in the Samans, and knowledge of the various deities associated with different types of Samans. Besides, one also needs to be conversant with grammar and pronunciation. This is a highly specialized branch of Vedic knowledge, which is essential to ensure the purity, sanctity and efficacy of the sacrifices. Some of the hidden and cryptic aspects Samans are discussed in this section. I have no doubt that the symbolism of Chandogya Upanishad is the most difficult to explain, for this very reason. We have seen that even the most experienced singers of Samans were often not conversant with the hidden aspects of the Samans. Hence, this verse emphasizes the importance of such knowledge, which is secret and taught only to qualified people. Those who possessed the knowledge were able to fulfill their wishes and those of their patrons. Hence they were able to enjoy good life and good food by the sheer power of their voice and their singing ability.

Chapter 2

Section 1

Meditation on the Whole Saman

1. aum samastasya khalu samna upasanam sadhu yatkhalu sadhu tat samety acaksate yad asadhu tad asameti.

1. Aum, meditation on the complete Saman is certainly good; whatever is certainly good, they call that Saman; and whatever is not good, they call it not-Saman (asama).

Notes: Upasana does not mean meditation alone. It means religious service, worship, attendance, adoration, sacrifice, or meditation. In the previous chapter we have seen comparison between various aspects of Saman and various aspects of creation. In this chapter, the emphasis is upon the symbolism and significance of Saman as a whole. The parts of Saman represent diversity in creation. Saman as a whole represents the unity and divinity of creation. Sama is sadhu. Sadhu means gentle, agreeable, peaceful, kind, compassionate, or conciliatory. Any spiritual or ascetic person who has these virtues and conquered his mind and body is known as sadhu. It is a positive state of mind which comes with self-awareness and inner purity. Since Saman is sadhu, meditation upon it, or the very act of singing it, leads to positive results. Asama is its opposite, means not good, not agreeable or not pleasant.

2. tad utapy ahuh samnainam upagad iti sadhunainam upagad ity eva tad ahuh asamnainam upagad ity asadhunainam upagad ity eva tadahuh.

2. Also, when people say thus, "He approached with Saman," what they mean is he approached with good in his heart, and when they say, "He approached without Saman" what they mean is he approached without good in his heart.

Notes: You can express good genuinely only when you have good in your heart. A person without good in his heart cannot sing Samans effectively, because the singing requires an attitude of goodness and sameness. Therefore, approaching with Saman means approaching with sameness and conciliatory attitude. This is usually in reference to a person approaching another in a conciliatory mood to settle their differences or disputes. Tradition recognizes four methods of reconciliation, namely sama or using gentle approach, dana or giving gifts, charity or bribes, bheda or aggravating the conflict by raising more objections and danda or using violent and coercive methods to settle a dispute. Saman is compared here to goodness itself. Approaching with Saman means approaching another with sameness or equanimity, without any ill will or aversion in the heart. This attitude is possible only in case of a sadhu, who has conquered his mind and heart and stabilized his intelligence.

3. athotapy ahuh sama no bateti yat sadhu bhavati sadhu batety eva tad ahuh asama no bateti yad asadhu bhavaty asadhu batety eva tad ahuh.

3. And when they say, "Truly this is Saman for us," when good is happening to them, what they mean is it is good for them; and when they say, "Truly that is not Saman for us," when good is not happening to them, what they means is it is not good for them.

4. sa ya etad evam vidvan sadhu samety upaste abhyaso ha yad enam sadhavo dharma a ca gacceyur upa ca nameyuh.

4. He who knowing thus meditates upon the Saman as good, all the qualities of a good person readily come to him, and (the merit arising out of them) accrues to him.

Section 2
The Fivefold Saman With Regard to Worlds

1. lokesu panca vidham samopasita: prithivi himkarah, agnih prastavo'ntariksam udgita, adityah pratiharo dyaur nidhanam ity urdhvesu.

1. With regard to the worlds, the Saman should be worshipped in five ways, the earth as the syllable Him, fire as Prastava, the mid-region as Udgita, the sun as Pratihara, and the heaven as Nidhana.

Notes: Samans have either four, five or seven aspects. most Samans begin with the staring sound Hin or Him. It is followed by the introductory song Prastava. The middle part is Udgita. The Penultimate part is called Pratihara. And the ending is called Nidhana. This is the fivefold Saman. In this section and in the subsequent ones, this fivefold Saman is compared to various aspects of Cosmic Reality. The worlds constitute the body of the Cosmic Person (Purusa). In this section the fivefold aspect of Saman in both ascending and descending orders are compared to the fivefold aspects of Purusha, in both ascending and descending orders. What does this imply? It suggests that creation or the Manifested Brahman Himself is a form of Saman only.

2. athavrittesu dyaur himkara adityah prastavo'ntariksam udgitho'gnih pratiharah prithivi nidhanam.

2. Now, in the descending order, the heaven as syllable HIM, the sun as Prastava, the mid-region as Udgita, fire as Pratihara, and the earth as Nidhana.

Notes: The previous verse is about the Saman with ascending notes and this one is about the Saman with descending notes. The previous one is about the upward journey of the souls from this world to the higher worlds and this one is about the return of the souls to the earth for rebirth.

3. kalpante hasmai loka urdhvas cavrittas ca ya etad evam vidvaml lokesu pancavidham samopaste.

3. *The worlds in their ascending and descending orders belong to him who, knowing thus, worships the Saman in the worlds in five ways.*

Notes: The knower of ascending and descend orders of Saman will be able to ascend to the ancestral world and return from there by the descending path to take another birth. He will not be able to exhaust his karmas or attain liberation, but he will be able to attain human birth in a pious family.

Section 3
The Fivefold Saman With Regard to Rain

1. vristau pancavidham samopasita purovato himkaro megho jayate sa prastavo varsati sa udgitho vidyotate stanayati sa pratihara.

1. *With regard to rain, the Saman should be worshipped in five ways, the winds before (rain) as the syllable HIM, the Prastava as the cloud formation, the rain fall as the Udgita, the lightning and thunder as the Pratihara.*

2. udgrihnati tan nidhanam varsati hasmai varsayati ha ya etad evam vidvan vristau pancavidham samopaste.

2. *And the ending (or withdrawal) as the Nidhana. Knowing thus whoever worships the Saman in these five ways, it rains for him and he can cause the rains to fall.*

Section 4
The Fivefold Saman With Regard to Water

1. sarvasv apsu pancavidham samopasita megho yat samplavate sa himkaro yadvarsati sa prastavo, yah pracyah syandante sa udgitho yah praticyah sa pratiharah samudro nidhanam.

1. *With regard to water, the Saman should be worshipped in five ways, the clouds that gather as the syllable HIM, the rain that falls as the Prastava, the water that flows eastwards as the Udgita, the water that flows westwards as the Pratihara, and the ocean as the Nidhana.*

2. na hapsu parity apsuman bhavati ya etad evam vidvan sarvasv apsu panca vidham samopaste.

2. *He will not die in water, indeed he becomes abundant with water, who knowing thus worships the Saman in five ways in all the waters.*

Section 5

The Fivefold Saman With Regard to Seasons

1. ritusu pancavidham samopasita vasanto himkarah grismah prastavo varsa udgitah sarat pratiharo hemanto nidhanam.

1. With regard to the seasons, the Saman should be worshipped in five ways; the spring as the syllable HIM, the summer as the Prastava, the rainy season as the Udgita, the Autumn as the Pratihara, and the winter as the Nidhana.

2. kalpante hasma ritava rituman bhavati ya etad evam vidvan ritusu pancavidham samopaste.

2. He controls the seasons and the seasons bring him riches who knowing thus worships the Saman in the seasons in five ways.

Section 6

The Fivefold Saman With Regard to Animals

1. pasusu panca vidham samopasit aja himkaro'vayah prastavo, gava udgitho'svah pratiharah puruso nidhanam.

1. With regard to animals, one should worship the Saman in five ways; the goats as the syllable HIM, the sheep as the Prastava, the cows as the Udgita, the horses as the Pratihara, and man as the Nidhana.

2. bhavanti hasya pasavah pasuman bhavati ya etad evam vidvan pasusu pancavidham samopaste.

2. Animals come to him and he becomes Rich with cattle, who knowing thus worships the Saman among the animals in five ways.

Section 7

The Fivefold Saman With Regard to Breaths

1. pranesu pancavidham parovariyah samopasita prano himkaro vak prastavah caksur udgitah srotram pratiharo mano nidhanam parovariyamsi va etani.

1. With regard to breaths, one should worship the most superior Saman in five ways; breath as the syllable HIM, speech as the Prastava, eyes as the Udgita, ears as the Pratihara, and the mind as the Nidhana. All these are superior to the other in the same order.

Notes: The reference is to the breaths, or the sense organs. The order is from the outer to the inner. Therefore, speech is mentioned as first and the Mind as the last.

2. parovariyo hasya bhavati parovariyaso ha lokan jayati ya etad evam vidvan pranesu pancavidham paro variyah samopasta iti tu pancavidhasya.

2. The highest and the most excellent happens to him, indeed, he attains the highest and the most excellent worlds, who knowing thus worships the Saman with regard to the senses in these five ways.

Section 8
The Sevenfold Saman With Regard to Speech

1. atha sapta vidhasya vaci sapta vidhm samopasita yat kim ca vaco humiti sa himkaro yat preti sa prastavo yadeti sa adih.

1. Now with regard to the sevenfold speech, one should meditate upon the Saman in the speech in seven ways: that speech which contains the syllable HIM as the syllable HIM, that which contains PRA as the Prastava, that which contains Ā as the Adi (Aum).

Notes: In the sevenfold Saman you find two additional parts, Adi and Upadrava. Both contain only a few syllables. Adi begins and ends with the utterance of Aum only. It precedes the Udgita, since the singing of the Udgita usually begins with the syllable Aum. In the Upadrava also only a few syllables or words are uttered. Of these seven parts of Saman, Prastava is sung by Prastotar, Udgita by Udgatar, Pratihara by Pratihartar priests. Nidhana is sung by all the three. Adi and Upadrava are also sung by the Udgatar.

2. yad uditi sa udgitho yat pratiti sa pratiharo yad upeti sa upadravo yann iti tan nidhanam.

2. That which contains UT as the Udgita, that which contains PRATI as the Pratihara, that which contains UPA as the Upadrava and that which contains NI as the Nidhana.

3. dugdhe'asmai vag doham yo vaco doho'nnavan annado bhavati ya etad evam vidvan vaci saptavidham samopaste.

3. Speech milks the milk of speech for him, who knowing thus meditates upon the Saman with regard to speech in these seven different ways. (With speech) he becomes Rik in food and enjoys eating food.

Notes: The message is clear. The knowledge of the Vedas should be complete. Singing a Saman is one aspect of it. Chandogya Upanishad derives its name mainly because it deals with Chhandas, the metrical aspect of singing various Samans. Chhandas is a subject (Vedanga) in itself. It teaches one how to sing the verses with varying rhythms and in specific meters. This knowledge is important because the heart of the Vedic mantras is pronunciation, which is repeatedly revered here and elsewhere as speech. One must know clearly the powers and the deities hidden in the Saman. How Saman should be sung on different occasions and in relation to various phenomena. One should know its parts and how, together, they make up a Saman. Those who possess this knowledge become adepts in sacrificial ceremonies and with their specialized knowledge attract abundance of various kinds.

Section 9

The Sevenfold Saman With Regard to the Sun

1. atha khalvamum adityam saptavidham samopasita sarvada samastena sama mam prati mam pratiti sarvena samastena sama.

1. One should worship the Saman in the sun in seven ways. The sun is the Saman because he is always the same (sama). He is always the same because everyone thinks, "He is looking at me. He is looking at me." Hence, he is the Saman.

Notes: The sun is impartial. He radiates light equally in all directions. The sun looks at everyone and observes everything. The sun does not choose or favor anyone or anything in particular. He is equal to all. Saman has a similar quality. When a Saman is sung, its sound reaches everyone. Saman does not reach out to anyone or anything in particular. The sound travels in all directions and reaches out to everyone. Hence, both the sun and Saman are equal to all.

2. tasminn imani sarvani bhutany anvayattan iti vidyat tasya yat purodayat sa himkaras tad asya pasavo'nvayattas tasmat te him kurvanti him karabhajino hy etasya samnah.

2. One should know that all beings are dependent upon him. That (sun) which is before the dawn is the syllable HIM and to that all animals are related. Therefore, they utter (the syllable) HIM. Truly they have their representation in the syllable HIM of that Saman.

Notes: Anvaya means related to, following, descended from, or connected. The syllable HIM is the first or the beginning aspect. It is the base or the support of the Saman. The animal world is the base or the support of life upon earth. Just as we nourish the gods, the animals nourish us.

3. atha yat prathamodite sa prastavas tadasya manusya anvayattas tasmatte prastuti kamah prasamsa kamah prastava bhajino hy etasya samnah.

3. Now that (sun) which appears first upon sunrise, is the Prastava. To that all humans are related. Therefore they desire praise and appreciation. Truly, they have their representation in the Prastava of that Saman.

4. atha yat samgavavelayam sa adih tad asya vayamsy anvayattani tasmat tany antarikse anaramban anyada'tmanam paripatanty adibhajini hy etasya samnah.

4. Now what is at the time of milking of the cows (when the calves join their mothers) that (sun) is the Adi (Aum). To that, the birds are related. Hence, the birds stay by themselves in the sky without support and fly here and there. Truly, they have their representation in the Adi of that Saman.

5. atha yat samprati madhyan dine sa udgitah tad asya deva anvayatth tasmat te sattamah prajapatyanam udgita bhajino hy etasya samnah.

5. Now, what appears at the midday, that (sun) is the Udgita. To that the gods are related. Therefore, they are the best progeny of Prajapati. Truly they have their participation in the Udgita of that Saman.

Notes: The gods are compared to the midday sun because they possess the brightest light or the best intelligence among the children of Prajapati.

6. atha yad urdhvam madhyandinat prag aparahnat sa pratiharas, tad asya garbha anvayattas tasmat te pratihrita navapadyante pratihara bhajino hy etasya samnah.

6. Now what is after midday but before afternoon, that (sun) is the Pratihara. To that all the embryos in the wombs are related. Therefore, on being conceived, they do not fall down. Truly they have their representation in the Pratihara of that Saman.

7. atha yad urdhvam aparahnat prag astamayat sa upadravah tad asyaranya anvayattah tasmat te purusam dristva kaksam svabhram ity upadravanty upadravabhajino hy etasya samnah.

7. Now, what is later than the afternoon but before the sunset, that (sun) is the Upadrava. To that, the dwellers of the forest are related. Therefore, upon seeing humans, they run into the forest as the hiding place. Truly, they have their representation in the Upadrava of the Saman.

Notes: Upadrava is the penultimate part. Hence it is compared to the evening or twilight, preceding the night, which is Nidhana. It is the time during which the birds and animals in the forests return to their abode. Upadrava also means trouble. The approach of the sunset means night is about to happen and for those who live in the forests, evening is an indication of the troubling times ahead and cause for concern.

8. atha yat prathamastamite tan nidhanam tad asya pitaro'n-vayattah tasmat tan nidadhati nidhana bhajino hy etasya samna evam khalvamumadityam saptavidham samo-paste.

8. Now that which appears first (the moon) at the time of sunset, that is Nidhana. To that all the ancestors are related. Therefore they rest them (the offerings made to the ancestors) in the Nidhana. Truly, they have their representation in the Nidhana of Saman. Thus, one should worship the Saman in the Sun in seven different ways.

Section 10

The Sevenfold Saman With Regard to Itself

1. atha khalv atma sammitam atimrityu sapta vidham samopasita himkara iti tryaksaram prastava iti tryaksaram tat samam.

1. Now, one should worship the Saman in relation to itself in seven ways, which results in the transcendence of death. The syllable HIM has three letters. The Prastava has three letters. That is the same (sama).

Notes: In the previous sections, the emphasis was on how to worship the Saman in relation to the worlds and other phenomena in creation. Now, the instruction is how to worship it in relation to itself. Him as three syllables and prastava (pra + sta+ va) also has three syllables. That makes them similar (sama).

2. adiriti dvyaksaram pratihara iti caturaksaram tata ihaikam tat samam.

2. Adi has two letters (ā + di). Pratihara has four letters (pra+ti+ha+ra). Taking one letter from here to there, that makes them equal (sama).

Notes: The meaning is when you subtract one letter from pratihara and add it to adi, they both become three lettered.

3. udgita iti tryaksaram upadrava iti caturaksaram tribhis tribhih samam bhavaty aksaram atisisyate tryaksaram tat samam.

3. Udgita has three (ut+gi+ta) has three letters. Upadrava has four letters (u+pa+dr+va). Three and three are equal. What is left over (va) is also a syllable (askhara)) with three letters (ak+sa+ra)) and that makes them equal.

4. nidhanam iti tryaksaram tat samam eva bhavati tani ha va etani dvavimsatir aksarani.

4. Nidhana has three letters. Therefore it is equal (to other syllables). Together they make up twenty two letters (of Saman).

5. eka vimsaty adityam apnoty ekavimso va ito'sav adityo dvavimsena param adityaj jayati tan nakam tad visokam.

5. With twenty one letters one attains the sun, for the sun is the twenty first. With the twenty second, one conquers what is beyond the sun, which is pure bliss and without sorrow.

Notes: Twelve months, five seasons, three worlds and the sun, constitute twenty one. The sun, here, denotes the end point of Time or Death and what is beyond Time is eternity or immortality. The twenty second letter is 'Ka' or pure bliss. With twenty one letters, one reaches the doors of the immortal world, but with twenty second one attains immortality and union with Brahman.

6. apnoti hadityasya jayam paro hasy aditya jayaj jayo bhavati, ya etad evam vidvan atma sammitam atimrityu sapta vidham samopaste samopaste.

6. He secures victory over the sun (time). Truly a victory higher than the victory over the sun comes to him who, knowing this thus, worships the Saman in seven ways, yes when he meditates upon the Saman thus.

Notes: Victory over the sun means winning the world of Brahman located in the sun.

Section 11

The Saman Hidden in the Senses

1. mano himkaro vak prastavas caksur udgitah srotram pratiharah prano nidhanam etad gayatram pranesu protam.

1. The mind is the syllable HIM, speech is Prastava, the eye is the Udgita, the ear is the Pratihara, breath is Nidhana. This is the Gayatra (Saman) woven in the (five) sense-organs.

Notes: Previously, we have studied the symbolic significance of fivefold and sevenfold Samans in general, without any reference to specific types of Samans. This section deals with specific types of Samans used in sacrificial ceremonies and their correlation with other objects found in creation. These Samans are used in the rituals in a specific order and the same order is followed here in describing them. Gayatra Saman is based upon the famous Gayatri mantra and it is used in certain morning rituals, such as the Jyotistoma sacrifices.

2. sa evam etad gayatram pranesu protam veda prani bhavati sarvam ayureti jyog jivati mahan prajaya pasubhir bhavati mahan kirtya mahamanah syat tad vratam.

2. He who thus knows this Gayatra interwoven in the five sense-organs becomes alive (through his sense organs), lives his full life, lives gloriously, attains greatness with progeny and cattle, and earns a great name for himself. He (who sings the Gayatra Saman) should be noble-minded. That is the rule.

Notes: Vratam means vow of observance, rule, norm, an ordinance, law, austerity, practice or resolve.

Section 12

The Rathantara Saman in the Fire

1. abhimanthati sa himkaro dhumo jayate sa prastavo jvalati sa udgitho'ngara bhavanti sa pratihara upasamyati tan nidhanam samsamyati tan nidhanam etad rathamtaram agnau protam.

1. One rubs the fire-sticks (to produce fire), it is the syllable Him. The smoke rises, that is the Prastava. It burns, that is the Udgita. The burning coals appear, that is the Pratihara. It becomes extinguished, that is the Nidhana. This is the Rathantara Saman woven in the Fire.

2. sa ya evam etad rathamtaram agnau protam veda brahmavarcasy annado bhavati sarvam ayureti jyog jivati mahan prajaya pasubhir bhavati mahan kirtya na pratyann agnim acamen na nisthivet tad vratam.

2. He who thus knows this Rathantara woven in the fire, develops the glow of Brahman and becomes an eater of food, lives his full life, lives gloriously, attains greatness with progeny and cattle, and earns a great name for himself. He (who sings the Rathantara Saman) should not sip water or spit before the fire. That is the rule.

Section 13

The Vamadeva Saman in the Coitus

1. upamantrayate sa himkaro jnapayate sa prastavah striya saha sete sa udgitah prati strim saha sete sa pratiharah kalam gaccati tan nidhanam param gaccati tan nidhanam etad vamadevyam mithune protam.

2. He invites, that is the syllable HIM; he proposes, that is the Prastava; he lies down along with the woman, that is the Udgita; he lies upon the woman, that is the Pratihara; time goes by, it comes to an end and he enters supreme (blissful) state, that is Nidhana. This is Vamadeva Saman woven in the coitus.

2. sa ya evam etad vamadevyam mithune protam veda mithuni bhavati mithunan mithunat prajayate sarvam ayureti jyog

jivati mahan prajaya pasubhir bhavati mahan kirtya na kamcana pariharet tad vratam.

2. *He who thus knows this Vamadeva woven in the coitus, becomes able for coitus, procreates from coitus to coitus, lives his full life, lives gloriously, attains greatness with progeny and cattle, and earns a great name for himself. He (who sings the Vamadeva Saman) should not avoid any woman (who desires coitus for the sake of procreation). That is the rule.*

Section 14
The Brhat Saman in the sun

1. udyan himkara uditah prastavo madhyamdina udgitho-'parahnah pratiharo'stam yan nidhanam etad brihad aditye protam.

1. The rising sun is the syllable HIM, the risen (sun) is the Prastava. The midday sun is the Udgita, the afternoon sun is the Pratihara. The setting sun is the Nidhana. This is the Brhat Saman woven in the sun.

2. sa ya evam etad brihadaditye protam veda tejasvy annado bhavati sarvam ayureti jyog jivati mahan prajaya pasubhir bhavati mahan kirtya tapantam na nindet tad vratam.

2. He who thus knows this Brhat (Saman) woven in the sun, becomes filled the vigor (of the sun) and an eater of food, lives his full life, lives gloriously, attains greatness with progeny and cattle, and earns a great name for himself. He (who sings the Brhat Saman) should not blame the scorching sun. That is the rule.

Section 15
The Vairupya Saman in the Clouds

1. abhrani samplavante sa himkaro megho jayate sa prastavo varsati sa udgitho vidyotate stanayati sa pratihara udgrihnati tan nidhanam etad vairupam parjanye protam.

1. The vapors assemble, that is the syllable HIM; clouds appear, that is the Prastava. The rain falls, that is the Udgita. When lightning and thunder are seen, that is the Pratihara. It stops, that is the Nidhana. This is Vairupya Saman woven in the cloud.

2. sa ya evam etad vairupam parjanye protam veda virupams ca surupams ca pasun avarundhe sarvam ayureti jyog jivati mahan prajaya pasubhir bhavati mahan kirtya varsantam na nindet tad vratam.

2. He who thus knows this Vairupya (Saman) woven in the cloud, acquires diverse types of cattle of beautiful forms, lives his full life, lives gloriously, attains greatness with progeny and cattle, and earns a great name for himself. He (who sings the Vairupya Saman) should not blame until the end when it is raining. That is the rule.

Section 16

The Vairaja Saman in the Seasons

1. vasanto himkaro grismah prastavo varsa udgitah sarat pratiharo hemanto nidhanam etad vairajam ritusu protam.

1. The spring is the syllable HIM, the summer is the Prastava, the rainy season is the Udgita, the Autumn is the Pratihara, the winter is the Nidhana. This is the Vairaja (Saman) interwoven in the seasons.

2. sa ya evam etad vairajam ritusu protam veda virajati prajaya pasubhir brahmavarcas ena sarvam ayureti jyog jivati mahan prajaya pasubhir bhavati mahan kirtya rtun na nindet tad vratam.

2. He who thus knows this Vairaja (Saman) woven in the seasons, flourishes with the abundance of progeny and cattle, and the light of Brahman, lives his full life, lives gloriously, attains greatness with progeny and cattle, and earns a great name for himself. He (who sings the Vairaja Saman) should not blame the seasons. That is the rule.

Section 17

The Sakavari Saman in the Clouds

1. prithivi himkaro'ntariksam prastavo dyaur udgitho disah pratiharah samudro nidhanam etah sakvaryo lokesu protah.

1. The earth is the syllable HIM, the sky is the Prastava, the heaven is the Udgita, the directions are the Pratihara, the oceans is the Nidhana. This is the Sakvari Saman woven in the worlds.

2. sa ya evam etah sakvaryo lokesu prota veda loki bhavati sarvam ayureti jyog jivati mahan prajaya pasubhir bhavati mahan kirtya lokan na nindet tad vratam.

2. He who thus knows this Sakvari (Saman) woven in the worlds, secures the best of these worlds, lives his full life, lives gloriously, attains greatness with progeny and cattle, and earns a great name for himself. He (who sings the Sakvari Saman) should not blame the worlds. That is the rule.

Section 18

The Revati Saman in the Beings

1. aja himkaro'vayah prastavo gava udgitho'svah pratiharah puruso nidhanam eta revatyah pasusu protah.

1. The goats are the syllable HIM, the sheep the Prastava, the cows the Udgita, the horses the Pratihara, humans the Nidhana.

Notes: Pasu means both an animal and a living being (jiva) who is subject to the impurities of egoism, attachment and delusion. The animal nature ends in the humans. Therefore they are rightly described as the Nidhana.

2. sa ya evam eta revatyah pasusu prota veda pasum anbhavati sarvam ayureti jyog jivati mahan prajaya pasubhir bhavati mahan kirtya pasun na nindet tad vratam. This is the Revati Saman woven in the living beings.

2. He who thus knows this Revati (Saman) woven in the beings becomes the possessor of beings, lives his full life, lives gloriously, attains greatness with progeny and cattle, and earns a great name for himself. He (who sings the Revati Saman) should not blame the beings. That is the rule.

Section 19

The Yajnayajniya Saman in the Limbs

1. loma himkaras tvac prastavo mamsam udgithosthi pratiharah majja nidhanam etad yajna yajniyam angesu protam.

1. The hair is the syllable HIM, the skin is the Prastava, the flesh the Udgita, the bone marrow the Nidhana. This is the Yajnayajniya Saman woven in the limbs.

2. sa ya evam etad yajna yajniyam angesu protam vedangi bhavati nangena vihurcati sarvam ayureti jyog jivati mahan prajaya pasubhir bhavati mahan kirtya samvatsaram majjno nasniyat tad vratam majjno nasniyad iti va.

2. He who thus knows this Yajnayajniya (Saman) woven in the limbs becomes the possessor of perfect limbs without any deformity in them, lives his full life, lives gloriously, attains greatness with progeny and cattle, and earns a great name for himself. The rule is for a year he (who sings the Yajnayajniya Sama) should not eat bone marrow, or better, he should not eat bone marrow at all.

Section 20

The Rajana Saman in the Deities

1. agnir himkaro vayuh prastava aditya udgitho naksatrani pratiharah candrama nidhanam etad rajanam devatasu protam.

1. The fire is the syllable HIM, the air is the Prastava, the sun is the Udgita, the sky is the Pratihara, the moon is the Nidhana. This is the Rajana Saman woven in the deities.

2. sa ya evam etad rajanam devatasu protam vedaitasam eva devatanam salokatam sarstitam sayujyam gaccati sarvam ayureti jyog jivati mahan prajaya pasubhir bhavati mahan kirtya brahmanan na nindet tad vratam.

2. He who thus knows this Rajana (Saman) woven in the deities attains the worlds of the deities, and sameness and oneness with them. He lives his full life, lives gloriously, attains greatness with progeny and cattle, and earns a great name for himself. He (who sings Rajana Saman) should not blame the brahmanas. That is the rule.

Section 21

The Saman Woven in All

1. trayi vidya himkaras traya ime lokah sa prastavo'gnir vayur adityah sa udgitho naksatrani vayamsi maricayah sa pratiharah sarpa gandharvah pitaras tan nidhanam etat sama sarvasmin protam.

1. The threefold knowledge is syllable Him; the triple worlds are the Prastava; fire, air and the sun are the Udgita; the stars, the birds and the sun-rays are the Pratihara; the serpents, celestial beings and the ancestors are the Nidhana. This is the Saman woven in all.

2. sa ya evam etat sama sarvasmin protam veda sarvam ha bhavati.

2. He who knows this thus as interwoven in all, becomes all

3. tadesa slokah yani pancadha trini trini tebhyo na jyayah param anyad asti.

3. Regarding this there is the verse, "That which is fivefold in threes and threes. There is nothing else superior to these other than them."

Notes: Saman is fivefold, starting with Him and ending with Nidhana. This fivefold Saman is found in three and three, which are described before, namely the triple worlds, the tripe deities of fire, air and the sun, the stars, the triple aspects of the mid-region: the sun rays and the birds, and so on.

4. yas tad veda sa veda sarvam sarva diso balim asmai haranti sarvam asmity upasita tad vratam tad vratam.

4. He who knows that, knows all. He obtains sacrificial offerings from all sides. One should meditate upon this, "I am all." That is the observance, yes it is the observance.

Section 22
Different Ways of Singing the Saman

1. vinardi samno vrine pasavyam ity agner udgitho'niruktah prajapater niruktah somasya mridu slaksnam vayoh slaksnam balavad indrasya krauncam brihaspater apadhvantam varunasya tan sarvan evopaseveta varunam tv eva varjayet.

1. I chose to offer the loud singing of Saman similar to the loud noise made by the animals, as the Udgita to fire. The one not so well pronounced to Prajapati, the one well pronounced to Soma, the smooth and excellent to Vayu, the strong and excellent to Indra, the heron-like to Brihaspati, the irregular or the unwholesome to Varuna. One should practice all these, discarding the one offered to Varuna.

Notes: The Samans are sung in various ways. Some are sung very loudly in high pitch, imitating the sounds of animals like the bellowing of bulls as in case of the Udgita addressed to fire. Some are sung with indistinct sounds as in case of the Samans addressed to Prajapati. Some are sung in clear voice with distinct sounds, such as the Gayatra Saman or others addressed to Soma. Some are sung in soft and smooth tones like the sound of a breeze as in case of the Samans addressed to Vayu. Some are sung with smooth, but with forceful effort, like a rolling thunder, as in case of the Samans addressed to Indra. Some are sung in the manner of a heron, as in case of the Samans addressed to Brihaspati. Some are sung in irregular and jarring fashion like the sound of metal as in case of hymns addressed to Varuna. The verse says that one should practice all these methods of singing, but avoid the kind of singing meant for Varuna. No specific explanation has been given why it should be so.

2. amritatvam devebhya agayanity agayet svadham pitribhya asam manusyebhyas trinodakam pasubhyah svargam lokam yajamanayannam atmana agayanity etani manasa dhyayann apramattah stuvita.

2. *One should sing thus thinking, "May I secure immortality for the gods through my singing, tasty food for the ancestors, hope for men, grass and water for the animals, heavenly world for the patrons of sacrifices, and food for oneself." Thus thinking about these in one's mind with full concentration, one should sing the eulogies carefully without making mistakes.*

Notes: The Samans serve many purposes, which are listed here, namely immortality for gods, food for ancestors to build their bodies, hope for men that they can fulfill their desires and secure peace and happiness here and now, water and fodder for the animals, heavenly world for those who perform sacrifices and food for oneself. All these are possible only when the Samans are sung properly according to established procedures and meters.

3. sarve svara indrasyatmanah sarva usmanah prajapater atmanah sarve sparsa mrityor atmanas tam yadi svares upalabhetendram saranam prapanno'bhuvam sa tva prati vaksyatity enam bruyat.

3. *All the vowels are the personification of Indra, all sibilants are the personification of Prajapati, all consonants are the personification of death. If someone criticizes a person for his vowels, he should tell him, "I have taken refuge in Indra and he will respond to you."*

Notes: Svara means voice, sound, tone and also a vowel, such as 'a' or 'e'. Usmana means the syllable pronounced with a hissing sound, such as 'sa' or 'ha'. It is also translated by some as spirant, a consonant pronounced by narrowing the vocal tract. They produce indistinct sounds. Hence they personify Prajapati who is also indistinct. The sparsas are consonants such as 'Ka.'

4. atha yady enam usmasupalabheta prajapatim saranam prapanno'bhuvam sa tva prati peksyat ity enam bruyad atha yady enam sparses upalabheta mrityum saranam prapanno'bhuvam sa tva prati dhaksyatity enam bruyat.

4. *If someone criticizes him for his sibilants, he should say, "I have taken refuge in Prajapati. He will smash you." Then, if someone criticizes him for his consonants, he should say, " I have taken refuge in death and he will burn you to ashes."*

5. sarve svara ghosavanto balavanto vaktavya indre balam dadaniti sarva usmano'grasta anirasta vivrta vaktavyah

prajapater atmanam paridadaniti sarve sparsa lesenanabhinihita vaktavya mrityor atmanam pariharaniti.

5. All the vowels should be uttered in a ringing tone, with great force, thinking, "May I give strength to Indra." All the sibilants should be uttered without swallowing (agrasta) or blurting out, but (in a free flowing manner) with an open passage between the tongue and the hard palate, thinking, "May I dedicate myself to Prajapati." All consonants should be pronounced slowly, without cluttering them, thinking, "May I free myself from Death."

Notes: All the vowels should be uttered with a ringing tone because the Samans addressed to Indra are meant to be sung with force and clarity.

Section 23

The Threefold Nature of Merit, Worlds and Aum

1. trayo dharma skandha yajno'dhyayanam danam iti prathamas tapa eva dvitiyo brahmacarya carya kulavasi tritiyo'tyantam atmanam acaryakule avasadayan sarva ete punyaloka bhavanti brahma samstho'mritatvam eti.

1. These are the three divisions of duty: sacrifice, study and charity. This is the first. Austerity is truly the second and the practice of celibacy (brahmacarya) as a student in the household of a teacher (gurukul) is the third. All these lead to the (ancestral) world of merit; but the one well established in Brahman attains immortality (that is becomes free from births and deaths).

Notes: The first three, duty, sacrifice and study are meant for the householders. Austerity is meant for those who retire to forests or secluded places and practice asceticism as a preparation for the stage of Sanyasa. The practice of celibacy is meant for those who study the Vedas as students under a master of the Vedas. These three categories of people do not attain liberation, but secure a place in the ancestral world by virtue of their good deeds. However, those take to Sanyasa or renunciation and remain firmly established in Brahman reach the world of Brahman and become liberated.

2. prajapatir lokan abhyatapat tebhyo abhitaptebhyas trayi vidya samprasravat, tam abhyatapat tasya abhitaptaya etany aksarani samprasrvanta bhur bhuvah svariti.

2. Prajapati subjected the worlds to the heat of penance (tapas). From them, following the penance thus performed, the triple knowledge emerged. He brooded upon it (the triple knowledge) and from them emerged the three syllables, Bhuh, Bhuvah, and Svah.

Notes: Triple knowledge refers to the triple Vedas. The Vedas were originally three. Hence, in many early Upanishads we do not find reference to the fourth Veda. The three syllables correspond to the three regions, bhuh (the earth), the bhuvah (the mid region) and svah (the sky).

3. tan ayabhyatapat tebhyo'bhitaptebhya aumkarah samprasravat tad yatha sankuna sarvani parnani samtrinnany evam omkarena sarva vak samtrinnomkara evedam sarvam omkara evedam sarvam.

3. He subjected the worlds to the heat of penance (tapas) and from them, following the penance thus performed, emerged the syllable AUM. Just as the stalk extends into all leaves (in the form of midriff), so does AUM extends into all speech (syllables). The syllable AUM is indeed all this, yes, the syllable AUM is all this.

Notes: How does Aum present in all speech? It is because Aum is the sound of breath. And breath is present in all sounds and speech we utter.

Section 24

How To Perform Soma Sacrifices Correctly

1. brahmavadino vadanti yad vasunam pratah savanam rudranam madhyam dinam savanam adityanam ca visvesam ca devanam tritiya savanam.

1. The exponents of Brahman declare that the morning extraction (of the Soma juice) belongs to the Vasus, the midday extraction to the Rudras and the evening extraction to the Adityas and the Visvadevas.

Notes: Savanah is a sacrifice involving the extraction of Soma juice and its offering and drinking. It also refers to ritual bathing or ablution.

2. kva tarhi yajamanasya loka iti sa yastam na vidyat katham kuryad atha vidvan kuryat.

2. Where then is the world (attained by) the sacrificer (through the sacrifice)? Without knowing it how can one perform the sacrifice? Only he who knows it should perform.

Notes: The fruit of the sacrifice goes to the deities mentioned in the previous verse. Then, what is the fate of the one who makes the offering? A sacrificer needs to know the correct answer to this so that he can strive correctly.

3. pura pratar anuvakasyopakaranaj jaghanena garhapatyasyodanmukha upavisya sa vasavam samabhigayati.

3. Before the beginning of the pre-dawn chant, sitting behind the garhyapatya fire, facing the north, he sings the Saman for the Vasus.

Notes: As per the tradition, a brahmana has to maintain three sacrificial fires in his house to perform daily sacrifices, namely Ahvaniya, Daksina and Garhapatya fires. Each has its own significance in the Vedic rituals.

4. lokadvaram apavarnu pasyema tva vayam rajyaya iti.

4. Open the door to the world and let us see you, so that we may gain the kingdom.

5. atha juhoti namo'gnaye prithiviksite lokaksite lokam me yajamanaya vindaisa vai yajamanasya loka etasmi.

5. Then he pours the libation saying, "Salutations to Agni, who dwells upon earth, who dwells in the world. Secure that world for me who is the sacrificer. It is the world of the sacrifice to which I shall go."

6. atra yajamanah parastad ayusah svaha pajahi parigham ity uktvottisthati; tasmai vasavah pratah savanam samprayacchanti.

6. "I shall go there at the end of my life." Then he pours the libation and says, "Take this, and remove the bolt (to the door that leads to the other world)." Having said this, he stands up. For him, the Vasus fulfill (the wish expressed in) the morning extraction.

7. pura madhyam dinasya savanasyopakaranaj jaghanena agnidhriyasyodanmukha upavisya sa raudram samabhigayati.

7. Before the beginning of the midday extraction, sitting behind the Agnidhariya fire, facing north, he sings the Saman meant for the Rudras.

8. lokadvaram apavarnu pasyema tva vayam vairajyaya iti.

8. Open the door to the world (of the sky or the mid region) and let us see you, so that we may gain the kingdom.

9. atha juhoti namo vayave antariksaksite lokaksite lokam me yajamanaya vindaisa vai yajamanasya loka etasmi.

9. Then he pours the libation saying, "Salutations to Vayu, who dwells in the sky, who dwells in the world, secure that world for me who is the sacrificer. It is the world of the sacrifice to which I shall go."

10. atra yajamanah parastad ayusah svahapajahi parigham ity uktvottisthati tasmai rudra madhyan dinam savanam samprayacchanti.

10. *"I shall go there at the end of my life." Then he pours the libation and says, "Take this, and remove the bolt (to the door of the other world)." Having said this, he stands up. For him, the Rudras fulfill (the wis expressed in) the midday extraction.*

11. pura tritiya savanasyopakaranaj jaghanenahavani yasyodanmukha upavisya sa adityamsa vaisvadevam samabhigaya iti.

11. Before the beginning of the third extraction, sitting behind the Ahavaniya fire, facing north, he sings the Saman for the Adityas and Visve Devas.

12. loka dvaram apavarnu pasyema tva vayam svarajyaya iti.

12. "Open the door to the world and let us see you, so that we may gain the kingdom (of heaven)."

13. adityam atha vaisvadevam lokadvaram apavarnu pasyema tva vayam samrajyaya iti.

13. That is the Saman chant for the Adityas. Now, to the Visvadevas, "Open the door to the world and let us see you, so that we may gain the kingdom (of heaven)."

14. atha juhoti nama adityebhyas ca visvebhyas ca devebhyo diviksidbhyo lokaksidbhyo lokam me yajamanaya vindata.

14. Then he pours the libation saying, "Salutations to the Adityas and to the Visvadevas, who dwell in the heaven, who dwell in the world, secure that world for me who is the sacrificer."

15. esa vai yajamanasya loka etasmy atra yajamanah parastad ayusah svaha pahata parigham ity uktvottisthati.

15. "I shall go there at the end of my life." Then he pours the libation and says, "Take this, and remove the bolt (to the door)." Having said this, he stands up.

16. tasma adityas ca visve ca devas tritiya savanam samprayacchanty esa ha vai yajnasya matram veda ya evam veda ya evam veda.

16. For him the Adityas and the Visvadevas fulfill (the wish expressed in) the third extraction. He knows the real purpose of the sacrifice, who knows this, yes, who knows it.

Notes: It is incorrect to presume that all sacrifices are meant for worldly ends. In this section we have seen that these morning, middya and evening prayers associated with the extraction of Soma are meant for attaining liberation.

Chapter 3

Section 1

The Sun as the Honey of Gods - Rigveda

1. aum asau va adityo devamadhu tasya dyaur eva tirascinavamsah antariksam apupah maricayah putrah.

1. Aum! Truly, the sun up there is honey of the gods. Of this, the heaven is the curved-beam (that holds the hive), the sky is the hive and the sun rays are the eggs.

Notes: What is honey in the context of these verses? It is whatever that gives you happiness, pleasure, delight and fulfillment. It is the sweetness of life, which is the result of good actions and pious life. This honey is gathered through the threefold duty mentioned before, namely sacrifice, study and charity in case of householders. Here, the sun is described as the honey of gods, he provides sweetness, strength and vigor to the gods. The sky is compared to the beehive because it is filled to the brim like the honey in a beehive with sweetness, light, vigor and energy of the Sun

2. tasya ye pranco rasmayas ta evasya pracyo madhunadyah rica eva madhukrita rigveda eva puspam ta amrita apasta va eta ricah.

2. The eastern rays of that sun are the honey cells on the eastern side. The Riks (hymns of the Rigveda) are the bees. The Rigveda is the flower. The sacrificial water is the nectar produced by the Riks.

Notes: The hymns of the Rigveda are compared to bees because when they are chanted loudly, they fly in the space, just like bees, gathering the sweetness (merit) and blessings for the sacrificer. The Rigveda itself is the source of the nectar of immortality. The nectar arises in the form of the sacrificial water. By offering it to the sun, a worshipper earns the right to enter the world of immortality.

3. etam rigvedam abhyatapams tasyabhitaptasya yasas teja indriyam viryam annadyam raso'ajayata.

3. They (the bees) performed penance (tapas) on the Rigveda (the flower). From that penance emerged as its sap fame, vigor, sense-organs, semen, food and health.

Notes: The rasah or the sap is the honey arising from the pressing of the Rigveda.

4. tad vyaksarat tad adityam abhito'srayat tad va etad yad etad adityasya rohitam rupam.

4. It (the sap) flowed out and took refuge in the Sun. Truly, that is what is in the sun in the form of red color.

Section 2

The Sun as the Honey of Gods - Yajurveda

1. atha ye'asya daksina rasmayas ta evasya daksina madhu nadyo yajumsy eva madhukrito yajurveda eva puspam ta amrita apah.

1. Now, the southern rays of that sun are the honey cells on the southern side. The Yajus (hymns of the Yajurveda) are the bees. The Yajurveda is the flower. The sacrificial water is the nectar produced by the Yajus.

2. tani va etani yajumsyetam yajurvedam abhyatapams tasyabhitaptasya yasas teja indriyam viryam annadyam rasojayata.

2. They (the bees) performed penance (tapas) on the Yajurveda (the flower). From that penance emerged as its sap (honey) fame, vigor, sense-organs, semen, food and health.

3. tad vyaksarat tad adityam abhito'srayat tad va etad yad etad adityasya suklam rupam.

3. It (the sap) flowed out and took refuge in the Sun. Truly, that is what is in the sun in the form of white color.

Section 3

The Sun as the Honey of Gods - Samaveda

1. atha ye.asya pratyanco rasmayasta evasya praticyo madhunadyah samany eva madhukritah samaveda eva puspam ta amrita apah.

1. The western rays of that sun are the honey cells on the western side. The Samans (hymns of the Yajurveda) are the bees. The Samaveda is the flower. The sacrificial water is the nectar produced by the Samans (bees).

2. tani va etani samany etam samavedam abhyatapams tasyabhitaptasya yasas teja indriyam viryam annadyam raso'ajayata.

2. They (the bees) performed penance (tapas) on the Samaveda (the flower). From that penance emerged as its sap (honey) fame, vigor, sense-organs, semen, food and health.

3. tad vyaksarat tad adityam abhito'srayat tad va etad yad etad adityasya krisnam rupam.

3. It (the sap) flowed out and took refuge in the Sun. Truly, that is what is in the sun in the form of dark color.

Section 4

The Sun as the Honey of Gods - Atharvaveda

1. atha ye'asyodanco rasmayas ta evasyodicyo madhunadyo'tharvangirasa eva madhu krita itihasa puranam puspam ta amrita apah.

1. Now, the northern rays of that sun are the honey cells on the northern side. The Atharvans (hymns of the Yajurveda) and the Angirasas are the bees. The Atharvaveda is the flower. The sacrificial water is the nectar produced by the Atharvans (bees).

2. te va ete'atharvangirasa etad itihasa puranam abhyatapams tasyabhitaptasya yasasteja indriyam viryam annady amraso'ajayata.

2. They (the bees) performed penance (tapas) on the Atharvaveda (the flower). From that penance emerged as its sap (honey) fame, vigor, sense-organs, semen, food and health.

3. tad vyaksarat tad adityam abhito'srayat tad va etad yad etad adityasya param krisnam rupam.

3. It (the sap) flowed out and took refuge in the Sun. Truly, that is what is in the sun in the form of a very dark color.

Notes: The colors of the sap produced from the pressing of the Rigveda, Yajurveda, Samaveda and Atharvaveda, which flowed into the sun, were red, white, black and very black respectively. These four represent the color of the morning sun, the midday sun, the twilight sun and the night. They also symbolize the practice of singing the hymns from the four Vedas during different times of the day. We may also regard them as the representative colors of the four sphere or worlds starting from the earth, namely the mortal world, the mid-region, the world of gods and the immortal heaven of Brahman.

Section 5

The Sun as the Honey of Gods - The Vedas

1. atha ye'asyordhva rasmayas ta evasyordhva madhunadyo guhya evadesa madhukrito brahmaiva puspam ta amrita apah.

1. Now, its upward rays are the upper honey cells. The secret teachings are the bees, Brahman is verily the flower and water is the nectar.

2. te va ete guhya adesa etad brahmabhyatapams tasyabhi-taptasya yasas teja indriyam viryam annadyam raso'ajayata.

2. They (the bees) performed penance (tapas) on Brahman (the flower). From that penance emerged as its sap (honey) fame, vigor, sense-organs, semen, food and health.

3. tad vyaksarat tad adityam abhito'srayat tad va etad yad etad adityasya madhye ksobhata iva.

3. It (the sap) flowed out and took refuge in the Sun. Truly, that is what flickers in the middle of the sun.

4. te va ete rasanam rasa veda hi rasah tesam ete rasah tani va etany amritanam amritani veda hy amritah tesam etany amritani.

4. Truly, these are the very saps of the saps. The Vedas are the saps and these are their saps. They are indeed the immortal nectars of the immortal nectars. The Vedas are indeed the immortal nectars and these are their immortal nectars.

Notes: The Upanishads constitute the secret teachings of the Vedas. They are truly the essence of the Vedas. Their knowledge leads to immortality. Whatever one can achieve through the chanting of the Vedic hymns during the sacrificial ceremonies, may also be achieved through the study of the Upanishads and the knowledge of Brahman. In the previous verses, the emphasis was on the importance of sacrificial actions. Here it is on the knowledge of Brahman contained in the Upanishads. Spiritual knowledge is subtle knowledge hidden in the Vedas. Hence it is considered the essence of the essences.

Section 6

The Vasus as the Nectar

1. tad yat prathamam amritam tad vasava upajivanty agnina mukhena na vai deva asnanti na pibanty etad evamritam dristva tripyanti.

1. That which is the first nectar, on that the Vasus (serpents) live with fire in their mouths. Truly these deities do not eat or drink, but are content with seeing the nectar.

Notes: The Vasus are described as the attendant deities of Indra, and in some scriptures, of Vishnu. They are said to be eight in number. Some lists include gods such as Agni, Prithvi, Vayu, and Soma also as Vasus.

2. ta etad eva rupam abhisam visanty etasmad rupad udyanti.

2. They enter into that (red) form, and with that form they rise.

3. sa ya etad evam amritam veda vasunam evaiko bhutvagninaiva mukhenaitad evamritam dristva tripyati sa ya etad eva rupam abhisamvisaty etasmad rupad udeti.

3. He who thus knows this nectar, becomes one of the Vasus, and with fire in the mouth, remains satisfied with seeing the nectar; and he too having entered that form arises from that form.

4. sa yavad adityah purastad udeta pascad astam eta vasunam eva tavad adhipatyam svarajyam paryeta.

4. As long as the sun rises in the east and sets in the west, so long will he enjoy the lordship and the kingdom of the Vasus.

Section 7
The Rudras as the Nectar

1. atha yad dvitiyam amritam tad rudra upajivantindrena mukhena na vai deva asnanti na pibanty etad evamritam dristva tripyanti.

1. That which is the second nectar, on that the Rudras (storm gods) live with the lightning of Indra in their mouths. Truly these deities do not eat or drink, but are content with seeing the nectar.

Notes: The Rudras are described in the Rigveda as the loyal companions of Rudra. Rudra literally means he who make others cry. They are variously described in the Vedas as the storm gods, the gods of vital breaths, who rule the middy sky and the middle part of the body. In the human body, they reside in the veins of the eye. In creation, they reside in the sky. They bring down tears from the eyes in case of beings and rains from the sky in case of the world.

2. ta etad eva rupam abhisam visanty etasmad rupad udyanti.

2. They enter into that form, and with that form they rise.

3. sa ya etad evam amritam veda rudranam evaiko bhutvendrenaiva mukhenaitad evamritam dristva tripyati sa etad eva rupam abhisamvisaty etasmad rupad udeti.

3. He who thus knows this nectar, becomes one of the Rudras, and with lightning in the mouth, remains satisfied with seeing the nectar; and he too having entered that form arises from that form.

4. sa yavad adityah purastad udeta pascad astam eta dvis tavad daksinata udetottarato'stam eta rudranam eva tavad adhipatyam svarajyam paryeta.

4. As long as the sun rises in the east and sets in the west, so long will he enjoy the lordship and the kingdom of the Rudras.

Section 8

The Adityas as the Nectar

1. atha yat tritiyam amritam tad aditya upajivanti varunena mukhena na vai deva asnanti na pibanty etad evamritam dristva tripyanti.

1. That which is the third nectar, on that the Adityas (solar gods) live with Varuna in their mouths. Truly these deities do not eat or drink, but are content with seeing the nectar.

Notes: The Adityas are the solar deities, said to be the sons of Aditi, the mother of gods. There are twelve in number.

2. ta etad eva rupam abhisam visanty etasmad rupad udyanti.

2. They enter into that form, and with that form they rise.

3. sa ya etad evam amritam vedadityanam evaiko bhutva varunenaiva mukhenaitad evamritam dristva tripyati sa etadeva rupam abhisamvisaty etasmad rupad udeti.

3. He who thus knows this nectar, becomes one of the Adityas, and with Varuna in the mouth, remains satisfied with seeing the nectar; and he too having entered that form arises from that form.

4. sa yavadadityo daksinata udetottarato'stam eta dvis tavat pascad udeta purastad astam etadityanam eva tavad adhipatyam svarajyam paryeta.

4. As long as the sun rises in the east and sets in the west, so long will he enjoy the lordship and the kingdom of the Adityas.

Section 9

The Maruts as the Nectar

1. atha yac caturtham amritam tan maruta upajivanti somena mukhena na vai deva asnanti na pibanty etad evamritam dristva tripyanti.

1. That which is the fourth nectar, on that the Maruts (wind gods) live with Soma in their mouths. Truly these deities do not eat or drink, but are content with seeing the nectar.

Notes: The Maruts are also storm gods or wind gods. They are attendants of Indra, the lord of the sky. They are said to be twenty seven, who are described in the Rigveda as violent and aggressive, with iron teeth, wielding golden weapons and riding golden cariots.

2. ta etad eva rupam abhisamvisanty etasmad rupad udyanti.

2. They enter into that form, and with that form they rise.

3. sa ya etad evam amritam veda marutam evaiko bhutva somena iva mukhenaitad evamritam dristva tripyati sa etad eva rupam abhisamvisaty etasmad rupad udeti.

3. He who thus knows this nectar, becomes one of the Maruts, and with Soma in the mouth, remains satisfied with seeing the nectar; and he too having entered that form arises from that form.

4. sa yavad adityah pascad udeta purastad astam eta dvistavad uttarata udeta daksinato'stam eta marutam eva tavad adhipatym svarajyam paryeta.

4. As long as the sun rises in the east and sets in the west, so long will he enjoy the lordship and the kingdom of the Maruts.

Section 10
The Sadhyas as the Nectar

1. atha yat pancamam amritam tat sadhya upajivanti brahmana mukhena na vai deva asnanti na pibanty etad evamritam dristva tripyanti.

1. That which is the fourth nectar, on that the Sadhyas live with Brahma in their mouths. Truly these deities do not eat or drink, but are content with seeing the nectar.

Notes: The Sadhyas are gods of commonality, who, according to the Mahabharata, were said to be born from Cosmic Person (Virat). They are described in the Vishnupurana as the grand children of Daksha Prajapati. They are variously described as the attendant deities of Indra and worshippers of Lord Siva.

2. ta etad eva rupam abhisam visanty etasmad rupad udyanti.

2. They enter into that form, and with that form they rise.

3. sa ya etad evam amritam veda sadhyanam evaiko bhutva brahmanaiva mukhenaitad evamritam dristva tripyati sa etadeva rupam abhisamvisaty etasmad rupad udeti.

3. He who thus knows this nectar, becomes one of the Sadhyas, and with Brahma in the mouth, remains satisfied with seeing the nectar; and he too having entered that form arises from that form.

4. sa yavad aditya uttarata udeta daksinato'stam eta dvistavad urdhvam udetavan astam eta sadhyanam eva tavad adhipatyam svarajyam paryeta.

4. As long as the sun rises in the east and sets in the west, so long will he enjoy the lordship and the kingdom of the Sadhyas.

Section 11
The Secret Teaching of Brahma

1. atha tata urdhva udetya naivod eta nastam eta ekala eva madhye sthata tadesa slokah.

1. Now, having risen high above, he neither rises nor falls. He remains in the middle; and regarding this there is this verse...

2. na vai tatra na nimloca nodiyaya kadacana; devas tenaham satyena ma viradhisi brahmaneti.

2. "It is not so (as it is here). There he does not rise, does not set even a little. O gods, by this truth may I not lose my position as a Brahmana."

Notes: The sun rises and sets in our world. We have days and nights, and death and birth because everything here is impermanent. It is not so in the immortal world of Brahman. There the sun neither rises nor sets and there is neither death nor rebirth. Everything is constant and fixed.

3. na ha va asma udeti na nimlocati sakrid diva haivasmai bhavati ya etam evam brahmopanisadam veda.

3. It does not rise and does not set, but remains as the day forever for him who knows thus this secret teaching of Brahma.

Notes: The divisions of time and duality do not exist in the realm of Brahman. Hence those who ascend into that world remain forever in light and bliss.

4. tadd haitad brahma prajapataya uvaca prajapatir manave manuh prajabhyah tadd haitad uddalakayarunaye jyesthaya putraya pita brahma provaca.

5. Brahma revealed this (knowledge of Brahman) to Prajapati, Prajapati to Manu, Manu to his progeny. This knowledge of Brahman was revealed to his eldest son, Uddalaka Aruni, by his father.

5. idam vava taj jyesthaya putraya pita brahma prabruyat pranayyaya vantevasine.

5. This should be taught only by a father who is like Brahma to his eldest son or to a meritorious student.

6. nanyasmai kasmai cana yady apy asma imam adbhih parigrihitam dhanasya purnam dadyad etad eva tato bhuya ity etad eva tato bhuya iti.

6. But not to anyone else even if he has been offered in charity the whole treasure-filled world surrounded by the oceans, saying, "Indeed this is greater than that, yes, this is greater than that."

Section 12

The Greatness of Gayatri

1. gayatri va idam sarvam bhutam yad idam kim ca vag vai gayatri vagva idam sarvam bhutam gayati ca trayate ca.

1. Truly, Gayatri is all this existence whatsoever that is here. Speech indeed is Gayatri for speech only sings and protects all this that exists here.

Notes: Verses such as these allude to the belief that the source of all manifestation was sound. Gayatri is not a reference to a particular mantra but a reference to the Gayatri meter which is the meter of all meters. It is the Brahman among the meters and the source of all Samans. As Shankara commented, it is the chosen vehicle for the teaching of Brahman. It is Gayatri, which carries our offerings to gods and it is Gayatri, which carries our prayers to the sun or Savitur. Speech is Gayatri because, like all the chants, it arises from speech only. All the hymns of the Vedas arise from speech only because with the help of speech only we are able to sing and chant. Speech protects because with the help of speech only we are able to defend ourselves and seek the protection of gods.

2. ya vai sa gayatriyam vava sa yeyam prithivy asyam hidam sarvam bhutam pratishthitam etam eva natisiyate.

2. That which is Gayatri, truly, is also the earth for whatever that exists here rests upon this only, but not beyond.

Notes: Gayatri is meant for the people of the earth. It rests upon earth, means its existence is here in this world, in the speech of the people, but not elsewhere. Since it is an earthly prayer, the earth only is its resting ground.

3. ya vai sa prithiviyam vava sa yadidam asmin puruse sariram asmin hime pranah pratishthita etad eva natisiyante.

3. That which is the earth, truly, is that which is the body of the Purusha, for it is in that the breath rests, but not beyond.

Notes: Gayatri rests in the breath of a being. Hence, just Gayatri is the earth, it is also the body.

4. yadvai tat puruse sariram idam vava tad yad idam asminn antah puruse hridayam asmin hime pranah pratisthita etad eva natisiyante.

4. That which is the body of the Purusha, truly, is that which is the heart in the Purusha, for it is in the heart the breath rests but not beyond.

5. saisa catuspada sadvidha gayatri tad etad ricabhyanuktam.

5. That Gayatri has four feet and six forms, thus it has been stated by a verse in the Rigveda.

Notes: Traditionally, it is believed that Gayatri meter (Chandas) has three feet of eight syllable each. However, the Chandogya Upanishad says it has four feet of six syllables each. According to Shankara, the six syllables represent the six manifestations, namely Speech, Purusha, the Earth, Body, Heart and the Breath. The Upanishad further states that from of Gayatri that we know, containing four feet of 24 syllables is actually one feet of Brahman or Purusha. The other three are in heaven. This is explained in the following verses.

6. etavan asya mahima tato jyayams ca purusah; pado'sya sarva bhutani tripad asyamritam diviti.

6. "Such is its greatness, greater than that is the Purusha. All beings are His one foot (or His one fourth). The (remaining) three are in the immortal heaven.

Notes: Gayatri is just not a meter. It is the four footed Brahman or Purusha Himself. Of that four feet, the entire creation constitute His one foot. The Gayatri that we sing here, having four feet of six syllables, has its support in speech. It represents just one foot of Para Brahman Gayatri. The other three have their support in Purusha and exist in the immortal heaven.

7. yadvai tad brahmetidam vava tadyoyam bahirdha purusad akaso yo vai sa bahirdha purusad akasah.

7. That which is Brahman, truly, is that space which is outside of Purusha; that space indeed is outside of Purusha

8. ayam vava sa yo'yamantah purusa akaso yo vai so'antah purusa akasah.

8. That (space outside of Purusha) is indeed whatever space within the Purusha, yes, whatever space that lies within the Purusha

9. ayam vava sa yo'yam antar hridaya akasas tad etat purnam apravarti purnam apravartinim sriyam labhate ya evam veda.

9. *That is the same as whatever space is within the heart. That is full and unchanging. He who knows it thus, attains full and unchanging prosperity.*

Section 13

The Five Openings of the Heart

1. tasya ha va etasya hridayasya panca devasusayah sa yo'sya pran susih sa pranan tac caksuh sa adityas tad etat tejo'nn-adyam ity upasita tejasvy annado bhavati ya evam veda.

1. *In this heart, there are five openings for the gods. Its eastern opening is Prana (in-breath or up-breath). That is the eye, that is the sun. One should meditate upon it as vigor and health. He who knows this becomes vigorous and healthy.*

Notes: This is about heart meditation upon Gayatri Brahman. The heart is where the Self gathers up the breaths before departing. The openings are the gates or doors through which he departs to the higher worlds. They are guarded by different breaths, such as prana, which is mentioned here as the protector of the eastern gate. By meditating upon this eastern gate, which leads to the sun, who is the provider of food and energy, one develops vigor and health. Similarly meditation upon different gates and different aspects of Gayatri Brahman leads to different results, which are explained in the subsequent verses.

2. atha yo'sya daksinah susih sa vyanah tac crotram, sa candramah tad etac cris ca yasas cety upasita sriman yasasvi bhavati ya evam veda.

2. *Now, its southern opening is Vyana (diffused breath). That is the ear, that is the moon. One should meditate upon it as prosperity and fame. He who knows this becomes prosperous and famous.*

3. atha yo'sya pratyan susih so'apanah sa vak so'agnih tad etad brahmavarcasam annadyam ity upasita brahma varcasy annado bhavati ya evam veda.

3. *Now, its western opening is Apana (down breath). That is the speech, that is the Fire. One should meditate upon it as the luster of Brahman and health. He who knows this becomes lustrous with the radiance of Brahman and healthy.*

4. atha yo'syodan susih sa samanah tan manah sa parjanyah tad etad kirtis ca vyustis cety upasita kirtiman vyustiman bhavati ya evam veda.

4. *Now, its northern opening is Samana (equalizing breath). That is the mind, that is Parjanyah (rain). One should meditate upon it as fame and prosperity. He who knows this becomes famous and prosperous.*

Note: vyusti means prosperity or praise. It is translated by some as beauty.

5. atha yo'syordhvah susih sa udanah sa vayuh sa akasas tad etad ojas ca mahas cety upasita ojasvi mahasvan bhavati ya evam veda.

5. *Now, its upper opening is Udana (out breath). That is the air, that is Space. One should meditate upon it as strength and greatness. He who knows this becomes strong and great.*

6. te va ete panca brahma purusah svargasya lokasya dvarapah sa ya etan evam panca brahmapurusan svargasya lokasya dvarapan veda asya kule viro jayate pratipadyate svargam lokam, ya etan evam panca brahmapurusan svargasya lokasya dvarapan veda.

6. *These, indeed, are the five Brahma Beings, doorkeepers of the heavenly world. He who knows these Brahma Being, the doorkeepers of the heavenly world, a hero is born in his family. He who knows these Brahma Beings, the doorkeepers of the heavenly world, himself attains the heavenly world.*

7. atha yad atah paro divo jyotir dipyate visvatah prsthesu, sarvatah prsthesu anuttamesuttamesu lokesu, idam vava tad yad idam asminn antah purse jyotih.

7. *Now, that light which shines brightly above the heaven, above the universe, above all, higher than the highest worlds, it is the same which is here within the person.*

Notes: The light of Brahman is the same as the light of the Self. One shines brightly high above and one shines brightly within.

8. tasyaisa dristih yatritad asmin sarire samsparsenosnimanam vijanati tasyaisa srutih yatraitat karnav apigrihya ninadam iva nadathur ivagner iva jvalata upasrinoti tad etad dristam ca srutam cety upasita caksus yah sruto bhavati ya evam veda ya evam veda.

8. *They are perceived thus: on touching the body one has the feeling of the warmth; on closing the ears one hears a rumbling, bellowing or crackling sound. One should meditate upon this as the seen and heard.*

He who knows this, will be perceived by others through their eyes and ears as beautiful and renowned, yes he who knows thus.

Section 14

Sandilya Vidya Regarding Brahman and Self

1. sarvam khalv idam brahma tajjalan iti santa upasita atha khalu kratumayah purusah yatha kratur asmiml loke puruso bhavati that etah pretya bhavati sa kratum kurvita.

1. Truly, all this here is Brahman. One should meditate upon it as tajjalan (the origin, continuation and the dissolution of the world). Now a person is indeed made of actions. As his actions in this world are, so does he become upon departing from here. Therefore let him perform (sacrificial) actions.

Notes: So far the emphasis was on the aspects of Brahman or His creation. Here the emphasis is directly upon Brahman Himself. Everything arises and dissolves in Brahman only. A person's life upon earth is determined by his actions, desires and intentions. As one thinks and acts, so does one become and so does become his world hereafter. Some translate kratu as will or resolve and interpret this verse accordingly. It seems the word is used here to denote sacrificial actions or obligatory duties performed out of desires, not to express mere exercise of will or resolve. Under the influence of desires, a person's will or resolve to do something or to attain something may actually becomes weak under some circumstances.

2. manomayah prana sariro bharupah satyasamkalpa akasatma sarvakarma sarvakamah sarvagandhah sarvarasah sarvam idam abhyatto'vaky anadarah.

2. Made of mental and breath bodies, with the form of light, with truthful resolve, with a self like the space, the source of all actions, all desires, all odors, all tastes, pervading all this here, without speech and without concern...

3. esa ma atmantar hridaye'aniyan vriher va yavad va sarsapad va syamakad va syamaka tandulad va isa ma atmantar hridaye jyayan prithivya jyayan antariksaj jyayan divah jyayanebhyo lokebhyah.

3. This (what has been described above) is my Self within my heart, smaller than a grain of rice, than a corn of barely, than a mustard seed, than a grain of millet or the kernel of a grain of millet. This is my Self within my heart, greater than the earth, greater than the sky, greater than the heaven, greater than these worlds.

4. sarva karma sarva kamah sarvagandhah sarvarasah sarvam idam abhyatto'vaky anadara esa ma atmantar hridaya etad brahma itam itah pretyabhisam bhavitasmiti yasya syat addha na vicikitsastiti ha smaha sandilyah sandilyah.

4. *All actions, all desires, all odors, all tastes, pervading all this, without speech and without concern, this is my self within my heart. He is that Brahman. Into him, upon departing from here, I shall enter. He who believes in this will not suffer from doubt. So said, Sandilya, yes thus he said.*

Notes: The doctrine described in this section is known as Sandilya Vidya. Its salient features are: 1. Brahman is the source of all. 2. Actions determine a person's life. 3. The Self is the same as Brahman. 4. The Self finally becomes one with Brahman.

Section 15
Brahman as the Imperishable Chest

1. antariksodarah koso bhumi budhno na jiryati diso hyasya sraktayo dyaur asyottaram bilam sa esa koso vasudhanas tasmin visvam idam sritam.

1. *With the atmosphere as its interior and the earth as its base, the chest does not decay. The quarters are its corners, the heaven is its lid above. That chest contains all the riches of the universe and in that rest all that is here.*

Notes: The whole creation, with the heaven as the upper lid, the mid-region as the interior and the earth as the base is compared to a treasure chest. What does it hold? It holds all the riches and the wealth of creation.

2. tasya praci dig juhur nama sahamana nama daksina rajni nama pratici subhuta namodici tasam vayur vatsah sa ya etam evam vayum disam vatsam veda na putrarodam roditi so'aham etam evam vayum disam vatsam veda ma putrarodam rudam.

2. *Its eastern quarter is called Juhu, the southern one Sahanama, the western one Rajni, and the northern one Subhuta. Of these, the air is the child. He who knows that this wind is the son of the quarters never weeps for his son. Truly, I know that the wind is the son of the quarters; (therefore) may I never weep for my son.*

Notes: Juhu is the sacrificial ladle with which the offerings are poured (juhoti) into the fire. According to Sankara the eastern quarter is called Juhu because the offerings are made towards the east. The southern direction is known as Sahamana. The world of Yama is located in the south where sinners go after departing from here to suffer punishments for their sinful actions. The western direction is known as Rajni because it is presided over by Varuna, the king (raja) or because the western sky bears red color during dusk. The northern direction is known as Subhuta because it is presided over by auspicious (su) and prosperous beings such as Isvara and Kubera. The person who knows that the wind is the son of the directions will never weep for his son because he knows how to secure longevity to his son by praying to the chest, using the prayers that are described in the subsequent verses.

3. aristam kosam prapadye 'muna'muna'muna pranam prapadye 'muna'muna'muna bhuh prapadye 'muna'muna'muna bhuvah prapadye 'muna'muna'muna svah prapadye 'muna'muna'muna.

3. I take refuge in the imperishable chest for so and so, so and so, so and so. I take refuge in the bhuh (earth) for so and so, so and so, so and so. I take refuge in the bhuvah (the mid region) for so and so, so and so, so and so. I take refuge in the Svah (heaven) for so and so, so and so, so and so.

Note: So and so should be substituted with the name of the son for whom the prayer is uttered.

4. sa yad avocam pranam prapadya iti prano va idam sarvam bhutam yad idam kim ca tam eva tat prapatsi.

4. When I said, "I take refuge in breath," breath is truly all this here that exists, whatever there is. It was in this I took refuge.

5. atha yad avocam bhuh prapadya iti prithivim prapadye antariksam prapadye divam prapadya ity eva tad avocam.

5. When I said, "I take refuge in Bhuh," what I meant was, "I take refuge in the earth, I take refuge in the atmosphere, I take refuge in the heaven."

6. atha yad avocam bhuvah prapadya ity agnim prapadye vayum prapadya adityam prapadya ity eva tada vocam.

6. When I said, "I take refuge in Bhuvah," what I meant was, "I take refuge in the fire, I take refuge in the air, I take refuge in the sun."

7. atha yada vocam svah prapadya ity rigvedam prapadye yajurvedam prapadye samavedam prapadya ity eva tada vocam tada vocam.

7. When I said, "I take refuge in Svah," what I meant was, "I take refuge in the Rigveda, I take refuge in the Yajurveda, I take refuge in the Samaveda."

Section 16

Daily Sacrifices Compared to Phases of Life

1. puruso vava yajnah tasya yani catur vimsati varsani tat pratah savanam catur vimsaty aksara gayatri gayatram pratah savanam tad asya vasavo'nvayattah prana vava vasavah ete hidam sarvam vasayanti.

1. Purusha, indeed, is the Sacrifice. Of him, his first twenty four years constitute the morning offering; the Gayatri (meter) has twenty-four letters; and Gayatri goes with the morning offering. The Vasus are related to this (offering) only. Indeed, the vital breaths are the Vasus, for it is they who cause everything here to exist.

Notes: Purusha, the person, is a sacrifice, in which he sacrifices the different phases of his own life as an offering. The whole life-span of a human being is compared to one day. The number 24 is specified because Gayatra Saman is chanted during morning offerings and it has 24 syllables. The morning offerings are made to Vasus, who are compared to the breaths in the body.

2. tam ced etasmin vayasi kim cid upatapet sa bruyat prana vasava idam me pratahsavanam madhyamdinam savanam anusamtanuteti maham prananam vasunam madhye yajno vilopsiyety uddhaiva tata ety agado ha bhavati.

2. In this age, if he suffers from any sickness, let him say, "O breaths, O Vasus, carry forward this morning offering of mine until the midday offering. May, I, the Sacrifice, is not cut off from the breaths and the Vasus. Then he recovers from his sickness and becomes full.

3. atha yani catuscatvarimsad varsani tan madhyam dinam savanam catus catvarimsad aksara tristup traistubham madhyam dinam savanam tad asya rudra anvayattah prana vava rudra ete hidam sarvam rodayanti.

3. Now, the next forty-four years constitute his middy offering; the Tristubh meter has forty-four letters; and Tristubh goes with midday offering. The Rudras are related to this (offering) only. Indeed, the vital breaths are the Rudras for it is they who cause everything here to cry.

Notes: According to Shankara, in this phase offerings have to be made to the Rudras because people tend to be cruel in the middle age.

4. tam ced etasmin vayasi kim cid upatapet sa bruyat prana rudra idam me madhyam dinam savanam tritiya savanam

anusamtanuteti maham prananam rudranam madhye yajno vilopsiyety udd haiva tata ety agado ha bhavati.

4. *In this age, if he suffers from any sickness, let him say, "O breaths, O Rudras, carry forward this morning offering of mine until the third daily offering. May, I, the Sacrifice, is not cut off from the breaths and the Rudras. Then he recovers from his sickness and becomes full.*

5. atha yany asta catvarimsad varsani tat tritiya savanam astacatvarimsad aksara jagati jagatam tritiya savanam tad asya ditya anvayattah prana vavaditya ete hidam sarvama dadate.

5. *Now, the next forty-eight years constitute his third daily offering; the Jagati meter has forty-eight letters; and Jatati goes with third daily offering. The Adityas are related to this (offering) only. Indeed, the vital breaths are the Adityas for it is they who take back all this here.*

6. tam ced etasmin vayasi kim cid upatapet sa bruyat prana aditya idam me tritiya savanam ayur anu samtanuteti maham prananam adityanam madhye yajno vilopsiyety udd haiva tata ety agado haiva bhavati.

6. *In this age if he suffers from any sickness, let him say, "O breaths, O Adityas, carry forward this morning offering of mine to the full span of life. May, I, the Sacrifice, is not cut off from the breaths and the Adityas. Then he recovers from his sickness and becomes full.*

7. etaddha sma vai tad vidvan aha mahidasa aitareyah sa kim ma etad upatapasi yo'ham anena na presyamiti sa ha sodasam varsasatam ajivat pra ha sodasam varsa satam jivati ya evam veda.

7. *Surely, this was what Mahidasa meant when he said, "Why do you afflict me thus when I am not going to die by it?" He lived one hundred and sixteen years. He, too, who knows this lives up to one hundred and sixteen years.*

Notes: Life is one long sacrifice. If a person lives a disciplined and virtuous life, performs his sacrificial duties and attends to his obligations and responsibilities that are specific to his profession or occupation, he has greater chances of living the full span of his life and attain his desired ends. This is the central theme of this section.

Section 17

The Life of a Person as a Sacrifice

1. sa yad asisisati yat pipasati yan na ramate ta asya diksah.

1. When one hungers, thirsts and abstains from pleasure, these are initiatory rites of the sacrifice.

Notes: These comparisons are based upon the same analogy that a human being is a sacrifice and his life is an offering. In the previous section the comparison was regarding the phases of life. Here it is regarding the actions. Initiatory rites involving fasting etc., cause pain and bodily discomfort. Hence painful experiences such as hunger, thirst and abstaining from pleasure are compared to them.

2. atha yad asnati yat pibati yad ramate tad upasadair eti.

2. When one eats, drinks and enjoys it is like one is observing the Upasadas.

Notes: In the Upasada ceremony, the worshippers are allowed to drink milk, which provides the much needed relief from the discomfort experienced during the initiatory rites. Hence, it is compared to eating, drinking and enjoying.

3. atha yad dhasati yaj jaksati yan maithunam carati stutasastrair eva tadeti.

3. When one laughs, eats and practices coitus, it is like one is chanting and reciting the Stuta and Sastra hymns.

Notes: The recitation of stuta hymns is accompanied by some singing and dancing. Hence they are compared to laughing, eating and dallying.

4. atha yat tapo danam arjavam ahimsa satyavacanam iti ta asya daksinah.

4. Austerity, charity, straightforwardness, non-injury and truthfulness, these are the gifts (earned by the sacrificer).

Notes: These are the results or the merit of a sacrifice. Hence, they are compared to the fee offered to the priests who perform the sacrifice. These are the results of good karmas, which ensure a good birth in the next life.

5. tasmad ahuh sosyaty asosteti punar utpadanam evasya tan maranam evavabhrithah.

5. Therefore, when they say, "shall give birth" and "has given birth," it is his rebirth. His death is the Avabhritha ceremony.

Notes: Sosyati and asosta are ritual terms related to pressing and extracting the soma juice during a soma sacrifice. They are used here to denote the conception and rebirth of a person in the sacrifice of life mentioned in the previous section (16.1).

6. tadd haitad ghora angirasah krisnaya devakiputra-yoktvovaca apipasa eva sa babhuva so'antavelayam etat trayam pratipadyetaksitam asi acyutam asi pranasamsitamasiti tatraite dve ricau bhavatah.

6. *After communicating this to Krishna, the son of Devaki, Ghora Angirasa also said the following, as he became free from thirst, "When the end approaches, one should take refuge in these three, 'You are imperishable (akistamasi); you are unchangeable (acyutamasi); and you are the very essence of the breath (pranasamsitamasi).'" On this there are these two verses from the Rigveda.*

7. ad itpratnasya retasah ud vayam tamasaspari jyotih pasyanta uttaram svah pasyanta uttaram devam devatra suryam aganma jyotir uttamam iti jyotir uttamam iti.

7. *Then they see the first morning germ of light that shines high above the sky. Perceiving the supreme light above the darkness (the seers say this) - seeing this light as our own, we reached the Sun, the god of gods, the highest light, yes the highest light.*

Notes: The first morning light emanating from the sun has been eulogized in the two verses (8.6.30 and 1.50.10) of the Rigveda described above. In the Vedic tradition, the Sun symbolizes Brahman, the God of gods, and the immortal world. Those who attain it would never return and take birth again. How is it attained? This is answered here. The sun is attained not physically but by realizing or seeing (as the seers have seen) that the Sun shining above the darkness and the Self shining within oneself are one and the same. Those who perform the sacrifice of life attain this light by reaching the sun.

Section 18
Twofold Meditation Upon Brahman

1. mano brahmety upasitety adhyatmam athadhi daivatam akaso brahmety ubhayam adistam bhavaty adhyatmam ca dhi daivatam ca.

1. *Meditating upon Brahman within the mind, this is (meditating) upon the Self (body). Meditating upon the sky as Brahman, this is (meditating) upon the gods. Thus (meditating) upon the Self (body) and meditating upon gods, this is said to be the twofold instruction.*

Notes: Adhi is a prefix to verbs. It means over, above or upon. Adhyatma means with regard to oneself or one's own body. Adhidaivata means with regard to the gods or the Divine Self. Adhyatmic meditation is practiced in the mind. The mind may be focused during meditation either upon the body or upon the Self. Adhyatmic meditation become adhidavic when we focus upon the organs in the body, instead of the whole body. The organs in the body are considered divinities. Therefore meditating upon the parts of body and meditating upon the gods mean the same.

2. tad etac catuspad brahma vak padah pranah padas caksuh padah srotram pada ity adhyatmam athadhidaivatam agnih

pado vayuh pada adityah pado disah pada ity ubhayam evadistam bhavaty adhyatmam caivadhidaivatam ca.

2. That Brahman (body) has four feet (quarters). Speech is one foot, breath is one foot, the eye is one foot, the ear is one foot. This is about the body. Now, with reference to the gods, Agni (fire) is one foot, Vayu (air) is one foot, Aditya (the sun) is one foot, the directions are one foot. This is the twofold instruction about the body and the gods.

Notes: Whether it is with regard to the horse sacrifice in the Brihadaranyaka Upanishad, here or elsewhere, in the Upanishads Brahman is generally described as a Cosmic Being having four feet (catuspad).

3. vag eva brahmanas caturthah padah so'agnina jyotisa bhati ca tapati ca bhati ca tapati ca kirtya yasasa brahma varcasena ya evam veda.

3. Speech indeed is the fourth foot of Brahman (the body). It shines and warms up with the light of Agni (fire). He who knows this, shines and warms up with name, fame and the luster of Brahman.

4. prana eva brahmanas caturthah padah sa vayuna jyotisa bhati ca tapati c bhati ca tapati ca kirtya yasasa brahma varcasena ya evam veda.

4. Breath indeed is the fourth foot of Brahman (the body). It shines and warms up with the light of Vayu (air). He who knows this, shines and warms up with name, fame and the luster of Brahman.

5. caksur eva brahmanas caturthah padah sa adityena jyotisa bhati ca tapati ca bhati ca tapati ca kirtya yasasa brahma varcasena ya evam veda.

5. The eye indeed is the fourth foot of Brahman (the body). It shines and warms up with the light of Aditya (the fire). He who knows this, shines and warms up with name, fame and the luster of Brahman.

6. srotram eva brahmanas caturthah padah sa digbhir jyotisa bhati ca tapati ca bhati ca tapati ca kirtya yasasa brahma varcasena ya evam veda ya evam veda.

6. The ear indeed is the fourth foot of Brahman (the body). It shines and warms up with the light of Directions (Quarters). He who knows this, shines and warms up with name, fame and the luster of Brahman.

Section 19

Separation of Worlds from the Cosmic Egg

1. adityo brahmety adesas tasyopavyakhyanam asad evedam agra asit; tat sad asit tat samabhavat tad andam niravartata tat samvatsarasya matram asayata tan nirabhidyata te andakapale rajatam ca suvarnam cabhavatam.

1. Aditya (the sun) is Brahman. This is the instruction and regarding it this is the explanation. In the beginning this was non-existent. Then the manifestation of that egg happened. It lay (dormant) for a year. It broke open and then appeared two eggshells, one silver and one gold.

Notes: Non-existence does not mean it never existed. It only means this world or the material universe was not there. Then the cosmic egg appeared. That cosmic egg was a reference to manifestation without names and forms and without duality and diversity.

2. tad yad rajatam seyam prithivi yat suvarnam sa dyaur yaj jarayu te parvata yad ulbam sa megho niharah ya dhamanayasta nadyah yad vasteyam udakam sa samudrah.

2. That which was the silver one is this earth; that which was golden one is the heaven. That which was the outer skin of the embryo is the mountains; that which was the vacuous material became is the mist with the clouds; what were the veins are the rivers; that which was the water within (embryonic fluid) is the ocean.

3. atha yat tad ajayata so'asav adityah tam jayamanam ghosa ululavo' nudatisthan sarvani ca bhutani sarve ca kamah tasmat tasyodayam prati pratyayanam prati ghosa ululavo'nuttisthanti sarvani ca bhutani sarve ca kamah.

3. Then that which was born from it was Aditya (the sun). When he was born, tumultuous shouts of joy arose; and all beings and desires arose. Therefore whenever the sun rises and sets, tumultuous shouts of joy arise; and all beings and all desires arise.

4. sa ya etam evam vidvan adityam brahmety upaste abhyaso ha yad enam sadhavo ghosa a ca gacceyur upa ca nimrederan nimrederan.

4. He who knowing thus meditates upon the sun as Brahman, pleasant shouts of joy will reach him, will continue to reach him and will continue to reach him.

Notes: The first morning light emanating from the sun has been eulogized in the two verses (8.6.30 and 1.50.10) of the Rigveda described above. In the Vedic tradition, the Sun symbolizes Brahman, the God of gods, and the lord of the immortal world. Those who attain it would never return and take birth again. How is it attained? This is answered in the next section. The sun is attained not physically but by realizing or seeing (as the seers have seen) that the Sun shining above the darkness and the Self shining within oneself are one and the same.

Chapter 4

Section 1

The Fame Of Raikva, The One With The Cart

1. aum, janasrutir ha pautrayanah sraddhadeyo bahudayi bahupakya asa sa ha sarvata avasathan mapayam cakre sarvata eva me'annamatsyantiti.

1. *Aum. It is said that the great grandson of Janasruti was a dedicated charitable person, and a generous giver of richly made food. He built resting places everywhere, wising "Everywhere, people will eat my food."*

2. atha hamsa nisayam atipetus tadd haivam hamso hamsam abhyuvada, ho ho'yi bhallaksa bhallaksa janasruteh pautrayanasya samam diva jyotir atatam tan ma prasanksis tat tva ma pradhaksid iti.

2. *Then one night some swans flew by (his residence). One swan said to another, "Ho! Ho! O! Bhallaksa, Bhallaksa, the radiance of Janasruti's great grandson has spread like the heaven. Do not touch it; otherwise it may burn you.*

3. tam u ha parah praty uvaca kam vara enam etat santam sayugvanam iva raikvam attheti yo nu katham sayugva raikva iti.

3. *The other replied to him, "How can you speak about him, being what he is, as if he were Raikva, the one with the cart?"*

"Who is this Raikva, the one with the cart?"

4. yatha kritaya vijitayadhareyah samyanty evam enam sarvam tad abhisamaiti yat kimca prajah sadhu kurvanti yas tad veda yatsa veda sa mayaitad ukta iti.

4. *"Just as in the game of dice throwing when all the lower numbers cast (by other players) belong to him who casts the Krita mark, so does whatever good others do goes to him who know what Raikva knows. This much I can say about him."*

Notes: In a kind of dice game played in ancient India, if any one got the Krta Cast, upon throwing the dice, he was entitled to receive all the lower casts. Krita cast was derived from the name Krita yuga. It bore the number four. The other casts, as per Shankara, were Treta, Dwapara and Kali bearing numbers three, two and one respectively. The knowledge that Raikva possessed was the knowledge of Brahman. Since the results of all sacrifices and meritorious acts accrued to Brahman only in the final analysis, the good karma of all people accrued to Raikva, the knower of Brahman, and also to those who possessed such knowledge.

5. tadu ha janasrutih pautrayana upasusrava sa ha samjihana eva ksattaram uvaca angare ha sayugvanam iva raikvam attheti yo nu katham sayugva raikva iti.

5. Now, Janasruti, the great grandson (of Janasruti), overheard this. Next day morning, when he woke up, he said to his attendant, "My friend, (this is what I heard from the swans), 'How can you speak about him, being what he is, as if he were Raikva, the one with the cart?'"

"Who is this Raikva, the one with the cart?"

6. yatha kritaya vijitayadhareyah samyanty evam enam sarvam tad abhisamaiti yat kimca prajah sadhu kurvanti yas tad veda yat sa veda sa mayaitad ukta iti.

6. "Just as in the game of dice throwing, when all the lower numbers cast (by other players) belong to him who casts the Krita mark, so does whatever good others does goes to him who know what Raikva knows. This much I can say about him."

7. sa ha ksattanvisya navidam iti pratyeyaya tam hovaca yatra-re brahmanasyanvesana tad enam arcceti.

7. The attendant went around looking for Raikva and returned saying, "I did not find him." Then he said to him, "Look for him where the brahmanas are usually found."

8. so'adhastac cakatasya pamanam kasamanam upopavivesa tam habhyuvada tvam nu bhagavah sayugva raikva ity aham hy ara iti ha pratijajne sa ha ksatt avidam iti pratyeyaya.

8. (Following the advice) he (finally) found a man beneath a cart, scratching his itch. He said to him, "O godman, are you Raikva, the one with the cart?" "Yes, I am." The attendant returned saying, "I have found him."

Section 2

Janasruti and Raikva - The offering of Gifts

1. tadu ha janasrutih pautrayanah satsatani gavam niskam asvatariratham tad adaya praticakrame tam habhyuvada.

1. Then Janasruti, the great grandson (of Janasruti) went to him with six hundred cows, a necklace, and a chariot drawn by mules, and said to him.

2. raikvemani sat satani gavam ayam nisko'yam asvatariratho'nu ma etam bhagavo devatam sadhi yam devatam upassa iti.

2. "Raikva, here are six hundred cows, a necklace, and a chariot drawn by mules. Godman, please teach me the deity you worship."

3. tamu ha parah pratyuvacaha haretva sudra tavaiva saha gobhir astv iti tad u ha punar eva janasrutih pautrayanah sahasram gavam niskam asvatariratham duhitaram tad adaya praticakrame.

3. Then the other replied to him, "O ignorant Sudra, keep your necklace, your chariot and the cows with yourself." Then the great grandson of Janasruti returned again with a thousand cows, a necklace, a chariot with mules, and his own daughter.

Notes: Sudra is a reference to an ignorant person, or a person who is not conversant with etiquette and manner. Raikva addressed him thus because Janasruti tried to exchange material things with knowledge.

4. tam habhyuvada raikvedam sahasram gavam ayam nisko'yam asvatariratha iyam jayayam gramo yasminn asse anv eva ma bhagavah sadhiti.

4. He said to him: "Raikva, here are a thousand cows, a necklace, a chariot with mules, this wife, and this (grant of the) village in which you live. Godman, please teach me."

5. tasya ha mukham upodgrihnann uvaca jaharemah sudra anenaiva mukhenalapayisyatha iti te haite raikvaparna nama mahavrisesu yatrasma uvasa sa tasmai hovaca.

5. Then holding her face with his hands (and looking at her), he said to "The Sudra has brought these. By this face alone you made me speak." Now, these were the villages called Raikvaparna among the Mahavrisas where he lived. Then he said to him.

Notes: Although Raikva was unimpressed by the gifts of wealth, cows and a chariot, he readily accepted the gift of a girl, who had an agreeable face and no birth defects. It is not clear why Raikva, who was a seer and a knower of Brahman appreciated the gift of a young girl who he though was looking good, while he refused to accept other gifts he was offered before.

Section 3

Air and Breath, the Absorbers

1. vayur vava samvargo yada va agnir udvayati vayum evapyeti yada suryo'stam eti vayum evapy eti yada candro'stam eti vayum evapyeti.

1. Air (Vayu) is indeed the absorber for when the fire exits, it ends up in the air; when the sun sets; it ends up in the air; and when the moon sets, it ends up in the air.

Notes: Now we know that the sun and the moon are not actually absorbed by air. They just disappear into air or the mid-region where air predominates.

2. yadapa uccusyanti vayum evapiyanti vayur hy evaitan sarvan samvrinkta ity adhidaivatam.

2. When the water dries up, it ends up in the air. Indeed, air consumes them all. This is with regard to the deities.

3. athadhyatmam prano vava samvargah sa yada svapiti pranam eva vag apyeti pranam caksuh pranam srotram pranam manah prano hy evaitan sarvan samvrinkta iti.

3. Now with reference to the body. Breath (prana) is indeed the absorber. When one sleeps, speech goes into the breath, sight goes into the breath, hearing goes into the breath, the mind goes into breath; indeed, breath consumes them all.

4. tau va etau dvau samvargau vayureva devesu pranah pranesu.

4. These two are indeed the absorbers, air among the gods, and breath among the organs.

5. atha ha saunakam ca kapeyam abhipratarinam ca kaksasenim parivisyamanau brahmacari bibhikse tasma u ha na dadatuh.

5. Once when Saunaka Kapeya and Abhipratarin Kaksaseni were waiting for their turn while food was being served, a celibate student begged them for food. They did not give him any.

Note: This story was introduced to illustrate the above teaching regarding the absorbers in the worlds and in the body. The two Brahmanas, who were well versed in the Vedas, ignored the student, although as Brahmanas, and as householders, they were obliged to offer him food. Shankara says they did it to test him and see how he would respond because they felt that he was proud of his knowledge.

6. sa hovaca: mahatmanas caturo deva ekah kah sa jagara bhuvanasya gopah tam kapeya nabhipasyanti martya abhipratarin bahudha vasantam yasmai va etad annam tasma etanna dattam iti.

6. He said: "The one deity who swallowed the four great ones, he, who is the guardian of the world, O Kapeya, the mortals do not see him. O Abhipratarin, although he dwells in many places, to whom all this food belongs, to him it has not been served."

Notes: The student said that the ultimate absorber of food both in the worlds and in the bodies was Prajapati only. People did not see him because he was indistinct and invisible. With this description, the student complained that the same Prajapati, who was in his body as the ultimate eater of food was not served by the two Brahmanas although they were aware of his presence.

7. tad u ha saunakah kapeyah pratimanvanah pratyeyaya atma devanam janita prajanam hiranya damstro babhaso'anasurah mahantam asya mahimanam ahuh anadyamano yad anannam atti iti vai vayam brahmacarinn idam upasmahe dattasmai bhiksam iti.

7. Then Saunaka Kapeya, pondering over this, went to him and said, "It is the Self among the gods, the creator of beings, with golden tusks, the eater, not without intelligence. They speak of his greatness as the greatest, because without being eaten, it eats even that which is not food. Thus, O student of the Vedas, we meditate upon it. Then he said (to his attendant), "Give him food."

8. tasma u ha daduh te va ete pancanye pancanye dasa santas tat kritam tasmat sarvasu diksv annam eva dasa kritam saisa viradannadi tayedam sarvam dristam sarvam asyedam dristam bhavaty annado bhavati ya evam veda ya evam veda.

8. They gave him food. Now these five and the other five make the ten and they are the highest. Further, in all the quarters, these ten are the food and the highest. This is Virat, the eater of food. By it all become visible. One who knows this sees all this and becomes an enjoyer of food, yes an enjoyer of food.

Notes: The first five are fire, air, the sun, the moon and the water, which are mentioned in the first verse of this section. They are with reference to the deities. The other five are mentioned in the third verse, namely breath, speech, eye, ear and the mind. They are with reference to the body.

Section 4

The Legend of Satyakama Jabala

1. satyakamo ha jabalo jabalam mataram amantrayam cakre brahmacaryam bhavati vivatsyami kim gotro nv aham asmiti.

1. It so happened, once Satyakama Jabala addressed his mother and said, "Mother, I wish to become a student of the Vedas. (Please tell me,) to which family name (gotra) I belong?"

2. sa hainam uvaca naham etad veda tata yad gotras tvam asi bahv aham caranti paricarini yauvane tvam alabhe saham etan na veda yad gotras tvam asi jabala tu namaham asmi satyakamo nama tvamasi sa satyakama eva jabalo bravitha iti.

2. She said to him: "My child, I do not know what your family name is. In my youthful days, when I moved about as a maid servant (among many families) then I got you. Hence, I do not know your family name. My name is Jabala and your name is Satyakama. You may therefore call yourself Satyakama Jabala.

3. sa ha haridrumatam gautamam etyovaca brahmacaryam bhagavati vatsyamy upeyam bhagavantam iti.

3. Thereupon, he went to Gautama Haridrumata and said to him, "O godman, I wish to become a student of the Vedas under you. May I become your student, O godman."

4. tam hovaca kim gotro nu somya, asiti sa hovaca nahametad veda bho yad gotro'ham asmy apriccam mataram sa ma pratyabravid bahv aham caranti paricarini yauvane tvam alabhe saham etan na veda yad gotras tvam asi, jabala tu namaham asmi satyakamo nama tvam asiti so'ham satyakamo jabalo'smi bho iti.

4. He said to him: "What is your family name my dear?" He replied, "I do not know revered sir, what my family name is. I asked my mother and she said, In my youthful days, when I moved about as a maid servant, then I got you. Hence, I do not know your family name. My name is Jabala and your name is Satyakama.' Therefore revered sir, I am Satyakama Jabala.

5. tam hovaca naitad abrahmano vivaktum arhati samidham somy ahar upa tva nesye na satyad aga iti tam upaniya krisanam abalanam catuhsata ga nirakrityovac imah somya

anusamvrajeti ta abhiprasthapayann uvaca nasahasrenavarteyeti sa ha varsaganam provasa ta yada sahasram sampeduh.

5. He said to him: "None but a true Brahmana would speak like this. Arrange for the fuel, I shall initiate you. You have not deviated from truth." After the initiation ceremony, he picked lean and weak cows numbering four hundred and said, " Take care of these, my dear." As he was leaving with them, he said to himself, "I shall not return without (they becoming) a thousand. " He lived for a number of years by which time they became a thousand.

Notes: Satyakama did not know his father's name or his family lineage. He only knew his mother's name, who said she worked in many houses and did not know who his father was actually. Yet, this knowledge did not deter Satyakama from returning to his teacher and telling him the truth, because he was determined to study under him and master the Vedas. The teacher accepted him as his student, appreciating his honesty and truthfulness. Upon being accepted by his teacher and entrusted with the task of taking care of the cows, he resolved to increase the number of cows. It shows that he was diligent in his duty, honest and virtuous. Satyakama became a Brahmana not by birth but by his character and inner purity.

Section 5

The One Foot of Brahman

1. atha hainam risabho'bhyuvada satyakama iti bhagava iti ha pratisusrava praptah somya sahasram smah prapaya na acaryakulam.

1. Then Risabha, (Vayu in the form of a bull), said to him, "Satyakama!"

He replied, " Yes, godman!"

"We have reached a thousand, lead us to the teacher's house."

2. brahmanas ca te padam bravan iti bravitu me bhagavan iti tasmai hovaca praci dik kala pratici dikkala daksina dik kalodici dik kalaisa vai somya catuskalah pado brahmanah prakasavan nama.

2. "I will declare to you one foot (quarter) of Brahman."

"Please declare so godman."

He said to him, "East, one direction, west one direction, south one direction, and north one direction. My dear, this one, indeed, is the four-quartered foot called the shining one (praksavah)."

Notes: The whole world, the earth, the mid region and the sky together is compared to one aspect of Brahman, having four sides. This shining one was described before as the belly of the treasure chest.

3. sa ya etam evam vidvams catuskalam padam brahmanah prakasavan ity upaste prakasavan asmiml loke bhavati prakasavato ha lokan jayati ya etam evam vidvams catuskalam padam brahmanah prakasavan ity upaste.

3. "Knowing thus, he who meditates upon the one four-quartered foot of Brahman as the shining one, becomes a shining one in this world. He conquers the radiant worlds, who knowing this meditates upon the one four-sided foot of Brahman as the shining one.

Section 6

The Second Foot of Brahman

1. agnis te padam vakteti sa ha svo bhute ga abhi prasthapayam cakara ta yatrabhi sayam babhuvus tatragnim upasamadhaya ga uparudhya samidham adhaya pascad agneh pran upopavivesa.

1. "Fire (Agni) will declare to you another foot (quarter) of Brahman." The next day, he took the cows out. When the evening approached, he lit a fire, tied the cows, dropped the fuel wood into the fire and sat down behind it, looking towards the east.

2. tam agnir abhyuvada satyakama iti bhagava iti ha pratisusrava.

2. Then Fire said to him, "Satyakama!"

He replied: "Yes, godman"

3. brahmanah somya te padam bravaniti bravitu me bhagavan iti tasmai hovaca prithivi kalantariksam kala dyauh kala samudrah kalaisa vai somya catuskalah pado brahmano'nantavan nama.

3. Fire said: "I will declare to you my dear one foot (quarter) of Brahman."

"Please declare so godman," he replied.

He said to him, "The earth, one direction, the mid-region one direction, the sky one direction, and the ocean one direction. My dear, this is indeed the one four-quartered foot called the Endless (anantavan)."

4. sa ya etam evam vidvams catuskalam padam brahmano'nantavan ity upaste anantavan asmimlloke. Bhavaty anantavato ha lokan jayati ya etam evam vidvams catuskalam padam brahmano'n antavan ity upaste.

4. *"Knowing thus, he who meditates upon the one four-quartered foot of Brahman as the Endless, becomes infinite in this world. He conquers the infinite worlds, who knowing this meditates upon the one four-sided foot of Brahman as the Endless.*

Section 7

The Third Foot of Brahman

1. hamsas te padam vakteti sa ha svobhute ga abhiprastha payam cakara ta yatrabhi sayam babhuvuh tatragnim upasamadhaya ga uparudhya samidham adhaya pascad agneh pranupopa- vivesa.

1. *"The swan (Aditya) will declare to you another foot (quarter) of Brahman." The next day, he took the cows out. When the evening approached, he lit a fire, tied the cows, dropped the fuel wood into the fire and sat down behind it, looking towards the east.*

2. tam hamsa upanipatyabhyuvada satyakama iti bhagava iti ha pratisusrava.

2. *Then the swan flew down to him and said, "Satyakama!"*

He replied: "Yes, godman"

3. brahmanah somya te padam bravaniti bravitu me bhagavan iti tasmai hovac agnih kala suryah kala candrah kala vidyut kalaisa vai somya catuskalah pado brahmano jyotisman nama.

3. *The swan said: "I will declare to you my dear one foot (quarter) of Brahman."*

"Please declare so godman," he replied.

He said to him, "The fire, one direction, the sun one direction, the moon one direction, and the lightning one direction. My dear, this is indeed the one four-quartered foot called the effulgent (jyotisman)."

4. sa ya etam evam vidvams catuskalam padam brahmano jyotisman ity upaste jyotisman asmiml loke bhavati jyotism-

ato ha lokan jayati ya etam evam vidvams catuskalam padam brahmano jyotisman ity upaste.

4. "Knowing thus, he who meditates upon the one four-quartered foot of Brahman as the effulgent, becomes effulgent in this world. He conquers the effulgent worlds, who knowing this meditates upon the one four-sided foot of Brahman as the effulgent.

Section 8
The Fourth Foot of Brahman

1. madguste padam vakteti sa ha svobhute ga abhiprasthapayam cakara ta yatrabhi sayam babhuvuh tatragnim upasamadhaya ga uparudhya samidham adhaya pascad agneh pran upopavivesa.

1. "A water bird (called Madgu) will declare to you another foot (quarter) of Brahman." The next day, he took the cows out. When the evening approached, he lit a fire, tied the cows, dropped the fuel wood into the fire and sat down behind it, looking towards the east.

2. tam madgur upanipatyabhyuvada satyakama, iti bhagava iti ha pratisusrava.

2. Then the water bird flew to him and said, "Satyakama!"

He replied: "Yes, godman"

3. brahmanah somya te padam bravaniti bravitu me bhagavaniti tasmai hovaca pranah kala caksuh kala srotram kala manah kalaisa vai somya catuskalah pado brahmana ayatanavannama.

3. The water bird said: "I will declare to you, my dear, one foot (quarter) of Brahman."

"Please declare so godman," he replied.

He said to him, "The breath, one direction, the eye one direction, the ear one direction, and the mind one direction. My dear, this is indeed the one four-quartered foot called the repository (ayatanvan)."

4. sa yai etam evam vidvams catuskalam padam brahmana ayatanavan ity upasta ayatanavan asmiml loke bhavaty ayatanavato ha lokan jayati ya etam evam vidvams catuskalam padam brahmana ayatanavan ity upaste.

4. *"Knowing thus, he who meditates upon the one four-quartered foot of Brahman as the Endless, becomes a repository in this world. He conquers the worlds bearing repositories, who knowing this meditates upon the one four-quartered foot of Brahman as the repositories.*

Section 9

The Importance of a Teacher

1. prapa ha caryakulam tamacaryo'bhyuvada satyakama iti bhagava iti ha pratisusrava.

1. He reached the teacher's house. The teacher said to him : "Satyakama."

He replied: "Yes, godman."

2. brahmavid iva vai somya bhasi ko nu tvanusasasety anye manusyebhya iti ha pratijajne bhagavams tv eva me kame bruyat.

2. The teacher said: "My dear you shine like the knower of Brahman. Who taught you?" "Other than humans; but godman, only you should teach me, this is my wish."

3. srutam hy eva me bhagavaddrisebhyah acaryadd haiva vidya vidita sadhistham prapatiti tasmai haitad evovaca atra ha na kin cana viyayeti viyayeti.

3. "For I have heard from godmen like you that knowledge learnt from a teacher alone helps one to attain the highest end." Then he spoke to him the same knowledge. Nothing was left out, yes nothing was left out.

Notes: Satyakama learned the knowledge regarding the four feet of Brahman from the bull, fire, the swan and the water bird respectively. They were the deities of the quarters they spoke. Satyakama willingly learned from them. Yet, he resolved to relearn it from his teacher because he believed his teacher was the best and the knowledge he taught would be the best. knowledge.

Section 10

Upakosala Receiving the Knowledge of Fires

1. upakosalo ha vai kamalayanah satyakame jabale brahmacaryam uvasa tasya ha dvadasa varsany agnin paricara sa ha smanyan antevasinah samavartayams tam ha smaiva na samavartayati.

1. *Upakosala son of Kamala dwelt as a student with Satyakama Jabala practicing celibacy, keeping the domestic fires alive for twelve years. However, his teacher did not let him leave while he allowed others return to their homes.*

2. tam jayovaca tapto brahmacari kusalam agnin paricacarin ma tvagnayah paripravocan prabruhy asma iti tasmai ha procyaiva pravasam cakre.

2. *His wife said to him, "This celibate student has become skilful through austerities and kept your domestic fires burning. Please teach him, so that the fires will not blame you. But he went away, without teaching him.*

Notes: The teacher's wife wanted him to repay the karmic debt, since the student stayed in their house and served them with the expectation of receiving instructions in return. This verse suggests that a teacher's wife often advised her husband in matters concerning his students welfare.

3. sa ha vyadhinanasitum dadhre tam acarya jayovaca brahmacarinn asana kim nu nasnas iti sa hovaca bahava ime asmin puruse kama nanatyaya vyadhibhih pratipurno'smi nasisyami iti.

3. *The student fell ill and resolved not to eat. The teacher's wife said to him, "O celibate student, eat. Why do not you eat?" He said, "In this person are many desires spreading in different directions. I am filled with frustrations. I shall take no food.*

4. atha hagnayah samudire tapto brahmacari kusalam nah paryacarid hantasmai prabravameti tasmai hocuh prano brahma kam brahma kham brahmeti.

4. *Thereupon the fires said among themselves "This celibate student, who has become skilful through austerities has looked after us very well. Let us teach him. They said to him.*

5. sa hovaca vijanamy aham yat prano brahma kam ca tu kham ca na vijanamiti te hocur yad vava kam tad eva kham yad eva kham tad eva kam iti pranam ca hasmai tad akasam cocuh.

5. *"Breath is Brahman, Ka is Brahman, Kha is Brahman."*

He said, "I know that breath is Brahman, but I do not know Ka or Kha."

Then they said: "What is ka that is kha, and what is kha that is ka. Then they taught him breath and its space.

Section 11

The Forms of Garhapatya Fire

1. atha hainam garhapatyo'nusasasa prithivy agnir annam aditya iti ya esa aditye puruso drisyate so'aham asmi sa evaham asmiti

1. *Then the Garhapatya fire instructed him, "Earth, fire, food and the sun (are my forms). The person seen in the sun, that is I am, that indeed is I am."*

2. sa ya etam evam vidvan upaste apahate papakrityam loki bhavati sarvam ayur eti jyog jivati nasyavara purusah ksiyante upa vayam tam bhunjamo'smims ca loke"musmims ca ya etam evam vidvan upaste.

2. *"He who knowing thus meditates (upon the Garhyapatya fire), destroys sin, attains this world, lives until the end of his lifespan, and lives gloriously. His descendents shall never perish. We serve him here and hereafter, whoever knowing thus meditates.*

Section 12

The Forms of Anvaharya Fire

1. atha hainamanvaharyapacano'nusasasapo diso naksatrani candrama iti ya esa candramasi puruso drisyate so'aham asmi sa evaham asmiti.

1. *Then the Anvaharya fire instructed him: "Water, the quarters, the stars, the moon (are my forms). The person seen in the moon, that is I am, that is I am indeed.*

2. sa ya etamevam vidvanupasteapahate papakrityam loki bhavati sarvamayureti jyogjivati nasyavarapurusah ksiyanta upa vayam tam bhunjamo'smimsca lokeamusmimsca ya etam evam vidvan upaste.=

2. *"He who knowing thus meditates (upon the Anvaharya fire), destroys sin, attains the world, lives until the end of his lifespan, and lives gloriously. His descendents shall never perish. We serve him here and hereafter, whoever knowing thus meditates.*

Section 13

The Forms of Ahvaniya Fire

1. atha hainam ahavaniyo'nusasasa prana akaso dyaur vidyuditi ya esa vidyuti puruso drisyate so'aham asmi sa evaham asmiti.

1. Then the Ahvaniya fire instructed him: "Breath, space, the sky, the lightning (are my forms). The person seen in the lightning, that is I am, that is I am indeed.

2. sa ya etam evam vidvan upaste apahate papakrityam loki bhavati sarvam ayur eti jyog jivati nasyavara purusah ksiyanta upa vayam tam bhunjamo'smims ca loke amusmims ca ya etam evam vidvan upaste.

2. "He who knowing thus meditates (upon the Ahvaniya fire), destroys sin, attains this world, lives until the end of his lifespan, and lives gloriously. His descendents shall never perish. We serve him here and hereafter, whoever knowing thus meditates.

Notes: Garhapatya, Anvaharya and Ahvaniya are the three domestic fires. They were kept in the house of a householder (grihasta) for performing domestic rituals and making daily offerings. Garhapatya was kept in the house. Anvaharya and Ahvaniya were kept on the southern and the eastern sides of the house respectively.

Section 14

The Purifying Knowledge of the Self

1. te hocuh upakosala isa somya te asmad vidyatma vidya ca caryas tu te gatim vaktety ajagama hasya caryas tam acaryo'bhyuvadopakosala iti.

1. Then they said, "Upkosala, my dear, this is the knowledge regarding us (the fires) and the Self. Your teacher will teach you their application. (Upon his return), the teacher said, " O Upkosala!"

2. bhagava iti ha pratisusrava brahmavida iva somya te mukham bhati ko nu tvanusasas eti ko nu manusisyad bhoh iti iha apeva nihnuta ime nunam idrisa anyadrisa itihagnin abhyude kim nu somya kila te.avocann iti

2. He replied, "Yes, godman."

The teacher said, "My dear your face is shining like that of a knower of Brahman. Who has given you the instruction?"

"Who would instruct me sir," he said. Then, as if he was concealing the fact, he said pointing to the fires, "Are not these fires now look different than what they were before?"

The teacher said, "Well my dear, what did they indeed tell you?"

3. idam iti ha pratijajne lokan vava kila somya te, avocann aham tu te tad vaksyami yatha puskara palasa apo na slisyanta evam evam vidi papam karma na slisyata iti bravitu me bhagavan iti tasmai hovaca.

3. "This," he replied.

The teacher said : "They have, indeed, taught you about the worlds, my dear. I will tell you this, just as water does not cling to a lotus leaf, so does no evil deed cling to the one who knows it."

He said: "Godman, please tell it me." To him, then he said.

Section 15

The Divine Path to the World of Brahman

1. ya eso'ksini puruso drisyata esa atma iti hovaca etad amritam abhayam etad brahmeti tad yady apy asmin sarpir vodakam va sincati vartmani eva gaccati.

1. "The person who is seen in the eye, it is the Self. This is immortal, without fear; this is Brahman. Therefore, even if one drops melted butter or water into this (eye) it trickles down from both sides."

2. etam samyadvama ity acaksata etam hi sarvani vamany abhisamyanti sarvany enam vamany abhisamyanti ya evam veda.

2. "This they call the unifier of all good things (samyadvama), for all good things go to him in union. Indeed, all good things go to him in union, who knows this."

3. esa u eva vamanih esa hi sarvani vamani nayati sarvani vamani nayati ya evam veda.

3. "This is also the carrier of good things (vamani). He carries all good things, who knows thus."

4. esa u eva bhamanir esa hi sarvesu lokesu bhati sarvesu lokesu bhati ya evam veda.

4. *"This is also the source of light (bhamani), for he shines in all worlds. He who knows this, shines in all the worlds."*

5. atha yad u caivasmin cavyam kurvanti yadi ca na arcisam evabhisambhavanty arciso'har ahna apuryamana paksam apuryamana paksad yan sad udann eti masams tan masebhyah samvatsaram samvatsarad adityam adityac candramasam candramaso vidyutam tat puruso'manavah sa enan brahma gamayaty esa devapatho brahmapatha etena pratipadyamana imam manavam avartam navartante navartante.

5. *"Now for him whether they perform cremation ceremony or not, he goes to the light (arcis), from light to the day, from day to the fortnight, from bright fortnight to the first six months during which the sun appears in the north, from the month to the year, from the year to the Sun, from the sun to the moon, from the moon to the lightning. There is that person who is not human. He takes them to Brahman. This is the path of gods (devapatha), the path to Brahman (brahmapatha). Following this path they do not return to this world of humans, yes, they do not return."*

Section 16

The Role of the Brahman Priest in a Sacrifice

1. esa ha vai yajno yo'yam pavate esa ha yannidam sarvam punati yadesa yannidam sarvam punati tasmadesa eva yajnastasya manasca vakca vartani.

1. *Truly, that which blows is the sacrifice, for by moving around he purifies all this. Because by moving around he purifies all this, therefore he is the sacrifice. Regarding that sacrifice, there are two ways (to perform them), by the mind and by speech.*

Notes: Pavate means blows or purifies. Both meaning are apt here and applicable to Vayu, the god of Air.

2. tayor anyataram manasa samskaroti brahma vaca hotadhvaryur udgita anyataram sa yatraupakrite pratar anuvake pura paridhaniyaya brahma vyavadati.

2. *Of them, one is performed through the mind by the Brahman priest; and the other is performed through speech by the Hotri, the Adhvaryu and the Udgatri priests. When the mooring recitation has begun, but before the concluding recitation is completed, if he speaks.*

Notes: In a sacrifice, the Brahman priest, who acts like a witnessing supervisor, remains silent, while keeping a close watch on the proceedings. He performs the sacrifice in his mind, while the other priests perform it with speech as they chant and sing. It is customary for the Brahman priest to remain silence throughout the sacrifice and not speak at all.

3. anyataram eva vartanim samskaroti hiyate'anyatara sa yathaikapad vrajan ratho vaikena cakrena vartamano risyaty evam asya yajno risyati yajnam risyantam yajamano'nurisyati sa istva papiyan bhavati.

3. He performs (the sacrifice) by the one only, while the other is rendered defective. As a man walking on one foot, or a carriage going on one wheel is deemed defective, his sacrifice is deemed defective, and with a defective sacrifice the sacrificer also becomes defective; yes, performing the sacrifice defectively as the sacrificer, he becomes the worst sinner.

Notes: If the Brahmana priest, who is the overseer and protector of the sacrifice, speaks during this phase of the sacrifice, then that part which is supposed to be performed with the mind becomes defective or broken. In other words of the two paths by which the offerings are supposed to reach Air, one is blocked, preventing the sacrificer to make his offerings to the deities. As a result, the sacrificer, because of the actions of the Brahman priest, incurs sin and thereby comes to grief.

4. atha yatropakrite prataranuvake na pura paridhaniyaya brahma vyavadaty ubhe eva vartani samskurvanti na hiyate'anyatara.

4. But if the Brahman priest does not speak after the morning recitation begins and until the concluding recitation, then they (the priest and the sacrificer) perform the sacrifice perfectly and neither of them is harmed.

Notes: This is the tradition. A Brahman priest takes a vow of silence and keeps that vow throughout the sacrifice. He will not utter a word until the conclusion of the sacrifice. In the end he performs expiatory functions to correct any mistakes other priests might have committed in the sacrifice. Like the air, the Brahman priest is absorber and purifier of the sacrifice. Hence, he should not commit mistakes himself.

5. sa yathobhayapad vrajan ratho vobhabhyam cakrabhyam vartamanah pratitisthaty evam asya yajnah pratitisthati yajnam pratitisthantam yajamano'nupratitisthati sa istva sreyan bhavati.

5. Just as a man walking on two legs and a chariot moving on two wheels, so is his sacrifice well supported. When the sacrifice is well supported, the sacrificer is well supported. Yes, by performing the sacrifice, he becomes excellent.

Section 17

The Methods of Rectifying a Sacrifice

1. Prajapatir lokan abhyatapat tesam tapyamananam rasan pravrihad agnim prithiv ya vayum antariksat adityam divah.

1. Prajapati subjected the worlds to penance. During the penance he extracted from them their saps (essences), fire (Agni) from the earth, air (Vayu) from the atmosphere and the sun (Aditya) from the sky.

2. sa etas tisro devata abhyatapat tasam tapyamananam rasan pravrihad anger rico vayor yajumsi samany adityat.

2. He subjected these three deities also to penance. During the penance he extracted their saps, the hymns of the Rigveda from fire, the hymns of the Yajurveda from air and the hymns of the Samaveda from the Sun.

3. sa etam trayim vidyam abhyatapat tasyas tapyamanaya rasan pravrihad bhur ity rigbhyo bhuvar iti yajurbhyah svar iti samabhyah.

3. He subjected the triple knowledge to penance. During the penance he extracted their saps, bhur from the hymns of the Rigveda, bhuva from the verses of the Yajurveda and svah from the verses of the Samaveda.

4. tad yad rikto risyed bhuh svaheti garhapatye juhuyad ricam eva tad rasena rcam viryena rcam yajnasya viristam samdadhati.

4. If the sacrifice is injured from the chanting of the Rig verses, let him offer an oblation into the Garhapatya fire, saying 'bhuh svaha.' Thus through this extraction of the Rik verses and through the vigor of the Rik verses, he should remedy the injury caused to the Rik sacrifice.

Notes: These expiatory functions have to be performed by the Brahman priest who has to maintain silence.

5. sa yadi yajusto risyed bhuvah svaheti daksinagnau juhuyad yajusam eva tad rasena yajusam viryena yajusam yajnasya viristam samdadhati.

5. If the sacrifice is injured from the chanting of the Yaju verses, let him offer an oblation into the southern fire, saying 'bhuvah svaha.' Thus through this extraction of the Yaju verses and through the vigor of the Yaju verses, he should remedy the injury caused to the Yaju sacrifice.

6. atha yadi samato risyet svah svahety ahavaniye juhuyat samnam eva tad rasena samnam viryena samnam yajnasya viristam samdadhati.

6. If the sacrifice is injured from the chanting of the Saman chants, let him offer an oblation into the Ahvaniya (western) fire, saying 'svah svaha.' Thus, through this extraction of the Saman chants and through the vigor of the Saman chants, he should remedy the injury caused to the Saman sacrifice.

7. tad yatha lavanena suvarnam samdadhyat suvarnena rajatam rajatena trapu trapuna sisam sisena loham lohena daru daru carmana.

7. Just as one binds the gold with salt, silver with gold, tin with silver, lead with tin, metal with lead, wood with metal or wood with leather.

8. evam esam lokanam asam devatanam asyas trayya vidyaya viryena yajnasya viristam samdadhati bhesajakrito ha va esa yajno yatraivamvid brahma bhavati.

8. So should one remedy the defects that happened in the performance of the sacrifice with the power of these three worlds, the three deities and the three Vedas. That sacrifice is well healed when it has a Brahman priest who knows this.

9. esa ha va udakpravano yajno yatraivamvid brahma bhavaty evamvidam ha va esa brahmanam anu gatha yato yata avartate tat tad gaccati.

9. Truly, that sacrifice is inclined towards the northern path, which has a Brahman priest who knows this. With regard to such a Brahman priest who knows this there is this song, "Wherever it fails, there he goes."

10. manavo brahmaivaika ritvik kurun asvabhiraksaty evam viddha vai brahma yajnam yajamanam sarvams ca rtvijo'bhiraksati tasmad evam vidam eva brahmanam kurvita nanevamvidam nanevamvidam.

10. The silent Brahman, the manava, like a Ritvik priest, protects the sacrifice like a mare, that is he protects the sacrifice, the sacrificer and all the other priests. Therefore, one should engage the one who knows this as the Brahman priest, not the one who does not know it, not the one who does not know it.

Chapter 5

Section 1

The Superiority of Breath to the Body

1. yo ha vai jyestham ca srestham ca veda jyesthas ca ha vai sresthas ca bhavati prano vava jyesthas ca sresthas ca.

1. Truly, he who knows the oldest and the best becomes the oldest and the best; and breath indeed is the oldest and the best.

Notes: For the fetus in the womb, breath comes first before the organs begin to appear. Speech comes only after he is born.

2. yo ha vai vasistham veda vasistho ha svanam bhavati vag vava vasisthah.

2. Truly, he who knows the most prosperous, becomes the most prosperous among his own (people); and speech indeed is the most prosperous.

Notes: A Brahmana becomes prosperous through speech because with speech only he performs sacrifices, pleases the gods and obtains gifts and blessings from the patrons.

3. yo ha vai pratistham veda prati ha tisthat yasmims ca loke amusmims ca caksur vava pratistha.

3. Truly, he who knows the support, becomes the support in this world and in the next. The eye indeed is the firm rest.

Note: Pratishta means support, foundation, basis, authority, honor and so on.

4. yo ha vai sampadam veda sam hasmai kamah padyante daivas ca manusas ca srotram vava sampat.

4. Truly, he who knows material success, his desires, both divine and human desires, succeed. The ear indeed is success.

5. yo ha va ayatanam vedayatanam ha svanam bhavati mano ha va ayatanam.

5. Truly, he who knows the abode, becomes an abode for his people. The mind indeed is the abode.

Notes: Alternate meanings for ayatanam are container, refuge, and receptacle.

6. atha ha prana aham sreyasi vyudire aham sreyanasmy aham sreyan asmiti.

6. *Now, the five senses quarreled among themselves about their superiority, saying, "I am superior, I am superior."*

7. te ha pranah prajapatim pitaram etyocur bhagavan ko nah srestha iti tan hovaca yasmin va utkrante sariram papisthataram iva drisyeta sa vah srestha iti.

7. *They went to Prajapati, their father and said, "Godman, who is the best among us?" He said to them, "By whose departure the body becomes the vilest, he is the best among you."*

Notes: The body of a living being becomes vile only when it dies. In other words, the organ has to be vital for its survival to be counted as superior.

8. sa ha vag uccakrama sa samvatsaram prosya paryetyovaca katham asakata rte maj jivitum iti yatha kala avadantah pranantah pranena pasyantas caksusa srinvantah srotrena dhyayanto manasaivam iti pravivesa ha vak.

8. *The speech departed and having stayed away for a year it returned and said, "How are you doing without me." "Like the dumb, "(they replied),"not speaking, but breathing with breath, seeing with the eyes, hearing with the ear, thinking with the mind. Thus (we lived)." The speech then went in.*

9. caksur hoccakrama tat samvatsaram prosya paryetyo-vaca katham asakata rte maj jivitum iti yathandha apasyantah pranantah pranena vadanto vaca srinvantah srotrena dhyayanto manasaivam iti pravivesa ha caksuh.

9. *The eye departed and having stayed away for a year it returned and said, "How are you doing without me." "Like the blind, "(they replied),"not seeing, but breathing with breath, speaking with the speech, hearing with the ear, thinking with the mind. Thus (we lived)." The eye then went in.*

10. srotram hoccakrama tat samvatsaram prosya paryetyovaca katham asakata rte maj jivitumiti yatha badhira asrinvantah pranantah pranena vadanto vaca pasyantas caksusa dhyayanto manasaivam iti pravivesa ha srotram.

10. *The ear departed and having stayed away for a year it returned and said, "How are you doing without me." "Like the deaf, "(they replied),"not hearing, but breathing with breath, speaking with the speech, seeing with the eye, thinking with the mind. Thus (we lived)." The ear then went in.*

11. mano hoccakrama tat samvatsaram prosya paryetyovaca katham asakata rte maj jivitumiti yatha bala amanasah pranantah pranena vadanto vaca pasyantas caksusa srinvantah srotrenaivam iti pravivesa ha manah.

11. The mind departed and having stayed away for a year it returned and said, "How are you doing without me." "Like the children without a mind, "(they replied),"not thinking, but breathing with breath, speaking with the speech, seeing with the eye, hearing with the ear. Thus (we lived)." The mind then went in.

12. atha ha prana uccikramisan sa yatha suhayah padvisasankun samkhided evam itaran pranan samakhidat tam habhisametyocur bhagavan edhi tvam nah srestho'si motkramir iti.

12. Now, the breath on the verge of departing leapt upward, tearing up the senses, just as a fine horse might leap upward tearing up the pegs to which it is tied. They gathered around him and said, "Godman, please stay. You are the best among us. Please do not depart from us."

13. atha hainam vag uvaca yad aham vasistho'smi tvam tad vasistho'sity atha hainam caksur uvaca yadaham pratisthasmi tvam tat pratistha siti.

13. Then speech said to him, "If I am the most prosperous, you are the most prosperous." The eye said to him, "If I am the support, you are the support."

14. atha hainam srotram uvaca yadaham sampad asmi tvam tat sampad asity atha hainam mana uvaca yad aham ayatanam asmi tvam tad ayatanam asiti.

14. The ear said to him: "If I am material success, you are material success." The mind said to him: "If I am the abode, you are the abode."

15. na vai vaco na caksumsi na srotrani na manamsity acaksate prana ity evacaksate prano hy evaitani sarvani bhavati.

15. And people do not call them speech, eyes, ears, or mind, but breath, for all these are breaths.

Notes: The superiority of the breath in the body is illustrated as here in the Brihadaranyaka Upanishad also with minor variations. Breath is superior because it is incorruptible. You may perform bodily functions such as seeing, hearting etc., with good or bad intentions. But as far as the breath is concerned, it is independent of your will or intention. Since breath is impervious to evil thoughts and negativity, you can use breath control (Pranayama) effectively to stabilize your mind and drive away the negative thoughts and impurities of your mind.

Section 2

A Mantha Rite to Attain Greatness

1. sa hovaca kim me annam bhavisyatiti yat kim cid idam a svabhya a sakunibhya iti hocuh tad va etada anasyannam ano ha vai nama pratyaksam na ha va evamvidi kimcana anannam bhavatiti.

1. He said: "What shall be my food?" They said, "Whatever that is here even from dogs to birds." Thus, this is the food for the breath. His name is clearly Ana (breath). To him who knows this there is nothing that is not food.

Notes: Breath is present in all living beings. It is the eater or absorber of food. Hence whatever food that is eaten by the beings, that becomes its food.

2. sa hovaca kim me vaso bhavisyatiy apa iti hocuh tasmad va etad asisyantah purastac coparistac cadbhih paridadhati lambhuko ha vaso bhavaty anagno ha bhavati.

2. He said: "What shall be my clothing?" They said, "Water." Therefore it is that when people are about to eat food, they cover it, before and after, with water." Thus he obtains his clothing and does not remain naked.

3. tadd haitat satyakamo jabalo gosrutaye vaiyaghrapadyayoktvovaca yady apy etac cuskaya sthanave bruyat jayerann evasmin cakhah praroheyuh palasaniti.

3. Having explained this to Gosruti, the son of Vyaghrapada, Satyakama Jabala said, "If one were to tell this to a dry stump, branches would grow, and leaves would spring from it."

4. atha yadi mahaj jigamised amavasyayam diksitva paurnamasyam ratrau sarvausadhasya mantham dadhimadhunorupamathya jyesthaya sresthaya svaha ity agnav ajyasya hutva manthe sampatam avanayet.

4. If one desires to attain greatness, having taken initiation (diksa) on the new moon day and then on the night of the full moon, he should stir a mixture of all kinds of herbs with curds and honey and pour clarified butter into the fire, saying; "Obeisance to the oldest and the best." Then he should throw all that remains into the mixture.

Notes: This and the following verses are about a rite called the Mantha Rite. A Mantha rite of a different type is mentioned in the last chapter of the Brihadaranyaka

Upanishad also. There, it is mentioned that the mixture has to be made in a mortar and transferred into a special vessel or cup made of Udumbara wood called Mantha.

5. vasisthaya svahety agnav ajyasya hutva manthe sampatam avanayet pratisthayai svahety agnav ajyasya hutva manthe sampatam avanayet sampade svahety agna vajyasya hutva manthe sampatam avanayed ayatanaya svahety agnav ajyasya hutva manthe sampatam avanayet.

5. Saying, "Obeisance to the richest," he should pour clarified butter on the fire. After that he should throw the remains into the mixture. Saying, "Obeisance to the firm support," he should pour clarified butter on the fire. After that he should throw the remains into the mixture. Saying, "obeisance to success," he should pour clarified butter on the fire. After that he should throw the remains into the mixture. Saying, "Obeisance to the abode," he should pour clarified butter on the fire. After that he should throw the remains into the mixture.

6. atha pratisripyanjalau mantham adhaya japaty amo namasy ama hi te sarvam idam sa hi jyesthah srestho rajadhipatih sa ma jyaisthyam sraisthyam rajyam adhipatyam gamayatv aham evedam sarvam asaniti.

6. Then moving aside and placing the mixture in his hands, he should recite, "By name, you are Ama for all this here exists in you. He is indeed the oldest and the best, the sovereign of the kings. May he lead me to become the oldest, the best, and the sovereign of the kings. May I be all this."

7. atha khalv etayarca pacca acamati tat savitur vrinimaha ity acamati vayam devasya bhojanam ity acamati srestham sarvadhatamam ity acamati turam bhagasya dhimah iti sarvam pibati nirnijya kamsam camasam va pascad agneh samvisati carmani va sthandile va vacamyamo'prasahah sa yadi striyam pasyet samriddham karmeti vidyat.

7. Then he eats, sipping water at every foot of this verse from the Rigveda, "We desire the Savitr." He sips (saying), "The food of the gods." He sips (saying), "The best and all supporting." He sips (saying)," We meditate upon the source of all." Here he drinks up the rest. Having cleansed the vessel or the cup, he lies down behind the fire, on a skin or on the ground, without speaking, without making any effort. Now, if he happens to see a woman, he should consider that he has succeeded in his effort.

8. tadesa sloko yada karmasu kamyesu striyam svapnesu pasyanti samriddhim tatra janiyat tasmin svapna nidarsane tasmin svapna nidarsane.

8. *Regarding this, there is this verse, "If during the sacrifices performed to fulfill certain desires one sees a woman in a dream, he should know that the dream is a proof of his fulfillment, yes the dream is a proof of that.*

Section 3

The Paths by Which Souls Travel upon Death

1. svetaketur haruneyah pancalanam samitim eyaya tam ha pravahano jaivalir uvaca kumar anu tvasisat pitety a nuhi bhagava iti.

1. *Svetaketu Aruneya went to the general assembly of the Pancalas. Pravahana Jaivali said to him: "Son, has your father instructed you?" Yes, godman," (he replied).*

2. vettha yadito'dhi prajah prayantiti na bhagava iti vettha yatha punar avartanta iti na bhagava iti vettha pathor devayanasya pitriyanasya ca vyavartana iti na bhagava iti.

2. *"Do you know where do people go from here?"*

"No, godman." "Do you know how they return?"

"No, godman."

"Do you know where the path of the gods and the path of the ancestors separate?"

"No, godman.".

3. vettha yathasau loko na sampuryata iti na bhagava iti vettha yatha pancamyam ahutav apah purusa vacaso bhavant iti naiva bhagava iti.

3. *"Do you know why the other world is never full?"*

"No, godman."

"Do you know why the fifth offering in the sacrifice is spoken of as a person?

"No, godman."

4. atha nu kim anusistho'vocatha yo himani na vidyat katham so'anusisto bruviteti sa hayastah pitur ardham eyaya tam hovaca ananusisya vava kila ma bhagavan abravid anu tvasisam iti.

4. *"Then why did you say you were instructed? Indeed, how could anyone who did not know these speak of himself as having been instructed?" Distressed, he went to his father's place and said, "Godman, without teaching me correctly, you said you had given me instruction."*

5. panca ma rajanyabandhuh prasnan apraksit tesam naikam canasakam vivaktumiti sa hovaca yatha ma tvam tada etan avadah yath aham esam naikam ca na veda yady aham iman avedisyam katham te navaksyam iti.

5. *"That king, an acquaintance, asked me five questions and I could not answer even one of them." The father said, "The questions of his just as you told me, I do not know any of them. If I had known them, why should I not have told you?"*

6. sa ha gautamo rajno'rdham eyaya tasmai ha praptayarham cakara sa ha pratah sabhaga udeyaya tam hovaca manusasya bhagavan gautama vittasya varam vrinitha iti sa hovaca tavaiva rajan manusam vittam yameva kumarasyante vacam abhasa-thas tam eva me bruhiti sa ha kriccri babhuva.

6. *Then Gautama went to the king's place. When he arrived there, the king paid him proper respects. In the morning he went to the people's assembly where the king was. He said to him, "Gautama, O godman, seek any material boon pertaining to the wealth of worldly people." He replied," Tell me about the questions, which you asked the young man." The king was perplexed.*

7. tam ha ciram vasety ajnapayam cakara tam hovaca yatha ma tvam gautam avado yatheyam na praktvattah pura vidya brahmanan gaccati tasmad u sarvesu lokesu ksatrasyaiva pras-asanam abhud iti tasmai hovaca.

7. *"Stay for a while," he ordered him. Then he said: "As to what you said, Gautama, this knowledge had never been imparted to any Brahmana before you, and thus far this teaching has remained in all the worlds with the warrior class (Khsatriyas only). " Then he spoke.*

Section 4

The Heaven as Sacrificial Fire

1. asau vava loko gautam agnih tasyaditya eva samid rasmayo dhumah, ahar arcih, candrama angarah naksatrani visphulingah.

1. *"That world, O Gautama, is verily the sacrificial fire; of that the sun is the fuel; its rays are the smoke, the day the flame, the moon the coals, the stars the sparks."*

2. tasminn etasminn agnau devah sraddham juhvati tasya ahuteh somo raja sambhavati.

2. *"In that fire, the gods pour the departed as their funeral libations. From this libation arises, Soma, the king."*

Section 5

The Rains as Sacrificial Fire

1. parjanyo vava gautam agnis tasya vayur eva samit abhram dhumah vidyud arcih asanir angara hradanayo visphulingah.

1. *"Prajanya, the god of rain, O Gautama, is verily the sacrificial fire; of that the air is the fuel; the cloud is the smoke, the lightning is the flame, the thunder the coals and the hail the sparks."*

2. tasminn etasminn agnau devah somam rajanam juhvati tasya ahuter varsam sambhavati.

2. *"In that fire the gods pour the kingly Soma as their libation. From this libation arises rain."*

Section 6

The Earth as Sacrificial Fire

1. prithivi vava gautam agnih tasyah samvatsara eva samit akaso dhumo ratrir arcih diso'ngara avantara diso visphulingah.

1. *"The earth, O Gautama, is verily the sacrificial fire; of that year is the fuel, the space is the smoke, the night the flame, the quarters the coals and the intermediate quarters the sparks."*

2. tasminn etasminn agnau deva varsam juhvati tasya ahuter annam sambhavati.

2. *"In that fire, the gods pour rain as their libation. From this libation arises food."*

Notes: Notes: Food is the means by which the returning souls enter the human body and from there into the semen through food.

Section 7
Man As Sacrifical Fire

1. puruso vava gautam agnih tasya vag eva samit prano dhumah jihvarcis caksur angarah srotram visphulingah.

1. *"Man, O Gautama, is verily the sacrificial fire; of that speech is the fuel, breath is the smoke, the tongue the flame, the eyes the coals and the ears the sparks."*

2. tasminn etasminn agnau deva annam juhvati tasya ahute retah sambhavati.

2. *"In that fire the gods pour food as their libation. From this libation arises semen."*

Notes: The souls reincarnate by entering into the semen. From there they enter into the womb of a female through sexual intercourse.

Section 8
Woman as Sacrificial Fire

1. yosa vava gautamagnih tasya upastha eva samit yadupamantrayate sa dhumah yonirarcih yadantah karoti te angara abhinanda visphulingah.

1. *"The woman, O Gautama, is verily the sacrificial fire; of that the middle part is the fuel, the hair is the smoke, the vagina is the flame, penetration is the coals and the pleasure the sparks."*

Notes: A similar symbolism is proposed in the Brihadaranyaka Upanishad.

2. tasminn etasminn agnau deva reto juhvati tasya ahuter garbhah sambhavati.

2. *"In that fire, the gods pour semen as their libation. From this libation arises the fetus."*

Notes: After they are transferred into the womb through sexual intercourse, each soul enters into a fetus, which will eventually grow into a fully developed body for its rebirth.

Section 9

Water the Fifth Libation

1. iti tu pancamyam ahutav apah Purusa vacaso bhavantiti sa ulbavrito garbho dasa va nava va masanantah sayitva yavad vatha jayate.

1. "Hence, the fifth libation of water happens to be called Man. This yolk, inside the womb, having rested there for ten or nine months, more or less, becomes born."

2. sa jato yavad ayusam jivati tam pretam distamito'gnaya eva haranti yata eveto yatah sambhuto bhavati.

2. "Having born, he lives for whatever lifespan he may have. When he is dead, his closest ones carry him, as destined, to the fire from where he came, from which he arose."

Section 10

The Two Paths to Liberation

1. tad ya ittham viduh; ye ceme aranye sraddha tapa ity upasate te arcisam abhisambhavanty arciso'harahna apuryamana-paksam apuryamana paksad yan sad udanneti masams tan.

1. "Those who knows this, those who practice austerities in deep forests, with great faith, go to light, from light to the day, from day to the bright fortnight, from the bright fortnight to those six months during which the sun travels towards the north."

2. masebhyah samvatsaram samvatsarad adityam adityac candramasam candramaso vidyutam tatpurusah manavah sa enan brahma gamayaty esa devayanah pantha iti.

2. "From these months (they go) to the year, from the year to the sun, from the sun to the moon, from the moon to the lightning. There (they meet) that Person who is not human. He leads them to Brahman. This is the path of the gods."

Notes: The gods are immortals. Gods like Indra, Varuna or Agni do not live in Brahman's world, but in a lower heaven ruled by Indra. Still it the path to Brahman is called the path of gods because those who reach this world become gods in their own right. They also qualify to become gods in the next time cycle.

3. atha ya ime grama istapurte dattam ity upasate te dhumam abhisambhavanti dhumad ratrim ratrer aparapaksam aparapaksad yan sad daksinaiti masamstannaite samvatsaramabhiprapnuvanti.

3. *"But those who live in villages, who practice sacrifices to fulfill their desires and indulge in acts of public good and charity, they enter smoke, from smoke to night, from night to the darker fortnight, from the darker fortnight to those six months in which the sun moves southwards. They do not reach the year."*

Notes: The world of smoke is not as bright or pure as the world of light and fire. The souls whose karmas are not cleared enter this world, since they are not yet freed from bondage and from the impurities of their minds and bodies. The description of their journey is couched in symbolism just as in previous verses. Going from day to fortnight, what does this mean? It means the souls remain in the space for this duration, travelling higher and higher as they ascend. It may also means that as the souls ascend higher and higher, the duration of their time changes. Thus, a night in earth's time becomes equal to a fortnight, a fortnight to six months and so on. The world of moon is always surrounded by night or darkness. Hence those who reach the moon, remain surrounded by night or darkness until their return. Their night gets prolonged for months and years. They remain surrounded by darkness, until they return from the world of ancestors. This progressive expansion of time is described here. Upon departing from this world, the souls enter into a region where the duration of a night becomes equal to the duration of a fortnight of earthly time, from there they go the region where the night becomes equal to the duration of six months of earthly time. The progress stops there. These souls never get a chance to enter the world where a day is equal to a year. That is the world of gods and the immortals. According to Hindu calendar, time is both cyclical and relative. A year in earth's time is equal to a day of gods; and a year of gods time is equal to a day of Brahma, the creator god, and so on.

4. masebhyah pitrilokam pitrilokad akasam akasac candramasam esa somo raja tad devanam annam tam deva bhaksayanti.

4. *"From months to the world of ancestors, from the world of ancestors to space, from space to the moon. That one is king Soma. That is food for the gods, which they eat."*

Notes: The verse implies that the gods eat the bodies of the souls who enter the world of ancestors. This cannot be taken literally, because the consequences of performing good actions upon earth cannot be evil. Gods do not eat the bodies of the departing souls. Rather they consume their karmic (casual) bodies, or the karmic fruit accrued from their meritorious actions. Just as we milk the cows and consume that milk, they milk the merit of our actions and consume them. They do it until the subtle bodies of the souls are fully worn out by Time, the ultimate devourer.

5. tasmin yavat sampatam usitvathaitam evadhvanam punarnivartante yathetam akasam akasad vayum vayu rbhutva dhumo bhavati dhumo bhutva'bhram bhavati.

5. "There upon, exhausting the wealth of their karmas, they return again, by the same path by which they go, to space, and from space to air. Having become air, they become smoke; and having become smoke, they become mist."

6. abhram bhutva megho bhavati megho bhutva pravarsati ta iha vrihiyava osadhi vanaspatayah tilamasa iti jayante, ato vai khalu durnisprapataram, yo yo hy annam atti yo retah sincati tadbhuya eva bhavati.

6. "Having become mist, they become clouds, having become clouds, they rain down. Then they are born as rice plants and corn plants, as herbs and trees, as sesame and bean plants. From here on their escape becomes difficult. For whoever person may eat the food, and begets offspring, he henceforth becomes like unto him."

7. tadya iha ramaniya carana abhyaso ha yatte ramaniyam yonim apadyeran brahmanayonim va ksatriyayonim va vaisyayonim vatha ya iha, kapuyacarana abhyaso ha yat te kapuyam yonim apadyeran sva yonim va sukara yonim va candalayonim va.

7. "Those whose conduct was pleasant will attain pleasant wombs, such as the wombs of Brahmanas, Kshatriyas, or Vaisyas; and those whose behavior was evil, will attain the wombs of the evil and the impure ones."

8. athaitayoh pathor na katarenacana tanimani ksudrany asakridavartini bhutani bhavanti jayasva mriyasvety etat tritiyam sthanam tenasau loko na sampuryate tasmaj jugupseta tad esa slokah.

8. "Now, the small creatures do not follow either of the two paths. Being small, they keep revolving, or shall we say, they live and die repeatedly. This is the third condition, by which the world is never be full of humans. Therefore (to avoid this condition) one should cultivate aversion. Regarding this there is this verse."

Notes: Not all souls attain human birth. Those who do not qualify for either of the paths mentioned before, go into the nether world which exists below the earth. They are born as worms and insects and they keep assuming these births repeatedly until their sins are washed away. For this very reason, although the souls are numerous, the world is never full.

9. steno hiranyasya suram pibamsca guros talpam avasan brahma ha caite patanti catvarah pancamas cacarams tairiti.

9. *"Who takes away the wealth that does not belong to him, who drinks intoxicating drinks, who disrespects a teacher's bed, who kills a brahmana, these four fall down and so does the fifth who moves in their company."*

10. atha ha ya etan evam pancagnin veda na saha tair apy acaran papmana lipyate suddhah putah punyaloko bhavati ya evam veda ya evam veda.

10. "Now, he who knows the five fires thus, he is not tainted by sin even if he moves in their company. Pure and clean, he reaches the world of the virtuous, he who know this, yes he indeed who knows this."

Section 11
Vaisvanara, the Eater of Food

1. pracinasala aupamanyavah satyayajnah paulusih indradyumno bhallaveyo janah sarkaraksyo budila asvatarasvis te hai te mahasala mahasrotriyah sametya mimamsam cakruh ko na atma kim brahmeti.

1. Pracinasala Aupamanyava, Satyayajna Paulusi, Indradyumna Bhallaveya, Jana Sarkaraksya, and Budila Asvatarasvi, these five great householders, renowned in the recitations of the Vedas, once gathered to enquire into what the individual Self was and what Brahman was.

2. te ha sampadayamcakruh uddalako vai bhagavanto'yam arunih sampratimam atmanam vaisvanaram adhyeti tam hantabhyagaccameti tam habhyajagmuh.

2. They reflected and said to themselves, "Godmen, Uddalaka Aruni has been presently studying this Self called the Universal Being (Vaisvanara). Let us go to him." They went to him.

3. sa ha sampadayamcakara praksyanti mamime mahasala mahasrotriyah tebhyo na sarvam iva pratipatsye hantaham anyam abhyanusasaniti.

3. He thought, "These great householders, well versed in Vedic knowledge are going to question me and I may not answer them all. Therefore, I shall direct them to another teacher."

4. tan hovaca asvapatirvai bhagavanto'yam kaikeyah sampratimam atmanam vaisvanaram adhyeti tam hantabhya gaccameti tam habhyajagmuh.

4. He said to them: "Godmen, Asvapati Kaikeya has been studying that Self, called the Universal Being. Let us go to him." They went to meet him.

5. tebhyo ha praptebhyah prithag arhani karayamcakara sa ha pratah samjihana uvaca: na me steno janapade na kardaryo na madyapo nanahitagnir na vidvan na svairi svairini kuto yaksyamano vai bhagavantah aham asmi yavad ekaikasma ritvije dhanam dasyami tavad bhagavadbhyo dasyami vasantu bhagavanta iti.

5. When they arrived, the king had made arrangements to receive them severally with honors. After waking up the next morning, he said, "In my rural republic there is no thief, no miser, no drunkard, no man who has not kept domestic fires in his house, no ignorant person, no adulterer, and therefore no question of any adulterous woman. Godmen, I am going to perform a sacrifice, and I give you as much wealth as I give to each Ritvij priest. Godmen, please stay."

6. te hocuh yena haivarthena purusas caret tam haiva vadet atmanam evemam vaisvanaram sampraty adhyesi tam eva no bruhiti.

6. They replied: "The purpose for which a man comes, first he should indeed speak that. Presently you know about the Self called the Universal Being. Please, tell us about him."

7. tan hovaca pratar van prativaktasmiti te ha samitpanayah pur-vahne praticakramire tan hanupaniyaivaitaduvaca.

7. He said, " I will answer your question in the morning." Therefore, the next day morning they went to him with fuel in their hands, and he, without performing the initiatory rites, said to them.

Notes: The king spoke to them about the Self without the initiatory rites because they were already well versed in the knowledge of the Vedas.

Section 12

Incomplete Worship of Brahman as Gods

1. aupamanyava kam tvam atmanam upassa iti divam eva bhagavo rajanniti hovaca: isa vai suteja atma vaisvanaro yam tvam atmanam upasse tasmat tava sutam prasutam asutam kule drisyate.

1. *"Aupamanyava, whom do you worship in your mind" "Gods only, O venerable king."* He said, *"You worship the Universal Beings in your mind as beings of pure light. Therefore, your family has seen plenty of suta, prasuta and asuta extractions.*

Notes: Sankara explains that Suta, Prasuta and Asuta are different types of Soma extractions offered during the sacrifices. Aupamanyava and his family members performed many such sacrifices and made copious offerings of Soma juice to the gods. By virtue of these meritorious acts, the members of his family ensured a place for themselves in the ancestral world, instead of the immortal world, which is open only to those who worship Brahman through austerities and meditation.

2. atsyannam pasyasi priyam atty annam pasyati priyam bhavaty asya brahmavarcasam kule ya etam evam atmanam vaisvanaram upaste mudha tvesa atmana iti hovaca murdha te vyapatisyad yan mam nagamisya iti.

2. *"You eat food and see what is pleasing. He eats food and sees what is pleasing. In the family of him whoever worships the Universal Being thus will have the radiance of Brahman. That however is only the head of the Self,"* he said, *"Your head would have surely fallen off if you had not come to me."*

Notes: Aupamanyava worshipped only the head of the Purusha (Brahman), not the Purusha Himself. That is, he worshipped the gods who constituted the head of Brahman, rather than Brahman fully. Since he did not have full knowledge of Brahman, king Asvapati remarked that his head would have fallen in shame during debates had he not come to him and learned the secret teaching.

Section 13

Incomplete Worship of Brahman as the Sun

1. atha hovaca satyayajnam paulusim pracinayogya kam tvam atmanam upassa ity adityam eva bhagavo rajann iti hovaca isa vai visvarupa atma vaisvanaro yam tvam atmanam upasse tasmat tava bahu visvarupam kule drisyate.

1. *Then he said to Satyayajna Paulusi, "Pracinayogya, whom do you worship in your mind as the Self?"*

"The Sun only, O venerable king."

He said, "You worship the Universal Being within yourself as the Universal Self. Therefore, your family has seen many forms of the Universal Being."

2. pravritto svatariratho dasi niskah atsy annam pasyasi priyam atty annam pasyati priyam bhavat yasya brahmavarcasam

kule ya etam evam atmanam vaisvanaram upaste caksuse tad atmana iti hovaca andho bhavisyah yan mam nagamisya iti.

2. *"Such as chariots with mules, maid servants, and gold necklaces. You eat food and see what is pleasing. He eats food and sees what is pleasing. In the family of him whoever worships the Universal Being thus will have the radiance of Brahman. That however is only the eye of the Self," he said, "Your would have surely become blind if you had not come to me."*

Notes: We have heard before that the being in the Sun was also the person in the eye. Satyayajna's family had worshipped Brahman as the person in the eye, not as the universal Being. Therefore, they had seen numerous manifestations of Brahman, but not Brahman Himself. That qualified them for a place in the ancestral world, but not in the immortal world. Because of this, Asvapati suggested that this partial or incomplete knowledge of Brahman would have kept him blind or ignorant about the truth of Brahman had he not come to him seeking knowledge.

Section 14
Incomplete Worship of Brahman as Breath

1. atha hovacendradyumnam bhallaveyam vaiyaghrapadya kam tvam atmanam upassa iti vayum eva bhagavo rajann iti hovaca: isa vai prithag vartmatma vaisvanarah yam tvam atmanam upasse tasma ttvam prithag balaya ayanti prithag rathasrenayo'nuyanti.

1. Then he said to Indradyumna Bhallaveya,"Vaiyaghrapadya, on what do you meditate as the Self" He said,

"On air only, O venerable king."

He said, "You worship the Universal Being within your own body as the one who moves in various ways. Therefore offerings will come to you in various ways and rows of chariots will follow you in various ways.

Notes: Vaiyaghrapadya worshipped the Self as breath in his own body that moved along diverse paths, but not as the Self itself. His method of worship would earn him wealth but not immortality.

2. atsyannam pasyasi priyamattyannam pasyati priyam bhavatyasya brahmavarcasam kule ya etamevamatmanam vaisvanaramupaste pranastvesa atmana iti hovaca pranasta udakramisyadyanmam nagamisya iti.

2. "You eat food and see what is pleasing. He eats food and sees what is pleasing. In the family of him whoever worships the Universal Being thus (as breath) will have the radiance of Brahman. That however is only the breath of the Self," he said, "Your breath would have departed from you if you had not come to me."

Section 15

Incomplete Worship of Brahman as Space

1. atha hovaca janam sarkaraksya kam tvam atmanam upassa ity akasam eva bhagavo rajann iti hovaca isa vai bahula atma vaisvanaro yam tvam atmanam upasse tasma ttvam bahulo'si prajaya ca dhanena ca.

1. Then he said to Janam Sarkaraksya, "On what do you meditate as the Self"

"On space only, O venerable king."

He said, "You worship the Universal Being within yourself as full. Therefore you are full in offspring and wealth.

2. atsyannam pasyasi priyamattyannam pasyati priyam bhavatyasya brahmavarcasam kule ya etamevamatmanam vaisvanaramupaste samdehastvesa atmana iti hovaca samdehaste vyasiryadyanmam nagamisya iti.

2. "You eat food and see what is dearer. He eats food and sees what is dearer. In the family of him whoever worships the Universal Being thus (as space) will have the radiance of Brahman. That however is only the body of the Self," he said, "Your body would have fallen off if you had not come to me."

Section 16

Incomplete Worship of Brahman as Water

1. atha hovaca budilam asvatarasvim vaiyaghrapadya kam tvam atmanam upassa ityapa eva bhagavo rajann iti hovacaisa vai rayir atma vaisvanaro yam tvam atmanam upasse tasmat tvam rayiman pustiman asi.

1. Then he said to Budila Aasvatarasvim, "Vaiyaghrapadya, on what do you meditate as the Self" "On water only, O venerable king." He said, "You worship the Universal Being within yourself as matter. Therefore you are endowed with wealth and strength ."

Notes: Rayi means either food or material wealth. Both arise from water only. Food is produced from rains, since they ensure good harvest. Where there are rains, there is wealth of grains and cattle. Therefore, water is the source of material wealth. Even the goddess Lakshmi, emerged out of water only during the churning of oceans.

2. atsy annam pasyasi priyam atty annam pasyati priyam bhavat yasya brahmavarcasam kule ya etam evam atmanam vaisvanaram upaste bastis tv esa atmana iti hovaca bastis te vyabhetsyad yan mam nagamisya iti.

2. *"You eat food and see what is dearer. He eats food and sees what is dearer. In the family of him whoever worships the Universal Being thus (as water) will have the radiance of Brahman. That however is only the bladder of the Self," he said, "Your bladder would have burst if you had not come to me."*

Section 17

Incomplete Worship of Brahman as the Support

1. atha hovaca uddalakam arunim gautama kam tvam atmanam upassa iti prithivim eva bhagavo rajann iti hovaca isa vai pratisthatma vaisvanaro yam tvam atmanam upasse tasmat tvam pratisthito'si prajaya ca pasubhisca.

1. *Then he said to Uddalaka Aruni, "Gautama, on what do you meditate as the Self"*

"On earth only, O venerable king." He said, "You worship the Universal Self within yourself as well settled. Therefore you are endowed with offspring and cattle.

2. atsy annam pasyasi priyam atty annam pasyati priyam bhavaty asya brahmavarcasam kule ya etam evam atmanam vaisvanaram upaste padau tv etav atmana iti hovaca padau te vyamlasyetam yan mam nagamisya iti.

2. *"You eat food and see what is dearer. He eats food and sees what is dearer. In the family of him whoever worships the Universal Being thus (as earth) will have the radiance of Brahman. That however is only the feet of the Self," he said, "Your feet would have withered away if you had not come to me."*

Section 18

Worshipping Brahman as the Self

1. tan hovaca: ite vai khalu yuyam prithag ivemam atmanam vaisvanaram vidvamso'annam attha yas tv etam evam pradesa-

matram abhivimanam atmanam vaisvanaram upaste sa sarvesu lokesu sarvesu bhutesu sarvesv atmasv annam atti.

1. *To them he said, "Verily, indeed you eat your food thinking of the Universal Being variously; but he who worships the Universal Being as the measure of the universe and identical with the Self eats food in all worlds, in all beings, and in all Selves.*

2. tasya ha va etasyatmano vaisvanarasya murdhaiva sutejah caksur visvarupah pranah prithagvartmatma samdeho bahulo bastir eva rayih prithivy eva padav ura eva vedih lomani barhir hridayam garhapatyo mano'nvaharyapacana asyam ahavaniyah.

2. *"Of that Universal Being, his head is pure light, eyes are the universal form, breath is what moves in various paths, body is what is full, bladder is verily the wealth, feet are verily the earth, chest is indeed the sacrificial altar, hair the sacred grass, heart the Garhapatya fire, mind the Anvaharya fire, and mouth the Ahavaniya fire.*

Notes: Vaisvanarah is the Cosmic Self, Purusa. His parts represent the diversity of creation. Worshipping His parts is not the same as worshipping Him. However, it has its own rewards. Pradesamatra, which is mentioned in the previous verse, means that which is measured by its state or location or parts with the help of the five senses and the mind. This is in reference to the manifested Brahman, Purusha.

Section 19

Making an Offering of Food to Prana

1. tad yad bhaktam prathamam agaccet tadd homiyam sa yam prathamam ahutim juhuyat tam juhuyat pranaya svaheti pranas tripyati.

1. *"Therefore that food which comes first as an offering, that is the burnt offering, fit to be poured into the sacrificial fire. He who burns that offering in the sacrificial fire first, should make that offering to the incoming breath (prana), Saying,"Svaha to the incoming breath." Then the incoming breath is satisfied."*

Notes: When one eats food, a small portion of it should be offered to gods first with a sprinkling of water, as if it is a burnt offering or an offering poured into the sacrificial fire of an Agnihotra sacrifice. How should that be offered? This verse says, it should be offered, saying Svaha, to the breath in the body, who is the carrier of food. It is a practice in Hindu tradition to offer the food one eats to gods before eating it. The same is mentioned in the Bhagavadgita also, which says that he who eats food without offering it to God, verily eats sin.

2. prane tripyati caksus tripyati caksusi tripyaty adityas tripyaty aditye tripyati dyaus tripyati divi tripyantyam yat kim ca dyaus ca adityas cadhitisthatas tat tripyati tasyanu triptim tripyati prajaya pasubhir annad yena tejasa brahmavarcasena iti.

2. *"If the incoming breath is satisfied, the eye is satisfied; if the eye is satisfied, the sun is satisfied; if the sun is satisfied, heaven is satisfied; if heaven is satisfied, whatever is under the heaven and under the sun is satisfied. Through their satisfaction he (the sacrificer) himself is satisfied with offspring, cattle, food, vigor, and the glow of Brahman."*

Section 20

Making an Offering of Food to Vyana

1. atha yam dvitiyam juhuyattam juhuyat vyanaya svaheti vyanastripyati.

1. *"Then, while making the second burnt offering, he should pour that offering into the sacrificial fire saying, "Svaha to the diffused breath (vyana). Then the diffused breath is satisfied."*

2. vyane tripyati srotram tripyati srotre tripyati candramastripyati candramasi tripyati disastripyanti diksu tripyantisu yatkimca disasca candramascadhitisthanti tattripyati tasyanu triptim tripyati prajaya pasubhirannadyena tejasa brahmavarcasena iti.

2. *"If the diffused breath is satisfied, the ear is satisfied; if the ear is satisfied, the moon is satisfied; if the moon is satisfied, the quarters are satisfied; if the quarters are satisfied, whatever is under the moon and under the quarters is satisfied. Through their satisfaction he (the sacrificer) himself is satisfied with offspring, cattle, food, vigor, and the glow of Brahman."*

Section 21

Making an Offering of Food to Apana

1. atha yam tritiyam juhuyat tam juhuyad apanaya svahety apanas tripyati.

1. *"Then, while making the third burnt offering, he should pour that offering into the sacrificial fire saying, "Svaha to the downward breath (apana). Then the downward breath is satisfied."*

2. apane tripyati vaktripyati vaci tripyantyam agnis tripyaty-agnau tripyati prithivi tripyati prithivyam tripyantyam yat kim ca prithivi cagnis cadhitisthatas tat tripyati tasyanu triptim tripyati prajaya pasubhir annadyena tejasa brahmavar-casena iti.

2. *"If the downward breath is satisfied, speech is satisfied; if speech is satisfied, fire is satisfied; if fire is satisfied, the earth is satisfied; if the earth is satisfied, whatever is under the earth and under the fire is satisfied. Through their satisfaction he (the sacrificer) himself is satisfied with offspring, cattle, food, vigor, and the glow of Brahman."*

Section 22
Worshipping Brahman with the Offering of

1. atha yam caturthim juhuyattam juhuyatsamanaya svaheti samanastripyati.

1. *"Then, while making the fourth burnt offering, he should pour that offering into the sacrificial fire saying, "Svaha to the equalizing breath (samana). Then the equalizing breath is satisfied."*

Notes: Samana is equalizing breath, with its seat in the cavity of the navel. It plays an important role in the digestion.

2. samane tripyati manas tripyati manasi tripyati parjanyas tripyati parjanye tripyati vidyut tripyati vidyuti tripyantyam yat kim ca vidyucca parjanyas cadhitisthathah tat tripyati tasyanu triptim tripyati prajaya pasubhir annad yena tejasa brahmavarcaseneti.

2. *"If the equalizing breath is satisfied, the mind is satisfied; if the mind is satisfied, Prajanya is satisfied; if Prajanya is satisfied, the lightning is satisfied; if the lightning is satisfied, whatever is under the lightning and under Prajanya is satisfied. Through their satisfaction he (the sacrificer) himself is satisfied with offspring, cattle, food, vigor, and the glow of Brahman."*

Notes: Prajanya is rain god. What is below Prajanya and the lightning is the earth and the mortal world.

Section 23
Making an Offering of Food to Udana

1. atha yam pancamim juhuyat tam juhuyat udanaya svahety udanas tripyati.

1. *"Then, while making the fifth burnt offering, he should pour that offering into the sacrificial fire saying, "Svaha to the upward breath (udana). Then the upward breath is satisfied.*

Notes: Udana rises up the throat and goes into the head.

2. udane tripyati tvak tripyati tvaci tripyantyam vayus tripyati vayau tripyaty akasas tripyaty akase tripyati yat kim ca vayus cakasas cadhitisthatah tat tripyati tasyanu triptim tripyati prajaya pasubhir annadyena tejasa brahmavarcasena.

2. *"If the upward breath is satisfied, the skin is satisfied; if the skin is satisfied, the air is satisfied; if the air is satisfied, the space is satisfied; if the space is satisfied, whatever is under the air and under the space is satisfied. Through their satisfaction he (the sacrificer) himself is satisfied with offspring, cattle, food, vigor, and the glow of Brahman."*

Section 24

The Importance of Correct Knowledge

1. sa ya idam avidvan agnihotram juhoti yathangaran apohya bhasmani juhuyat tadrik tat syat.

1. *"If, without knowing this, one offers a libation to fire, it would be just like a man removing the burning coals and pouring his libations on the ashes.*

2. atha ya etad evam vidvan agnihotram juhoti tasya sarvesu lokesu sarvesu bhutesu sarvesv atmasu hutam bhavati.

2. *"But he who offers the libations knowing it thus, he makes the offerings to all the worlds, to all the beings and to all the selves.*

3. tad yathesikatulamagnau protam praduyeta ivam hasya sarve papmanah praduyante ya etad evam vidvan agnihotram juhoti.

3. *"Just as the fibers of the isika plant are readily burnt when thrown into the fire, so are his sins burnt whoever knowing it thus pours the libations into the fire.*

4. tasmad u haivamvid yady api candalayoccistam prayacced atmani haivasya tad vaisvanare hutam syad iti tad esa slokah.

4. *"Further, knowing it thus, if one were to offer the leftover of his food to a grossly impure person, it would be offered in his digestive fire (vaisvanara). On this there is the following verse.*

5. yatheha ksudhita bala mataram pary upasata evam sarvani bhutany agnihotram upasata ity agnihotram upasata iti.

5. *"As the hungry children sit here around their mother, so do all beings sit around the sacrificial fire, yes they do sit around the sacrificial fire."*

Chapter 6

Section 1

Uddalaka Aruni's Teaching to Svetaketu

1. aum, svetaketur haruneya asa tam ha pitovaca svetaketo vasa brahmacaryam na vai somya asmat kulino'nanucya brahma bandhur iva bhavatiti.

1. Aum. There lived Svetaketu Aruneya. To him, his father said, "You should study, practicing celibacy. Truly, dear there is none in our family tree, who has not learned (the Vedas) and was a brahmana just by relation only.

Notes: One becomes a true Brahmana only by studying and learning the Vedas, not otherwise.

2. sa ha dvadasa varsa upetya caturvimsati varsah sarvan vedan adhitya mahamana anucanamani stabdha eyaya tamha pitovaca; svetaketo yan nu somya idam mahamana anucanamani stabdho'sy uta tam adesam apraksyah.

2. Having begun his studies at the age of twelve and studied all the Vedas, at the age of twenty four he returned home, filled with pride and arrogance, thinking that he had become a great scholar. His father said to him, "Svetaketu you are so full of pride and arrogance, thinking that you are well read. Have you asked for that teaching?"

3. yenasrutam srutam bhavaty amatam matam avijnatam vijnatam iti katham nu bhagavah sa adeso bhavatiti.

3. "By which what cannot be heard is heard, what cannot be thought is thought, what cannot be known is known?"

"Godman, what is that instruction?"

4. yatha somyai ekena mritpindena sarvam mrinmayam vijnatam syad vacarambhanam vikaro namadheyam mrittikety eva satyam.

4. "Just as, my dear, by one ball of clay all that is made of clay is known, the difference being only the name arising from words. The underlying truth is that it is all clay.

5. yatha somyai ekena lohamanina sarvam lohamayam vijnatam syad vacarambhanam vikaro namadheyam loham ity eva satyam.

5. "Just as, my dear, by one nugget of gold all that is made of gold is known, the difference being only the name, arising from the words. The underlying truth it is all gold.

6. yatha somyi ekena nakhanikrintanena sarvam karsnayasam vijnatam syad vacarambhanam vikaro namadheyam krisnayasam ity eva satyam evam somya sa adeso bhavatiti.

6. "Just as, my dear, by one pair of nail clippers all that is made of iron is known, the difference being only the name arising from the words. The underlying truth it is all iron. Thus, my dear, is that instruction."

7. na vai nunam bhagavantas ta etad avedisuh yadd hy etad avedisyan katham me navaksyann iti bhagavams tv eva me tad bravitviti tatha somya iti hovaca.

7. "No, those Godmen did not know it; if they had known, why would they not have told me? Godman, please tell me that."

"So be it, my dear," he said,

Notes: Svetaketu learned the lower knowledge of the Vedas. He learned how to perform the sacrifices and chant the mantras. But he did not receive proper instruction in the secret teachings of the Upanishads.

Section 2

How Creation Manifested

1. sad eva saumya idam agra asid ekam evadvitiyam; tadd haika ahuh asad evedam agra asid ekam evadvitiyam tasmad asatah sajjayata.

1. "In the beginning, my dear, there was that one Being only, without a second. Others say, in the beginning there was that Non-Being, one only, without a second; and from that Non-Being the Being was born.

2. kutastu khalu saumya ivam syad iti hovaca katham asatah sajjayeteti; sat tv eva saumya idam agra asid ekam evadvitiyam.

2. "But, how could it be so my dear?" he said. "How could Being be born of Non-Being? Indeed, my dear, this was Being only in the beginning, one, without a second."

Notes: Uddalaka Aruni presented here a counter viewpoint held by the Vaisesikas, or the materialists, who argued that creation emerged from nothing (Non-Being) and no creator (Being) was responsible for it. The Purva Mimansakas also held similar opinion as they focused upon the procedural aspects of sacrifice and its symbolism rather than its source and origin, while the Vedantins clearly recognized a creator God. Uddalaka concurred with this opinion validated by the Vedas that Isvara (Being) was responsible for it. Although He did not manifest, the Being was still there in the beginning in a state similar to that sleep, in which we are there but still not there.

3. tad aiksata bahu syam prajayeyeti tat tejo'srijata: tat teja aiksata bahu syam prajayeyeti tad apo'srijata, tasmad yatra kvaca socati svedate va purusah tejasa eva tad adhyapo jayante.

3. It thought, "May I become many, may I grow further." It created brilliance (fire in the sun). That brilliance thought, "May I become many, may I grow further." It created water. Therefore, whenever a person is heated by brilliance he perspires; water is produced from brilliance (fire).

4. ta apa aiksanta bahvyah syama prajayemahiti ta annam asrijanta tasmad yatra kva ca varsati tad eva bhuyistham annam bhavaty adbhya eva tad adhy annadyam jayate.

4. Water thought, "May I become many, may I grow further." It created food (earth). Therefore, whenever it rains upon earth, food is produced upon earth abundantly. Thus eatable food is produced from water only.

Section 3

Threefold Origin of Beings

1. tesam khalv esam bhutanam triny eva bijani bhavanty andajam jivajam udbhijjam iti.

1. Of the living beings, there are only three origins, those produced from eggs, those produced by living beings and those produced from root bearing seeds.

2. seyam devataiksata hantaham imas tisro devata anena jivenatman anupravisya namarupe vyakaravaniti.

2. That Being thought, "Let me enter into these three divinities as the embodied Self and let me differentiate into various names and forms."

3. tasam trivritam trivritam ekaikam karavan iti seyam devatamas tisro devata anena iva jivenatman anupravisya namarupe vyakarot.

3. *"Let me make each of them threefold,"(thinking thus) the Being entered into those three Divinities as the embodied Self and developed names and forms.*

Notes: Each of them became threefold because of the triple gunas that were activated at the time of creation.

4. tasam trivritam trivritam ekaikam akarodyatha tu khalu saumya imas tisro devatas trivrit trivrid ekaika bhavati tan me vijanihiti.

4. *"He made each of them threefold. How each of these three divinities became threefold, that, my dear, now you learn from me.*

Section 4

The Triple Qualities of Creation

1. yad agne rohitam rupam tejasas tad rupam yac cuklam tad apam yat krisnam tad annasya apagad agner agnitvam vacarambhanam vikaro namadheyam trini rupanity eva satyam.

1. *That form which is bright red in fire is the form of bright light; that which is white is water; that which is black is food. Thus disappears the quality of fire from fire, as a modification of words in name only, arising from speech. But the truth is, the forms are only three.*

2. yad adityasya rohitam rupam tejasas tad rupam yac cuklam tad apam yat krisnam tad annasya apagad adityad aditya tvam vacarambhanam vikaro namadheyam trini rupanity eva satyam.

2. *That form which is glowing red in the sun is the form of bright light; that which is white is water; that which is black is food. Thus disappears the characteristic of the sun from the sun, as a modification of words in name only. But the truth is, the forms are only three.*

3. yac candramaso rohitam rupam tejasas tad rupam yac cuklam tad apam yat krisnam tad annasya apagac candrac candra tvam vacarambhanam vikaro namadheyam trini rupanity eva satyam.

3. *That form which is glowing red in the moon is the form of bright light; that which is white is water; that which is black is food. Thus disappears the characteristic of the moon from the moon, as a modification of words in name only. But the truth is, the forms are only three.*

4. yad vidyuto rohitam rupam tejasas tad rupam yac cuklam tad apam yatkrisnam tad annasya apagad vidyuto vidyut tvam vacarambhanam vikaro namadheyam trini rupanity eva satyam.

4. *That form which is glowing red in the lightning is the form of bright light; that which is white is water; that which is black is food. Thus disappears the characteristic of lightning from lightning, as a modification of words in name only. But the truth is, the forms are only three.*

5. etadd ha sma vai tad vidvamsa ahuh purve mahasala mahasrotriya na no'dya kascana srutam amatam avijnatam udaharisyatiti hy ebhyo vidamcakruh.

5. *Indeed it was this the great householder and learned people knew in the past when they declared the same saying, "None can mention to us anything that we have not heard, we have not perceived or we have not known." And they knew everything from these (three) only.*

6. yad u rohitam ivabhud iti tejasas tad rupam iti tad vidam cakruhyad u suklam ivabhud ity apam rupam iti tad vidam cakruh yad u krisnam ivabhud ity annasya rupam iti tad vidam cakruh.

6. *Whatever appeared red, they knew it was the form of bright light. Whatever appeared white, they knew it was the form of water; whatever appeared black, they knew it was the form of food (earth).*

Notes: Tejas means fire. All physical forms are essentially made up of fire, water and the earth. Air and space cannot be heard, seen or known through the senses. Hence they are not mentioned. However, these two are also present in the body, but only in a subtle form. The three forms are also represented by the triple gunas, namely the sattva, rajas and tamas symbolized here as the fire, the water and the earth.

7. yad avijnatam ivabhud ity etasam eva devatanam samasah iti tad vidam cakruh yatha tu khalu saumya imas tisro devatah purusam prapya trivrid trivrid ekaika bhavati tanme vijanihiti.

7. *Whatever seemed unknown, they knew was a combination of these three divinities only. Now, learn from me, my dear, how each of these three divinities become threefold when they gain hold of a person.*

Section 5

Threefold Nature of Food, Water and Fire

1. annam asitam tredha vidhiyate tasya yah sthavistho dhatus tat purisam bhavati yo madhyamas tan mamsam yo'nisthas tan manah.

1. Food becomes threefold when eaten; its elemental part becomes feces; its middle part flesh and its subtlest part becomes the mind.

2. apah pitas tredha vidhiyante tasam yah sthavistho dhatus tan mutram bhavati yo madhyamas tal lohitam yo'nisthah sa pranah.

2. Water becomes three fold when drunk; its elemental part becomes urine; its middle portion blood, its subtlest part becomes breath.

3. tejo'sitam tredha vidhiyate tasya yah sthavistho dhatus tad asthi bhavati yo madhyamah sa majja yo'nisthah sa vak.

3. Fire (in the food suc as butter or oil) becomes three fold when taken into the body; its elemental part becomes bone its middle portion marrow, its subtlest part becomes speech.

4. annamayam hi somya manah apomayah pranah tejomayi vag iti bhuya eva ma bhagavan vijnapayatv iti tatha somyeti hovaca.

4. Truly, by food only my dear the mind (is formed); by water the breath; by fire the speech. "Godman, explain to me again." "Surely my dear," he said.

Section 6

The Subtle Aspects of Food, Water and Fire

1. dadhnah somya mathyamanasya yo'nima sa urdhvah samudisati tat sarpir bhavati.

1. Regarding the curd, my dear, through churning the subtlest part rises up and becomes butter.

2. evam eva khalu saumya annasyasyamanasya yo'nima sa urdhvah samudisati tanmano bhavati.

2. In the same manner, my dear, when eaten, the subtlest part of the food rises up and becomes the mind.

3. apamsomya piyamananam yo'nima sa urdhvah samudisati sa prano bhavati.

3. When drunk, my dear, the subtlest part of the water rises up and becomes breath.

4. tejasah ssaumya asyamanasya yo'nima sa urdhvah samudisati sa vagbhavati.

4. When consumed, my dear, the subtlest part of the fire rise up and becomes speech.

5. annamayam hi saumya mana apomayah pranah tejomayi vagiti bhuya eva ma bhagavan vijnapayatv iti tatha somyeti hovaca.

5. Truly, by food only my dear the mind (is formed); by water the breath; by fire the speech. "Godman, explain to me again." "Surely my dear," he said.

Section 7
The Connection Between Food and Memory

1. sodasa kalah somya purusah pancadasahani masih kamam apah piba apomayah prano na pibato viccetsyata iti.

1. Sixteen parts, my dear, has a man. Do not eat for fifteen days, but drink as much water as you can. Breath is made up of water and you will be not be separated from breath if you drink water.

2. sa ha pancadasahani nasa atha hainam upasasada kim bravimi bho ity ricah saumya yajumsi samaniti sa hovaca na vai ma pratibhanti bho iti.

2. For fifteen days, he remained without food. Then, he returned to his father and said, "What should I say?"

"Chant the Riks, Yajus and the Samans."

He said, "They are not coming to me."

3. tam hovaca, yatha saumya mahato'bhya hitasyaiko'ngarah khadyotamatrah parisistah syat tena tato'pi na bahu dahet evam saumya te sodasanam kalanam eka kalatisista syat tayaitarhi vedan nanubhavasy asan atha me vijnasyasiti.

3. He said, "My dear, just as a little ember, only of the size of a firefly, when left out of a large fire cannot burn any more, so also my dear, is the case (of the body) if one part only is left out of the sixteen. Hence you were unable to recollect the Vedas. Now eat; then you will understand me."

4. sa hasatha hainam upasasada tam ha yat kimca papracca sarvam ha pratipede.

4. Then he ate and returned to him. This time, whatever he asked, he was able to answer all.

5. tam hovaca yatha somya mahato'bhyahitasyaikamangaram khadyotamatram parisistam tam trinairupasamadhaya prajvalayettena tato'pi bahu dahet.

5. He said, "Just as my dear a little ember only of the size of a firefly, when left out of a large fire can be flared up again by covering it with grasses and made to burn more than the original fire."

6. evam somya te sodasanam kalanam eka kalatisistabhut sa nnenopasamahita prajvali taya itarhi vedan anubhavasy anna mayam hi saumya mana apomayah pranas tejomayi vag iti tadd hasya vijajnav iti vijajnav iti.

6. "So also my dear, the one part left out of the sixteen parts was flared up and made to burn more by food. Because of that you were able to remember the Vedas. Thus, by food only my dear the mind (is formed); by water, the breath; by fire, the speech." Then he understood what he said; yes he did understand it.

Section 8

The Being as the Source of All Beings

1. uddalako harunih svetaketum putram uvaca svapnantam me saumya vijanihiti yatraitat purusah svapiti nama sata saumya tada sampanno bhavati svamapito bhavati tasmad enam svapitity acaksate svam hy apito bhavati.

1. Uddalaka Aruni said to his son Svetaketu: "Learn from me, my dear, what happens at the end of the dream state. When a person goes into that state, my dear, which goes by the name sleep, he reaches perfection, he goes into himself. Therefore, they say he is in himself (svapiti) because he has gone into himself.

2. sa yatha sakunih sutrena prabaddho disam disam patitvanyatrayatanam alabdhva bandhanam evopasrayata evam eva khalu saumya tan mano disam disam patitvan yatrayatanam alabdhva pranam evopasrayate prana bandhanam hi saumya mana iti.

2. *Just as a bird that is tied to a string struggles to fly in all directions and then finding no resting place elsewhere settles down at the very place where it is tied, so my dear the mind after flying in different directions and finding no resting place elsewhere settles down in breath. For the mind, my dear, is bound to breath only.*

3. asanapipase me saumya vijanihiti yatraitat puruso'sisisati nama apa eva tad asitam nayante tad yatha gonayo'svanayah purusanaya ity evam tad apa acaksate asanayeti tatritaccungam utpatitam saumya vijanihi nedam amulam bhavisyatiti.

3. *Learn from me, my dear, what hunger and thirst are. When a person is hungry, as it is called, water is carrying away what has been eaten (by him). Therefore, just as they speak of a cowherd, a horseman or a leader of men, they speak of water as the leader of food.*

4. tasya kva mulam syad anyatrannat evam eva khalu saumya annena sungenapo mulam anviccadbhih saumya sungena tejo mulam anvicca tejasa saumya sungena sanmulam anvicca sanmulah saumya imah sarvah prajah sadayatanah sat pratisthah.

4. *Where else could be its root other than food? So also, my dear, for the sprout called food consider water is the root; for the sprout called water, my dear, consider fire is the root; for the sprout called fire, my dear, consider the Being is the root. All these beings, my dear, have their root in the Being. They reside in the Being; they are established in the Being.*

5. atha yatraitat purusah pipasati nama teja eva tat pitam nayate tad yatha gonayo'svanayah purusanaya ity evam tat teja acasta udanyeti tatraitad eva sungam utpatitam saumya vijanihi nedam amulam bhavisyatiti.

5. *Now, when a person is thirsty, as it is generally called, fire carries away what has been drunk. Therefore, just as they speak of a cowherd, a horseman or a leader of men, they speak of fire as the leader of water. Therefore, my dear, know this (body) to be the offshoot that has sprouted; this (body) could not be without a root.*

6. tasya kva mulam syad anyatra adbhya adbhih saumya sungena tejo mulam anvicca tejasa saumya sungena san mulam anvicca sanmulah saumya imah sarvah prajah sadayatanah satpratistha yatha tu khalu saumya imas tisro devatah purusam prapya trivrit trivridekaika bhavati tad uktam purastad eva bhavaty asya saumya purusasya prayato van manasi sampadyate manah prane pranas tejasi tejah parasyam devatayam.

6. Where else could be its root other than water? So also, my dear, for the sprout called water consider fire is the root; for the sprout called fire, my dear, consider the Being is the root. All these beings, my dear, have their root in the Being. They reside in the Being; they are established in the Being. And how each of these three divinities, my dear, when they reach man become threefold has been explained (to you before). When, my dear, a person departs from here, his speech merges into his mind, his mind into his breath, his breath into fire and fire into the Supreme Deity.

7. sa ya eso'nima aitad atmyam idam sarvam tat satyam sa atma tat tvam asi svetaketu iti bhuya eva ma bhagavan vijnapayatv iti tatha somyeti hovaca.

7. Now that which is the subtle essence, in it all that exists here has its self. That is the True. That is the Self; and Svetaketu, That you are.

"Godman, teach me more."

"Be it so, my dear," he said.

Section 9

The Self as the Essence of All Beings

1. yatha somya madhu madhu krito nististhanti nanatyayanam vriksanam rasan samavaharam ekatam rasam gamayanti.

1. Just as the bees, my dear, create honey by collecting the sap of various trees and then reducing them into one sap.

2. te yatha tatra na vivekam labhante amusyaham vriksasya raso'asmy amusyaham vriksasya raso'asmity evam eva khalu saumya imah sarvah prajah sati sampadya na viduh sati sampadyamaha iti.

2. *And just as these juices have no intelligence to known that "I am the sap of this tree, or I am the sap of that tree," so also, my dear, all these beings, when they join with the Supreme Being, do not know that they have joined with the Supreme Being.*

3. ta iha vyaghro va simho va vriko va varaho va kito va patango va damso va masako va yad yad bhavanti tad abha-vanti.

3. *Whatever creatures are here, be it a lion, a wolf, a boar, a worm, a fly, a gnat, or a mosquito, that they become again.*

4. sa ya eso'nim aitad atmyam idam sarvam tat satyam sa atma tat tvam asi svetaketo iti bhuya eva ma bhagavan vijnapayatviti tatha somyeti hovaca.

4. *Now that which is the subtle essence, in it all that exists here has its self. That is the True. That is the Self; and Svetaketu, That you are."*

"Godman, teach me more."

"Be it so, my dear," he said.

Section 10

The Self as the Subtle Essence

1. imah saumya nadyah purastatpracyah syandante pascat praticyastah samudrat samudram evapiyanti sa samudra eva bhavati ta yatha tatra na viduh iyam aham asmi iyam aham asmiti.

1. *These rivers, my dear, the eastern ones flow eastwards, and the western ones flow westwards. From the ocean into the ocean they flow, and indeed thereby become the ocean itself. Just as these rivers, when they are in the ocean, do not know, "I am this river or that."*

2. evam eva khalu saumya imah sarvah prajah sata agamya na viduh sata agaccamaha iti ta iha vyaghro va simho va vriko va varaho va kito va patango va damso va masako va yad yad bhavanti tad abhavanti.

2. *In the same manner, my dear, all these creatures, all these beings, when they join with the Supreme Being, do not know that they emerge from the Supreme Being, do not know, "We have emerged from the Supreme Being." Whatever creatures are here, be it a lion, a wolf, a boar, a worm, a fly, a gnat, or a mosquito, that they become again.*

3. sa ya eso'nim aitad atmyam idam sarvam tat satyam sa atma tat tvam asi svetaketo iti bhuya eva ma bhagavan vijnapayatv iti tatha somyeti hovaca.

3. *Now that which is the subtle essence, in it all that exists here has its self. That is the True. That is the Self; and Svetaketu, That you are.*

"Godman, teach me more."

"Be it so, my dear," he said.

Section 11

The Self as the Root of All Beings

1. asya somya mahato vriksasya yo mule abhyahanyat jivan sravedyo madhye abhyahanyat jivan sravet yo'gre'abhyah anyat jivan sravet sa esa jiven atmananuprabhutah pepiyamano modamanas tisthati.

1. *Of this large tree, my dear, if one were to strike at its root, it would bleed, but live; if one were to strike in the middle, it would bleed, but live; if one were to strike at the top, it would bleed, but live. Pervaded by the living Self, the tree stands firm, drinking water and rejoicing.*

2. asya yad ekam sakham jivo jahaty atha sa susyati dvitiyam jahaty atha sa susyati tritiyam jahaty atha sa susyati sarvam jahati sarvah susyati.

2. *Of that tree, if life departs from one branch, that branch dries up; if it leaves the second branch, that branch dries up; if it leaves the third branch, that branch dries up. If it leaves the whole (tree), everything dries up.*

3. ,evam eva khalu saumya viddhiti hovaca, jivapetam vava kiledam mriyate na jivo mriyate iti sa ya eso'nima aitad atmyam idam sarvam tat satyam sa atma tat tvam asi svetaketo iti bhuya eva ma bhagavan vijnapayatv iti tatha evam eva khalu saumya viddhiti hovaca iti hovaca.

3. *"Know that, even this to be the same, my dear," he said. "Verily, indeed, this (body) dies when it is without the living Self; but the living Self does not die. Now that which is the subtle essence, in it all that exists here has its self. That is the True. That is the Self; and Svetaketu, That you are."*

"Godman, teach me more."

"Be it so, my dear," he said.

Section 12

An Example of Seed in Reference to the Self

1. nyagrodhaphalam ata aharet idam bhagava iti bhinddhiti bhinnam bhagava iti kimatra pasyasity anvya ivema dhana bhagava ity asamangaikam bhinddhiti bhinna bhagava iti kimatra pasyasiti na kimcana bhagava iti.

1. *"Bring from a fruit from that Nyagrodha tree."*

"Here it is, godman."

"Break it."

"It is broken, godman."

"What do you see in there?"

"These very small seeds, godman."

"Break one of them."

"It is broken, godman."

"What do you see there?"

"Nothing whatsoever, godman."

2. tam hovaca: yam vai saumya etam animanam na nibhalayasa etasya vai saumya eso'nimna evam mahan nyagrodhas tisthati sraddhatsva saumyeti.

2. *He said: "My dear, that minute one which you do not perceive there, truly, my dear, from that very minute thing this large Nyagrodha tree comes into existence. Have faith, my dear."*

Notes: The minute thing (the living Self) cannot be seen because it is subtle and beyond the senses. The Self cannot be perceived or validated by the senses through direct experience (pratyaksa). This has been explained before also. Since the Self was subtle and could not be reached with the senses, Uddalaka Aruni asked his son to have faith (sraddha) in what he was told because only through faith one could realize the transcendental Self. The same teaching continues in the next section also.

3. sa ya eso'nim aitad atmyam idam sarvam tat satyam sa atma tat tvam asi svetaketo iti bhuya eva ma bhagavan vijnapayatviti tatha somyeti hovaca.

3. *That which is minute, in it all that exists here has its self. That is the True. That is the Self; and Svetaketu, That you are.*

"Godman, teach me more."

"Be it so, my dear," he said.

Section 13
An Example of Salt in Reference to the Self

1. lavanam etad udake avadhay atha ma pratar upasidatha iti sa ha tatha cakara tam hovaca yad dosa lavanam udake avadha anga tad ahareti tadd havamrisya na viveda; yatha vilinam evam.

1. Put this salt in the water and then wait for me until the morning. He did as he was told. Then he said to him, "That salt, which you put in the water last night, bring it to me." He looked for it, but could not find it, since it was completely dissolved.

2. angasyantad acameti katham iti lavanam iti madhyad acameti kathamiti lavanam ity antad acameti katham iti lavanam ity abhiprasyaitad atha mopasidatha iti tadd ha tatha cakara tac casvat samvartate tam hovaca: atra vava kila tat saumya na nibhalayase atraiva kileti.

2. "Taste it from this end. How is it?"

"It is salty."

"Taste it from the middle. How is it?"

"It is salty"

"Taste it from the other end. How is it?"

"It is salty."

"Throw it away and come to me."

He did so, (saying), "It is always the same."

Then he said, "Truly, my dear, here (in this body) also, you do not perceive the Being, although it is there.

Notes: In previous section Uddlaka Aruni taught his son that the Self was subtle and minute (anima). Here he said that it was imperceptible and all pervasive.

3. sa ya eso'nimaitad atmyam idam sarvam tat satyam sa atma tat tvam asi svetaketo iti bhuya eva ma bhagavan vijnapayatv iti tatha somyeti hovaca.

3. *That which is minute, in it all that exists here has its self. That is the True. That is the Self; and Svetaketu, That you are.*

"Godman, teach me more."

"Be it so, my dear," he said.

Section 14

The Importance of a Teacher in Liberation

1. yatha saumya purusam gandharebhyo'bhinaddhaksam aniya tam tato'tijane visrijetsa yatha tatra pran vodan vadharan va pratyan va pradhmayitabhinaddhaksa anito'bhinaddhakso visristah.

1. *Just as my dear one might take a person away from the Gandhara with his eyes covered and leave him in a place that is devoid of people and just as that person would turn towards the east, north, or west and south, "I have been brought here with my eyes covered and left here with my eyes covered."*

Notes: Gandhara is the name of a place.

2. tasya yathabhinahanam pramucya prabruyad etam disam gandhara etam disam vrajeti sa gramad gramam priccan pandito medhavi gandharan evopasampadyeta ivam evehacaryavan puruso veda tasya tavad eva ciram yavan na vimoksye atha sampatsya iti.

2. *"And just as one might remove his blindfold and say, "Gandhara is in this direction, go in this direction," whereby, having been informed and capable of judgment, enquiring from village to village, he would eventually reach Gandhara exactly in the same manner in this world does that person who has a teacher know, "I shall be here so long as I am not liberated and attained perfection."*

Notes: When you do not know and cannot see, you have to rely upon others who know or who have seen. A teacher is therefore important and necessary in our spiritual education. He opens our eyes to the hidden truths. He dispels the ignorance of his disciples and prepares them for liberation or self-realization. He teaches them how to cultivate inner purity and discern the Self within.

3. sa ya eso'nima aitad atmyam idam sarvam tat satyam sa atma tat tvam asi svetaketo iti bhuya eva ma bhagavan vijnapayatviti tatha somyeti hovaca.

3. That which is minute, in it all that exists here has its self. That is the True. That is the Self; and Svetaketu, That you are.

"Godman, teach me more."

"Be it so, my dear," he said.

Section 15

Awareness in the Final Moments Of Death

1. purusam saumya, utopatapinam jnatayah paryupasate janasi mam janasi mam iti tasya yavanna van manasi sampadyate manah prane pranas tejasi tejah parasyam devatayam tavajjanati.

1. If a person, my dear, is sick, his relatives gather around him and ask, "Do you know me? Do you know me?" Of that, as long as his speech is not merged in his mind, his mind in breath, breath in fire and fire in the Supreme Being, he knows them.

Notes: Awareness lasts as long as a person is alive and conscious and his vital functions, such as speech, thinking, breathing, digestion and resting, are normal.

2. atha yadasya van manasi sampadyate manah prane pranas tejasi tejah parasyam devatayamatha na janati.

2. Now, when his speech is merged in his mind, his mind in breath, breath in fire, and fire in the Supreme Being, then he does not know them.

Notes: Death is common to all. Whether they are ignorant or liberated, eventually everyone dies. However, life after death is different from person to person. There is rebirth for those who desire things and live selfishly. There is liberation for those who renounce their desires and live austerely in the contemplation of Brahman. A liberated person goes to the world of Brahman and becomes immortal; while a worldly person, who has not freed himself from passions and desires, leaves behind his elemental body and goes to the world of ancestors from where he returns after a certain time to continue his existence upon earth.

3. sa ya eso'nim aitad atmyam idam sarvam tat satyam sa atma tat tvam asi svetaketo iti bhuya eva ma bhagavan vijnapayatviti tatha somyeti hovaca.

3. That which is minute, in it all that exists here has its self. That is the True. That is the Self; and Svetaketu, That you are.

"Godman, teach me more."

"Be it so, my dear," he said.

Section 16

The Self as the Truth

1. purusam saumya uta hastagrihitam anayanty apaharsit steyam akarsit parasum asmai tapata iti sa yadi tasya karta bhavati tata evanritam atmanam kurute so'anritabhisam-dho'nritenatmanam antardhaya parasum taptam pratigrihnati sa dahyate'atha hanyate.

1. My dear, they take away a person, seizing him by his hand, (saying), "He has stolen, he has taken away what does not belong to him, heat the axe for him." If he has done that he makes himself untruthful. Then being untruthful to himself and covering himself with falsehood, when he holds the heated axe, he is burnt and he is killed.

Notes: It was customary in ancient times to ask a person charged with a crime of stealing etc., to prove his innocence by holding a hot metal object such as an axe. If it burnt him, it was a proof that he was guilty. Otherwise innocent.

2. atha yadi tasyakarta bhavati tat eva satyam atmanam kurute sa satyabhisandhah satyenatmanam antardhaya parasum taptam pratigrihnati sa na dahyate atha mucyate.

2. But if he did not do that (theft), then he is verily true to himself. Then being truthful and having covered himself by truth, when he holds the heated axe, then he is not burnt, and he is released.

3. sa yatha tatra na dahyeta itad atmyam idam sarvam tat satyam sa atma tat tvam asi svetaketo iti tadd hasya vijajnav iti vijajnav iti.

3. Just as that person (who is truthful) who is not burnt is That which is the Self for all this here. That is the True. That is the Self; and Svetaketu, That you are. He understood what he said, yes, he understood it.

Notes: The state of the Self is the same as the truthful person, who is not burnt. It is true (sat). Therefore it is indestructible and it cannot be burnt. A person who attains the true Self also becomes eternal and indestructible.

Chapter 7

Section 1

Meditation upon the Names of Brahman

1. adhihi bhagava iti hopasasada sanatkumaram naradah tam hovaca: yad vettha tena mopasida tatas ta urdhvam vaksyamiti sa hovaca.

1. Narada said, approaching Sanatkumara, "Godman, teach me." He said, "Come nearer and tell me what you know. Then I will tell you what is higher than that."

2. rigvedam bhagavo'dhyemi yajurvedam samavedam atharvanam caturtham itihasa puranam pancamam vedanam vedam pitryam rasim daivam nidhim vakovakyam ekayanam devavidyam brahmavidyam bhutavidyam ksatravidyam naksatravidyam sarpadevajanavidyam etad bhagavo'dhyemi.

2. "Godman, I know the Rigveda, the Yajurveda, the Samaveda, the Atharvaveda as the fourth, the epics and the Puranas as the fifth, the Veda of the Vedas (grammar), the knowledge of making sacrificial offerings to ancestors, the knowledge of numbers and drawing birth carts, the science of predicting divine actions, the knowledge of treasures, logic, ethics, knowledge of gods, knowledge of Brahman, knowledge of spirits, knowledge of weapons, astronomy, knowledge of serpents and poisons, knowledge of celestial beings, all this I know Godman."

3. so'aham bhagavo mantravid evasmi natmavit srutam hy eva me bhagavad drisebhyah tarati sokam atmavid iti so'aham bhagavah socami tam ma bhagavan sokasya param tarayatv iti tam hovaca yad vai kim caitad adhyagistha, namaivaitat.

3. "However, godman, I know only the knowledge of chants, but I do not know the Self. I heard from Godmen like you that he who knows the Self transcends sorrow. Godman, I am in sorrow. Please, godman, take me beyond this sorrow of mine." He said to him, "Whatever you have studied is about names only."

Notes: Narada was a great sage. Yet, it appears from this verse that he lacked the knowledge of Self. He had the knowledge of scriptures, but no realization of the Self. Hence, he was in distress. His teacher, Sanatkumara, having ascertained the extent of his knowledge and his prior education, confirmed to him that whatever he knew about the Self was its names and forms, but not its very essence.

4. nama va rgvedo yajurveda samaveda atharvanas caturtha itihasapurana pancamo vedanam vedah pitryao rasir daivo, nidhir vakovakyam, ekayanam, devavidya, brahmavidya, bhutavidya, ksatravidya, naksatravidya, sarpadevajanavidya namavaitat, namopassveti.

4. *"The Rigveda is a name. So also the Yajurveda, the Samaveda, the Atharvaveda as the fourth, the epics and the Puranas as the fifth, the Veda of the Vedas (grammar), the knowledge of making sacrificial offerings to ancestors, the knowledge of numbers and drawing birth carts, the science of predicting divine actions, the knowledge of treasures, logic, ethics, knowledge of gods, knowledge of Brahman, knowledge of spirits, knowledge of weapons, astronomy, knowledge of serpents and poisons, knowledge of celestial beings. All this (knowledge) about names only. Meditate upon the name."*

5. sa yo nama brahmety upaste yavan namno gatam tatrasya yatha kamacaro bhavati yo nama brahmety upaste: 'sti bhagavo namno bhuya iti namno vava bhuyo'stiti; tan me bhagavan bravitv'iti.

5. *"He who meditates upon the names of Brahman, has the freedom to act so far as the names go, he who meditates upon names of Brahman." "Godman, is there anything better than the name?" "Yes, there is something greater than name."Godman, please tell me that."*

Notes: What the teacher meant was that he who had the knowledge of the names and the freedom to act within the sphere of that knowledge. That is, he could meditate upon those names and fulfill his desires. and gain some insight But there was a still a higher knowledge, which would lead to greater freedom and accomplishment and that he decided to teach him.

Section 2

Speech as Brahman

1. vag va va namno bhuyasi vag va rigvedam vijnapayati yajurvedam samavedam atharvanam caturtham itihasapuranam pancamam vedanam vedam pitryamvrasim daivam nidhim vakovakyam ekayanam devavidyam brahmavidyam bhutavidyam ksatravidyam sarpadevajanavidyam divam ca prithivim ca vayum cakasam capas ca tejas' ca devams' ca manusyams' ca pasums' ca vayamsi ca trina vanaspatin svapadany akitapatangapipilakam dharmam cadharmam ca satyam canritam ca sadhu ca sadhu ca hridayajnam ca hridayajnam ca

yad vai van na bhavisyan na dharmo nadharmo vyajnapayisyan na satyam nanritam na sadhu nasadhu na hridayajno nahridayajno vag evaitat sarvam vijnapayati vacam upassveti.

1. *"Speech is verily greater than the name. By speech alone Rigveda is made known. So also the Yajurveda, the Samaveda, the Atharvaveda as the fourth, the epics and the Puranas as the fifth, the Veda of the Vedas (grammar), the knowledge of making sacrificial offerings to ancestors, the knowledge of numbers and drawing birth carts, the science of predicting divine actions, the knowledge of treasures, logic, ethics, knowledge of gods, knowledge of Brahman, knowledge of spirits, knowledge of weapons, astronomy, knowledge of serpents and poisons, knowledge of celestial beings, heaven, earth, air, ether, water, fire, gods, men, cattle, birds, herbs, trees, all beasts down to worms, flies, and ants; the right and the wrong; the true and the untrue, the good and the bad, the pleasant and the unpleasant. Truly, if there were no speech, neither right nor wrong would be known, neither the true nor the false, neither the good nor the bad, neither the pleasant nor the unpleasant. Speech makes us understand all this. Meditate upon speech."*

2. sa yo vacam brahmety upaste yavad vaco gatam tatrasya yatha kamacaro bhavati yo vacam brahmety upaste'asti bhagavah vaco bhuya iti vaco vava bhuyo'stiti tan me bhagavan bravitviti.

2. *"He who meditates upon speech as Brahman, has freedom to act so far as the speech goes, he who meditates upon speech as Brahman." "Godman, is there anything better than the speech?" "Yes, there is something greater than speech.""Godman, please tell me that."*

Notes: Speech is greater than the names, because names are known through speech.

Section 3

The Mind as Brahman

1. mano vava vaco bhuyo yatha vai dve vamalake dve va kole dvau vaksau mustiranubhavatyevam vacam ca nama ca mano'nubhavati sa yada manasa manasyati mantranadhiyiyetyathadhite karmani kurviyetyatha kurute putramsca pasumscecceyetyatheccata imam ca lokamamum cecceyetyatheccate mano hyatma mano hi loko mano hi brahma mana upassveti.

1. *"Mind is truly greater than speech. Just as a closed first holds two amalaka or two kola or two aksa fruits, the mind holds speech and*

name. If a man holds in his mind the thought of reading the sacred hymns, he reads them; if he thinks of performing any actions, he performs them; if he desires in his mind to have sons and cattle, he desires for them; if has desire in his mind for this world and Brahman, he desires for them. Mind is indeed the Self, mind is the world, mind is Brahman. Meditate upon the mind."

Notes: Mind gives us the ability to reflect upon what we know or learned. Therefore mind is better than speech because it enhances the quality of our learning as well as understanding.

2. sa yo mano brahmety upaste yavan manaso gatam tatrasya yatha kamacaro bhavati yo mano brahmety upaste; asti bhagavay manaso bhuya iti manaso vava bhuyo'stiti; tanme bhagavan bravitv iti.

2. *"He who meditates upon mind as Brahman, has freedom to act so far as the mind goes, he who meditates upon mind as Brahman.""Godman, is there anything better than mind?""Yes, there is something greater than mind.""Godman, please tell me that."*

Section 4

Intention as Brahman

1. samkalpo vava manaso bhuyanyada vai samkalpayate atha manasyat yatha vacam irayati tam u namnirayati namni mantra ekam bhavanti mantresu karmani.

1. *"Will, truly, is better than the mind; for by the will only a man thinks in his mind, sends it forth as speech, sends it forth as a name. In name, the sacred hymns become one and in the sacred hymns, actions (become one)."*

2. tani ha va etani samkalpaikayanani samkalpatmakani samkalpe pratisthitani samaklipatam dyavaprithivi samakalpetam vayus cakasam ca samakalpantapas ca tejas ca tesam sam kliptyai varsam samkalpate varsasya samkliptya annam samkalpate, annasya sam kliptyai pranah samkalpante prananam sam kliptyai mantrah samkalpante mantranam sam kliptyai karmani samkalpante karmanam samkliptyai lokah samkalpate lokasya sam kliptyai sarvam samkalpate sa esa samkalpah samkalpam upassveti.

2. *"All these indeed centre in the will, have will as their source (Self), and abide in the will. By the will only heaven and earth, by the will*

only air and space, by the will only water and fire. By their will, rain intends. By the will of rain, food intends. By the will of food, breath intends. By the will of breath, the sacred hymns intends, by the will of sacred hymns, the sacrifices intends, by the will of sacrifices, the world intends. By the will of the world, everything becomes intended. This is how the will works. Meditate upon the will."

Notes: Samkalpa means will, resolve or intention. With the help of samkalpa one gives shape to one's thoughts and desires. The exercise of will or intention requires the use of discretion or intelligence. It is vital for practicing austerities, self-restraint and discipline. Without samkalpa one cannot practice renunciation (sanyasa) or withstand the rigors of self-discipline. Therefore will or intention is superior to mere thought.

3. sa yah samkalpam brahmety upaste samkliptanvai sa lokan dhruvan dhruvah pratisthitan pratisthito'vyathamanan avyatha mano'bhisidhyati yavat samkalpasya gatam tatrasya yatha kamacaro bhavati yah samkalpam brahmety upaste; asti bhagavah samkalpadbhuya iti samkalpad vava bhuyo'stiti tan me bhagavan bravitviti.

3. *"He who meditates upon the will as Brahman truly attains the worlds he has willed for himself, being constant, the constant worlds, being stable and undisturbed, stable and undisturbed worlds. As far as his will goes thus far he has the freedom to act, he who meditates upon the will as Brahman." "Godman, is there anything better than the will?" "Yes, there is something greater than will." "Godman, please tell me that."*

Section 5
The Discerning Mind as Brahman

1. cittam va va samkalpad bhuyah yada vai cetayate'tha samkalpayate atha manasyaty atha vacam irayati tam u namnirayati namni mantra ekam bhavanti mantresu karmani.

1. *"The discerning mind is better than will. When one thinks, then one wills, then one holds it in mind, then one sends its forth as speech, and one sends it forth as a name. In name, the sacred hymns become one and in sacred hymns, actions (become one)."*

Notes: Citta has several meanings. In a wider sense it means discernment and total mind and body awareness. In a restricted sense it means the mind or consciousness. We are able to discern or distinguish things in our citta only. We may also translate it as reason or intelligence, but actually these are aspects of citta, which is definitely more than mere thought.

2. tani ha va etani cittaikayanani cittatmani citte pratisthitani tasmad yady api bahu vida citto bhavati nayam astity evainam ahuh yad ayam veda yadva ayam vidvan nettham acittah syad ity atha yady alpavic cittavan bhavati tasma evota susrusante cittam hy evaisam ekayanam cittam atma cittam pratistha cittam upassveti.

2. "All these indeed centre in the discerning mind, have the discerning mind as their source, and abide in the discerning mind. Therefore, if a man is well learned but not intelligent, whatever he may know, people say he is nobody. If he knew, he would not be so thoughtless. However, if he is intelligent, even though he knows little, people would be inclined to listen to him gladly. Truly, the discerning mind is the centre, the discerning mind is the self, and the discerning mind is the support of all this. Meditate upon the discerning mind."

3. sa yas cittam brahmety upaste cittan vai sa lokan dhruvan dhruvah pratisthitan pratisthito'vyathamanan avyathamano'- bhisidhyati yavac cittasya gatam tatrasya yatha kamacaro bhavati yas cittam brahmety upaste; asti bhagavah cittad bhuya iti cittad va va bhuyo'stiti tan me bhagavan bravitv iti.

3. "He who meditates upon the discerning mind as Brahman truly attains the worlds he has willed for himself, being constant, the constant worlds, being stable and undisturbed, stable and undisturbed worlds. As far as his discerning mind goes thus far he has the freedom to act he who meditates upon the discerning mind as Brahman." "Godman, is there anything better than discerning mind?" "Yes, there is something greater than discerning mind." "Godman, please tell me that."

Section 6

Meditation as Brahman

1. dhyanam va va cittad bhuyo dhyayativa prithivi dhyayativa antariksam dhyayativa dyauh, dhyayantivapoh, dhyayantiva parvatah devamanusyah tasmad ya iha manusyanam mahattam prapnuvanti dhyanapadamsa ivaiva te bhavanty atha ye'lpah kalahinah pisuna upavadinas te atha ye prabhavo dhyanapadamsa ivaiva te bhavanti dhyanam upassveti.

1. "Meditation is better than thought. The earth meditates as it were, and so do the mid-region, the heaven, the water, the mountains, gods and men. Therefore, he who attains greatness among men here upon earth, seems to have attained a portion of (greatness arising from) meditation. Thus, while small and unskilled people are quarrelsome, abusive and slandering, great men seem to have attained a portion of (the greatness of) meditation. Meditate upon meditation."

2. sa yo dhyanam brahmety upaste yavad dhyanasya gatam tatrasya yatha kamacaro bhavati yo dhyanam brahmety upaste; asti, bhagavah dhyanad bhuya iti dhyanad va va bhuyo'stiti tanme bhagavan, bravitviti.

2. "He who meditates upon meditation as Brahman, has freedom to act as far as meditation goes, he who meditates upon meditation as Brahman." "Godman, is there anything better than meditation?""Yes, there is something greater than meditating." "Godman, please tell me that."

Section 7
Learned knowledge as Brahman

1. vijnanam va va dhyanad bhuyah vijnanena va rigvedam vijanati yajurvedam samavedam atharvanam caturtham itihasapuranam pancamam vedanam vedam pitryamrasim daivam nidhim vakovakyam, ekayanam devavidyam brahmavidyam bhutavidyam ksatravidyam naksatravidyam sarpadevajanavidyam divam ca prithivim ca vayum cakasam capasca tejas ca devams' ca manusyams' ca pasums' ca vayamsi ca trinavanaspatincvapadany akitapatanga pipilakam dharmam cadharmam ca satyam canritam ca sadhu casadhu ca hridayajnam ca hridayajnam cannam ca rasam cemam ca lokam amum ca vijnanenaiva vijanati vijnanam upassveti.

1. "Learned knowledge is certainly better than meditation. By learned knowledge only one understands the Rigveda, the Yajurverda, the Samaveda the Atharvaveda as the fourth, the epics and the Puranas as the fifth, the Veda of the Vedas (grammar), the knowledge of making sacrificial offerings to ancestors, the knowledge of numbers and drawing birth carts, the science of predicting divine actions, the knowledge of treasures, logic, ethics, knowledge of gods, knowledge of Brahman, knowledge of spirits, knowledge of weapons, astronomy, knowledge of serpents and poisons, knowledge of celestial beings, heaven, earth, air, ether, water, fire, gods, men, cattle, birds, herbs, trees, all beasts down to worms, flies, and ants; the right and the wrong; the true and the untrue, the good and the bad, the pleasant and the unpleasant. All this is known by learned knowledge only. Meditate upon learned knowledge."

Notes: Vijnanam means learned knowledge, material knowledge, empirical knowledge, worldly knowledge, or knowledge acquired through study, perception and memory. It is inferior to the higher knowledge (jnanam) arising from self-realization but superior to ignorance and delusion.

2. sa yo vijnanam brahmety upaste vijnanavato vai sa lokanj-nanavato'bhisidhyati yavad vijnanasya gatam tatrasya yatha kamacaro bhavati yo vijnanam brahmety upaste, asti bhagavo vijnanadbhuya iti vijnanad va va bhuyo'stiti tan me bhagavan bravitviti.

2. *"He who meditates upon learned knowledge as Brahman, truly attains the worlds of learned knowledge. He has freedom to act as far as learned knowledge goes, he who meditates upon learned knowledge as Brahman." "Godman, is there anything better than learned knowledge?" "Yes, there is something greater than learned knowledge." "Godman, please tell me that."*

Section 8

Strength as Brahman

1. balam vava vijnanad bhuyo'pi ha satam vijnanavatam eko balavana kampayate sa yada bali bhavaty athotthata bhavaty uttisthan paricarita bhavati paricarann upasatta bhavaty upasidandrasta bhavati srota bhavati manta bhavati boddha bhavati karta bhavati vijnata bhavati balena vai prithivi tisthati balenantariksam balena dyauh balena parvata balena devamanusya balena pasavas ca vayamsi ca trinavanaspatayah svapadany akitapatangapipilakam balena lokas tisthati balam upassveti.

1. *"Strength is better than wisdom. One strong person indeed makes a hundred men of wisdom shake in fear. When a person is strong, he rises in power. If he rises, he serves wise people. When he serves (wise people), he becomes their follower. When he follows, he becomes a seer, he becomes a listener, he becomes a thinker, he becomes a perceiver, he becomes doer, he becomes a person of wisdom. By strength indeed the earth rests on its foundation, by strength the mid-region, by strength the sky, by strength the mountains, by strength gods and men, by strength cattle, birds, grass and plants, all animals down to the worms,*

files and ants. By strength, the world rests on its foundation. Meditate upon strength."

2. sa yo balam brahmety upaste yavad balasya gatam tatrasya yatha kamacaro bhavati yo balam brahmety upaste, asti bhagavo balad bhuya iti balad va va bhuyo'stiti tan me bhagavan bravitviti.

2. "He who meditates upon strength as Brahman, he has freedom to act as far as strength goes, he who meditates upon strength as Brahman." "Godman, is there anything better than strength?" "Yes, there is something greater than strength." "Godman, please tell me that."

Section 9
Food as Brahman

1. annam vava balad bhuyah tasmad yady api dasa ratrir nasniyat yadyu ha jivet atha va adrasta srotamantaboddha karta vijnata bhavaty atha annasyayai drasta bhavati srota bhavati manta bhavati boddha bhavati karta bhavati vijnata bhavaty annam upassveti.

1. "Food is better than strength. Therefore if a man abstains from food for ten days, although he is alive, he becomes one who cannot see, who cannot hear, who cannot think, who cannot know, who cannot act and who cannot discern. But upon eating food, he becomes one who can see, who can hear, who can think, who can know, who can act and who can discern. Meditate upon food."

2. sa yo'nnam brahmety upaste, annavato vai sa lokan panavato'bhisidhyati yavad annasya gatam tatrasya yatha kamacaro bhavati yo'nnam brahmety upaste, asti bhagavo'nnadbhuya ity annad va va bhuyo'stiti tan me bhagavan bravitviti.

2. "He who meditates upon food as Brahman, truly he attains the worlds of food and drink. He has freedom to act as far as food goes, he who meditates upon food as Brahman." "Godman, is there anything better than food?" "Yes, there is something greater than food." "Godman, please tell me that."

Section 10

Water as Brahman

1. apo va va annad bhuyah tasmad yada suvristir na bhavati vyadhiyante prana annam kaniyo bhavisyatiti yatha yada suvristir bhavaty anandinah prana bhavanty annam bahu bhavisyatiti apa evema murta yeyam prithivi yad antariksam yad dyauh yat parvatah yad deva manusyah yat pasavas ca vayamsi ca trina vanaspatayah svapadany akita patanga pipilakam apa evema murtah apa upassveti.

1. "Water, truly is better than food. Therefore when there is insufficient rain, the living beings will be distressed by the thought that food will be insufficient; but when there is sufficient rain they rejoice in the hope that food will be abundant. Water only assumes these forms and becomes the earth, the mid-region, the heaven, the mountains, god and men, cattle, birds, plants and trees, all animals down to the worms, flies and ants. Water indeed is all these forms. Meditate upon water."

2. sa ya apo brahmety upasta apnoti sarvan kaman triptiman bhavati yavad apam gatam tatrasya yatha kamacaro bhavati yo'po brahmety upaste, asti bhagavah, adbhyo bhuya ity adbhyo vava bhuyo'stiti; tanme bhagavan bravitviti.

2. "He who meditates upon water as Brahman, truly he attains all his desires and becomes satisfied. He has freedom to act as far as water goes, he who meditates upon water as Brahman." "Godman, is there anything better than water?" "Yes, there is something greater than water." "Godman, please tell me that."

Section11

Fire As Brahman

1. tejo va va adbhyo bhuyah tasmad va etad vayum agrihyakasam abhitapati tad ahuh, nisocati nitapati varsisyati va iti teja eva tat purvam darsayitvathapah srijate tad etad urdhvabhis ca tirascibhis ca vidyudbhih ahradas caranti; tasmad ahuh: vidyotate stanayati varsisyati va iti teja eva tat purvam darsayitvatha'pah srijate: teja upassveti.

1. "Fire, truly, is better than water. Fire united with air, heats up the sky. Then people say, it is hot, it is scorching hot, it is going to rain. Thus, showing this mark first, fire creates water. So also, lightening appears, flashing above and across the sky, along with thunders. Therefore people say, there is lightning, there is thunder, and it is going to rain. After showing this mark first, fire creates water. Meditate upon fire."

2. sa yas tejo brahmety upaste tejasvi vai sa tejasvato lokan bhasvato'pahatatamaskan abhisidhyati, yavat tejaso gatam tatrasya yatha kamacaro bhavati yas tejo brahmety upaste; asti bhagavah tejaso bhuya iti; tejaso vava bhuyo'stiti; tanme bhagavan bravitv iti.

2. *"He who meditates upon fire as Brahman, truly, being radiant himself, attains radiant worlds that are bright and free from darkness. He has freedom to act as far as fire goes, he who meditates upon fire as Brahman." "Godman, is there anything better than fire?" "Yes, there is something greater than fire." "Godman, please tell me that."*

Section 12

1. akaso vava tejaso bhuyan: akase vai suryacandramasav ubhau vidyun naksatrany agnih akasenahvayaty akasena srinoty akasena pratisrinoty, akase ramate, akase na ramate, akase jayate; akasam abhijayate akasam upassveti.

1. *"Space, truly, is better than fire. For in space only exist both the sun and the moon, the lightning, the stars, fire. Through space one extends speech, through space one hears, through space one replies. In space, only one enjoys (the objects) or does not enjoy. In space all are born and into space all extend. Meditate upon space."*

Notes: That which supports is always superior to what is supported. Space supports the whole creation. It also pervades the whole creation. It is often compared to Brahman himself, since it is subtle, indefinable and infinite. Hence it is superior to all the objects mentioned before as the aspects of Brahman, such as air, water etc.

2. sa ya akasam brahmety upasta akasavato vai sa lokan prakasavato' sambadhan urugayavato'bhisidhyati yavad akasasya gatam tatrasya yatha kamacaro bhavati ya akasam brahmety upaste, asti bhagava, akasadbhuya iti; akasad va va bhuyo'stiti; tanme bhagavanbravitv iti.

2. *"He who meditates upon space as Brahman, truly, attains spacious and radiant worlds that are unconstrained, wide and extending. He has freedom to act as far as space goes, he who meditates upon space as Brahman." "Godman, is there anything better than space?" "Yes, there is something greater than space." "Godman, please tell me that."*

Section 13

Memory as Brahman

1. smaro va va akasad bhuyah tasmad yady api bahava asirann asmaranto naiva te kamcana srinuyuh na manviran, na vijaniran yada vava te smareyuh atha, srinuyuh, atha manvirann atha vijaniran, smarena vai putran vijanati, smarena pasun smaram upassveti.

1. *"Memory, truly, is better than space. Therefore, when many people assemble and if they lack memory, they would not hear anyone, they would not think, and they would not know. Through memory, one knows one's sons, through memory, one's cattle. Meditate upon memory."*

Notes: Memory or recollection is superior because without memory it is not possible to identify any of the objects mentioned before as Brahman. We are able to recognize even space as space because of memory only.

2. sa yah smaram brahmety upaste, yavat smarasya gatam tatrasya yatha kamacaro bhavati yah smaram brahmety upaste, asti bhagavah smarad bhuya iti smarad va va bhuyo'stiti tan me bhagavan bravitviti.

2. *"He who meditates upon memory as Brahman, has freedom to act as far as space goes, he who meditates upon memory as Brahman." "Godman, is there anything better than memory?" "Yes, there is something greater than memory." "Godman, please tell me that."*

Section 14

Hope as Brahman

1. asa va va smarad bhuyasy aseddho vai smaro mantran adhite karmani kurute putrams ca pasums ceccata imam ca lokam amum ceccata asam upassveti.

1. *"Hope is better than memory. Kindled with hope, memory chants the sacred hymns, performs sacrifices, desires sons, cattle, this world and the other. Meditate upon hope."*

2. sa ya asam brahmety upaste asayasya sarve kamah samridhyanty amogha hasyasiso bhavanti yavad asaya gatam tatrasya yatha kamacaro bhavati ya asam brahmety upaste, asti bhagava asaya bhuya ityasaya vava bhuyo'stiti tan me bhagavan bravitviti.

2. *"He who meditates upon hope as Brahman, all his desires are fulfilled by hope, his prayers do not go unheard. He, has freedom to act as far as hope goes, he who meditates upon hope as Brahman." "Godman, is there anything better than hope?" "Yes, there is something greater than hope." "Godman, please tell me that."*

Section 15

Breath as Brahman

1. prano va va asaya bhuyan yatha va ara nabhau samarpita evam asmin prane sarvam samarpitam pranah pranena yati pranah pranam dadati pranaya dadati prano ha pita prano mata prano bhrata pranah svasa prana acaryah prano brahmanah.

1. *"Breath, truly, is better than hope. As the spokes of a wheel are bound to the hub, so does everything is bound to the breath. By breath moves life. Breath gives life to life. It gives life to those that breath. Breath is the father, breath is the mother, breath is the brother, breath is the sister, breath is the teacher and breath is the Brahmana."*

2. sa yadi pitaram va mataram va bhrataram va svasaram vacaryam va brahmanam va kimcid bhrisamiva pratyaha dhiktvastvity evainam ahuh pitriha vai tvam asi matriha vai tvam asi bhratriha vai tvam asi svasriha vai tvam asi, acaryaha vai tvam asi brahmanaha vai tvam asiti.

2. *"If someone were to respond inappropriately to his father, mother, brother, sister, teacher or a Brahmana, then people say, "Shame on you. You are a slayer of father, a slayer of mother, a slayer of brother, a slayer of sister, a slayer of teacher, a slayer of a Brahmana."*

3. atha yady apy enan utkranta pranan sulena samasam vyatisamdahet naivainam bruyuh pitrihasiti na matrihasiti na bhratrihasiti na svasrihasiti na acaryahasiti na brahmanahasiti.

3. *"But when breath departs from them, and if one were to poke them with a stick and burn them to pieces, no one would say, "You are a slayer of father, a slayer of mother, a slayer of brother, a slayer of sister, a slayer of teacher, a slayer of a Brahmana."*

4. prano hy evaitani sarvani bhavati sa va esa evam pasyann evam manvanah evam vijanann ativadi bhavati tam ced bruyuh ativady asity ativady asmiti bruyat napahnuvita.

4. *"Breath is all this. Truly, he who sees this, thinks about this, knows this, becomes an excellent speaker. Even when people say to him, 'You are an excellent speaker,' he should say, 'I am indeed an excellent speaker.' He should not deny it."*

Section 16
Truth and Speech

1. esa tu va ativadati yah satyenativadati so'aham bhagavah satyenativadaniti satyam tv eva vijijnasitavyamiti; satyam bhagavo vijijnasa iti.

1. *"But, truly, he is an excellent speaker, who excels in speaking truth." "Godman, may I become an excellent speaker of truth?" "Indeed, (for that) one must wish to know the truth." "Godman, I wish to know the truth."*

Notes: Narada wished to know whether the instruction was complete and they arrived at truth. because in many teachings breath was extolled as superior to all the organs in the body. His teacher indicated that there was still more to know to arrive at the truth of Brahman.

Section 17
Understanding and Truth

1. yada vai vijanatyatha satyam vadati navijanan satyam vadati vijanann eva satyam vadati vijnanam tv eva vijijnasitavyam iti vijnanam, bhagavo, vijijnasa iti.

1. *"Truly, when one understands, then one speaks the truth. He who does not understands does not speak truth. Only he who understands speaks the truth. This understanding one must wish to understand." "Godman, I wish to understand the understanding."*

Section 18
Thinking and Knowing

1. yada vai manute, atha vijanati namatva vijanati matvaiva vijanati matis tv eva vijijnasitavyeti; matim bhagavo vijijnasa iti.

1. *"When one thinks, then one understands. He who does not think, does not understand. Only he who thinks, understands. This thinking one must wish to understand." "Godman, I wish to know about thinking."*

Section 19

Faith and Thought

1. yada vai sraddadhaty atha manute nasraddadhan manute sraddadhad eva manute sraddha tv eva vijijnasitavyeti; sraddham bhagavo vijijnasa iti.

1. "When one has faith, one thinks. He who does not have faith, does not think. Only he who has faith thinks. This faith one must wish to understand." "Godman, I wish to understand faith."

Section 20

Steadfast Service and Faith

1. yada vai nististhaty atha sraddadhati nanististhan sraddadhati nististhann eva sraddadhati nistha tv eva vijijnasitavyeti; nistham, bhagavo vijijnasa iti.

1. "When one serves (a teacher) steadfastly, then one has faith. He who does not serve steadfastly, does not have faith. Only he who serves steadfastly has faith. This steadfast service, one must wish to know." "Godman, I wis to know about service."

Section 21

Action and Steadfast Service

1. yada vai karoty atha nististhati nakritva nististhati kritvaiva nististhati kritistveva vijijnasitavyeti kritim bhagavo vijijnasa iti.

1. "When one acts, then one does service. He who does not act, does not perform service. Only he who acts does the service. This action one must wish to know." "Godman, I wish to know about action (that leads to service)."

Notes: The emphasis here is not any type of action, but upon actions performed sacrificially and selflessly as part of one's obligatory duty.

Section 22

Happiness and Actions

1. yada vai sukham labhate atha karoti nasukham labdhva karoti sukhameva labdhva karoti sukham tv eva vijijnasitavyamiti sukham bhagavo vijijnasa iti.

1. *"When one gains happiness, then one performs actions. He who does not gain happiness, does not perform actions. Only he who gains happiness performs actions. This happiness, you must wish to know." "Godman, I wish to know about happiness."*

Section 23
The Infinite as Happiness

1. yo vai bhuma tat sukham nalpe sukham asti bhumaiva sukham bhuma tv eva vijijnasitavya iti bhumanam bhagavo vijijnasa iti.

1. *"That which is infinite is happiness. There is no happiness in the finite. The infinite alone is happiness. This infinite, you must wish to know." "Godman, I wish to know the infinite."*

Section 24
The Difference Between Finite and Infinite

1. yatra nanyat pasyati nanyac crinoti nanyad vijanati sa bhumatha yatranyat pasyaty anyac crinoty anyad vijanati tad alpam yo vai bhuma tad amritam atha yadalpam tan martym sa bhagavah kasmin pratisthita iti sve mahimni yadi va na mahimniti.

1. *"Where nothing else is seen, nothing else is heard nothing else is known, that is the infinite. Where anything else is seen, anything else is heard, anything else known, that is finite. The infinite is immortal. The finite is mortal.""Godman, in what does the infinite rest?" "In its own greatness, or (perhaps) not in its greatness."*

Notes: The creation is finite. It is characterized by duality, while, Brahman, the infinite is free from all duality. In the infinite nothing else is perceived, heard or known. It is indeterminate. Hence, no one knows where the infinite rests.

2. goasvam iha mahimety acaksate hastihiranyam dasabharyam ksetrany ayatananiti naham evam bravimi bravimiti hovacanyo hy anyasmin pratisthita iti.

2. *"In this world, they speak of the cows, the horses, elephants, gold, slaves, wives, farmland and houses as greatness. I am not speaking about this greatness," he said. "For in that case one rests in another."*

Notes: The greatness (mahima) of Brahman is not dependent upon certain conditions or qualifiers, which is the case with us. For us greatness is an attribute. It is not our natural state, but arises under certain conditions. Brahman is greatness itself, without a second.

Section 25

The Ego and the Self

1. sa evadhastat sa uparistat sa pascat sa purastat sa daksinatah sa uttaratah sa evedam sarvam ity athato'hamkaradesa eva, aham evadhastat aham uparistad aham pascat aham purastat aham daksinatah aham uttaratah aham evedam sarvamiti.

1. *"That indeed is below. That is above. That is behind. That is in front. That is to the south. That is to the north. That is indeed all this. Now follows the instruction regarding the self-sense (ego). "I am below. I am above. I am behind. I am in front. I am to the south. I am to the north. I am indeed all this."*

Notes: The infinite is explained from two perspectives, one objectively as That in contrast to oneself, and the other subjectively as oneself, in a state of self-absorption, without the notion of duality or otherness (anyatvam).

2. athata atmadesa eva atmaivadhastat atmoparistat, atma pascat, atma purastat, atma daksinata atmottaratah, atmaivedam sarvam iti sa va esa evam pasyann evam manvana evam vijanann atmaratir atmakrida atmamithuna atmanandah sa svarad bhavati tasya sarvesu lokesu kamacaro bhavati atha ye anyathato viduh, anyarajanas te ksayyaloka bhavanti tesam sarvesu lokesv akamacaro bhavati.

2. *"Now, next, the instruction regarding the Self. The Self is below. The Self is above. The Self is behind. The Self is in front. The Self is to the south. The Self is to the north. The Self indeed is all this. Truly, he who sees this, who thinks this, who knows this, has pleasure in the Self, takes delight in the Self, is united with the Self and rejoices in the Self. He becomes a ruler of heaven. In all the worlds, he becomes free to do whatever pleases him. But they who know differently from this are ruled by others in the perishable worlds and they are not free to do whatever pleases them."*

Notes: The knowledgeable ones are free to act in all the worlds whatever pleases them because they are not bound by karma. The same is not true in case of those who are bound to the mortal worlds.

Section 26

The Self as the Source of All

1. tasya ha va etasyaivam pasyata evam manvanasya, evam vijanata atmatah prana atmata asatmatah smara atmata akasa atmatas tejah, atmata apa atmata avirbhavatirobhavau atmato'nnam atmato balam atmato vijnanam atmato dhyanam atmatas cittam atmatah samkalpa atmato mana atmato vac atmato nama atmato mantra atmatah karmany atmata evedam sarvam iti.

1. *"For him who sees thus, who thinks thus, who knows thus, from Self arises the breath, from the Self arises hope, from the Self arises memory, from the Self arises the space, from the Self arises fire, from the Self arises water, from the Self arises manifestation and dissolution, from the Self arises food, from the Self arises strength, from the Self arises discerning knowledge, from the Self arises meditation, from the Self arises thought, from the Self arises intention, from the Self arises the mind, from the Self arises the name, from the Self arises sacred hymns, from the Self arises (sacrificial) actions. Indeed, from Self only all this arises."*

2. tad esa slokah: na pasyo mrityum pasyati na rogam nota duhkhatam; sarvam ha pasyah pasyati sarvam apnoti sarvasa. iti, sa ekadha bhavati, tridha bhavati pancadha saptadha navadha caiva punas caikadash smritah satam ca dasa caikas ca sahasrani ca vimsatih aharasuddhau sattvasuddhau dhruva smritih smriti lambhe sarvagranthinam vipramoksas tasmai mridita kasayaya tamasah param darsayati bhagavan sanatkumarah tam skanda ityacaksate tam skanda ityacaksate.

2. *"Regarding this, there is this verse. He who sees this does not see death, nor sickness, nor even sorrow. He who sees this sees all and obtains everything everywhere. He who exists as One becomes threefold, fivefold, sevenfold, and nine-fold. Then again, He is said to be elevenfold, and hundred and tenfold, and a thousand and twentyfold. When nourishment is pure, sattva is pure and memory becomes firm. With firm memory, all the knots of the heart are loosened. To such a one, who has his impurities removed, godman Sanatkumara sowed Narada what is beyond of darkness. They call him Skanda, yes, they call him Skanda."*

Notes: Threefold, fivefold etc., suggests the parts of the body as well as parts of creation. They refer to the manifestation of diversity by Brahman, the One. This verse also speaks about the importance of purity in self-transformation, a concept that is central to classical yoga and other methods of spiritual practice.

Chapter 8

Section 1

The Body as the City of Brahman

1. Hari Aum, atha yad idam asmin brahmapure daharam pundarikam vesma daharo'sminn antarakasah tasmin yad antah tad anvestavyam tad va va vijijnasitavyamiti.

1. Hari Aum! Now, there, in this city of Brahman, is a subtle Palace in the form of a white lotus flower. In that is subtle space. Now what lies in that inner subtle space, that should be sought after and known.

2. tam ced bruyuh yad idam asmin brahmapure daharam pundarikam vesma daharo'sminn antarakasah kim tad atra vidyate yad anvestavyam yad va va vijijnasitavyam iti.

2. If they should say to him, "What lies within the subtle inner space inside the subtle lotus flower that lies within the subtle abode in the city of Brahman, which should be sought after and known?

3. sa bruyat yavan va ayam akasah tavan eso'ntarhridaya akasah ubhe asmin dyavaprithivi antar eva samahite ubhav agnisca vayus ca suryacandramasav ubhau vidyun naksatrani yac casyehasti yacca nasti sarvam tad asmin samahitam iti.

3. He should say, "As far as this (outer) space extends, so far is that space in the heart. Both the earth and the heaven are inside it, both fire and air, both the sun and the moon, both the lightning and the stars. Whatever there is of him, and whatever is not, all that is contained in it."

4. tam ced bruyuh asmimsced idam brahmapure sarvam samahitam sarvani ca bhutani sarve ca kama yadaitaj jara vapnoti pradhvamsate va kim tato'tisisyata iti.

4. If they should say to him, "If everything that exists is contained in this city of Brahman, all beings and all desires, then what remains when old age overtakes it or when it perishes?"

5. sa bruyat nasya jarayaitaj jiryati na vadhenasya hanyata etatsatyam brahmapuram asmin kamah samahitah esa atmapahata papma vijaro vimrityur visoko vijighatso'apipasah satyakamah satyasamkalpo yatha hy eveha praja anvavisanti

yathanusasanam yam yam antam abhikama bhavanti yam janapadam yam ksetrabhagam tam tam evopa jivanti.

5. Then he should say, "By the aging of this, that does not age; by the death of this, that is not killed. That is the true city of Brahman. In it are all desires contained. It is the Self, without sin, without aging, without death, without sorrow, without hunger, without thirst, with true desires and true intentions. Just as here on earth, people follow the laws to which they are subject and depend upon the province and upon the piece of land where they live (for their livelihood).

Notes: As per Shankara, these suggestions are meant for the teachers who have to respond to the questions asked by the students, who are implied in these verses as "they." These answers are also meant for people whose understanding of Brahman is rather poor or dull.

6. tad yatheha karmajito lokah ksiyata evam evamutra punya-jito lokah ksiyate tadya ihatmanam anuvidya vrajanty etams ca satyan kaman tesam sarvesu lokesv akamacaro bhavaty atha ya ihatmanam anivudya vrajanty etams ca satyan kaman tesam sarvesu lokesu kamacaro bhavati.

6. Just as here on earth the world earned through actions perishes, so perishes in the other world, the place secured by good actions. Those who depart from here without knowing the Self and their true desires, for them there is no freedom from duty in all the worlds. But those who depart from here, having realized the Self and those true desires, for them there is freedom to act in all the worlds.

Notes: Those who achieve self-realization are free from all duties and obligations. There is no rebirth for them.

Section 2

The Desires of a Self-Realized Person

1. sa yadi pitrilokakamo bhavati samkalpad evasya pitarah samuttisthanti tena pitrilokena sampanno mahiyate.

1. If he happens to desire the world of forefathers, by his mere intention, his forefathers come to him; and having gained the world of forefathers, he remains happy and great.

Notes: The will or intention of a self-realized person is so strong that whatever he intends happens.

2. atha yadi matrilokakamo bhavati samkalpad evasya matarah samuttisthanti tena matrilokena sampanno mahiyate.

2. *Now, if he happens to desire the world of mothers, by his mere intention, his mothers come to him; and having gained the world of mothers, he remains happy and great.*

3. atha yadi bhratrilokakamo bhavati samkalpad evasya bhratarah samuttisthanti tena bhratrilokena sampanno mahiyate.

3. *Now, if he happens to desire the world of brothers, by his mere intention, his brothers come to him; and having gained the world of brothers, he remains happy and great.*

4. atha yadi svasrilokakamo bhavati samkalpad evasya svasarah samuttisthanti tena svasrilokena sampanno mahiyate.

4. *Now, if he happens to desire the world of sisters, by his mere intention, his sisters come to him; and having gained the world of sisters, he remains happy and great.*

5. atha yadi sakhilokakamo bhavati samkalpad evasya sakhayah samuttisthanti tena sakhilokena sampanno mahiyate.

5. *Now, if he happens to desire the world of friends, by his mere intention, his friends come to him; and having gained the world of friends, he remains happy and great.*

6. atha yadi gandhamalyaloka kamo bhavati samkalpad evasya gandhamalye samuttisthatastena gandhamalyalokena sampanno mahiyate.

6. *Now, if he happens to desire the world of perfumes and garlands, by his mere intention, perfumes and garlands come to him; and having gained the world of perfumes and garlands, he remains happy and great.*

7. atha yady annapanalokakamo bhavati samkalpad evasyannapane samuttisthatah tena annapanalokena sampanno mahiyate.

7. *Now, if he happens to desire the world of food and drinks, by his mere intention, food and drinks come to him; and having gained the world of food and drinks, he remains happy and great.*

8. atha yadi gitavaditralokakamo bhavati samkalpadevasya gitavaditre samuttisthatastena gitavaditralokena sampanno mahiyate.

8. *Now, if he happens to desire the world of songs and music, by his mere intention, songs and music come to him; and having gained the world of songs and music, he remains happy and great.*

9. atha yadi strilokakamo bhavati samkalpad evasya striyah samuttisthanti tena strilokena sampanno mahiyate.

9. *Now, if he happens to desire the world of women, by his mere intention, women come to him; and having gained the world of women, he remains happy and great.*

10. yam yam antam abhikamo bhavati yam kamam kamayate so'asya samkalpad eva samuttisthati tena sampanno mahiyate.

10. *"Whatever object he desires, whatever that is desirable he desires, all that comes to him by his mere intention; and having obtained it, he remains happy and great.*

Section 3

True Desires and False Desires

1. ta ime satyah kama anritapidhanah tesam satyanam satam anritam apidhanam yo yo hyasyetah praiti na tamiha darsanaya labhate.

1. *These are true desires, concealed by what is false. Although the desires are true, they are concealed by what is false. Therefore, whoever departs from here, him we cannot get to see.*

Notes: The implication is that a self-realized person also desires, but his desires are pure and not covered by falsehood. Hence, what he wills or desires, happen. Now what is the falsehood? It is not explained, but we have to understand that it is the attachment, the impurities of guans, ignorance, lust, fear, envy, delusion, egoism, selfishness etc.

2. atha ye casyeha jiva ye ca preta yac canyad iccan na labhate sarvam tad atra gatva vindate, atra hyasyaite satyah kama anritapidhanah tad yathapi hiranyanidhim nihitam aksetrajna upary upari sancaranto na vindeyuh evam evemah sarvah praja ahar ahar gacchantya etam brahmalokam na vindanty anritena hi pratyudhah.

2. *Now those (people) of him, whether they are alive or dead, whatever else is there which one desires but does not attain, all that one finds upon going there (into the space in the heart). Since our true desires are concealed by what is false, just like the people who do not know the field, walk over a hidden gold treasure repeatedly and yet do not find it,*

so do the creatures go into the world of Brahman day after day and yet do not know it since they are carried away by untruth.

Notes: The truth, the Self, is hidden in the heart; we visit it every day in our sleep, and yet because we are subject to ignorance, we cannot perceive it.

3. sa va esa atma hridi tasyaitad eva niruktam hridy ayam iti tasmadd hridayam ahar ahar va evam vitsvargam lokam eti.

3. Truly, the Self is in the heart. Of that, this is the etymological explanation. Hridayam means hridi, in the heart, and ayam means this is. Hence it is called hridayam. He who knows this goes day by day into the heavenly world.

4. atha ya esa samprasado'smac carirat samutthaya param jyotir upasampadya svena rupenabhinispadyata esa atmeti hovaca etad amritam abhayam etad brahmeti tasya ha va etasya brahmano nama satyam iti.

4. Now that serene Being, having risen from this body, and having reached the supreme light, becomes united with his own form. That is the Self, he said. That is immortal, without fear; that is Brahman; of that Brahman, the name is the True.

5. tani ha va etani trinyaksarani satiyam iti tad yat sat tad amritam atha yat ti tan martyam atha yad yam tenobhe yaccati yad anenobhe yaccati tasmad yam ahar ahar va evam vit svargam lokam eti.

5. These, indeed, are the three syllables of the word satyam. Sat is that which is the immortal. Ti is the mortal. Yam is that by which one binds both. Because with it one holds both together, therefore it yam. He who knows this goes day after day into the heaven (in the heart).

Notes: Sat is the subject. Ti is the object. Yam is the seeing or enjoying, which brings the two into an empirical relationship that characterizes our existence upon earth. Sat is the Self. Ti the objective world and knowing or seeing the object is what connects them. This is the state of duality, the truth of our existence, the means by which the Self is bound to the world.

Section 4

The Self as the Bridge and the Boundary of the Worlds

1. atha ya atma sa setur vidhritir esam lokanam asambhedaya naitam setum ahoratre tarato na jara na mrityurna soko na suk-

ritam na duskritam sarve papmano'to nivartante, apahata-papma hyesa brahmalokah.

1. Now that Self is the bridge, and the boundary that keeps the worlds apart. Day and night do not cross that bridge, nor old age, nor death and suffering, nor good deeds and bad deeds. All evil things turn away from it, for this world of Brahman is free from evil.

2. tasmad va etam setum tirtvandhah sann anandho bhavati viddhah sann aviddho bhavaty upatapi sann anupatapi bhavati tasmad va etam setum tirtvapi naktam ahar evabhinispadyate sakrid vibhato hy evaisa brahmalokah.

2. Therefore, truly, upon crossing that bridge, a blind person is no longer blind, a wounded person is no longer wounded, a suffering person no longer suffers. Therefore, upon crossing that bridge, night, indeed, becomes day for the world of Brahman is illuminated forever.

3. tad ya evaitam brahmalokam brahmacaryenanuvindanti tesam evaisa brahmalokah tesam sarvesu lokesu kamacaro bhavati.

3. But only those attain the world of Brahman by practicing celibacy. To them only belongs the world of Brahman. For them there is freedom in all worlds to act.

Notes: Shankara defines brahmacharya as renouncing all desires for women.

Section 5
Brahmacharya as a Sacrifice

1. atha yad yajna ity acaksate brahmacaryam eva tad brahmacaryena hy eva yo jnata tam vindate, atha yadcistam ity acaksate brahmacaryam eva tad brahmacaryena hy evestvatmanam anuvindate.

1. Now what people call sacrifice, that really is brahmacharya. Only by brahmacharya does one obtains that world. Now what people call worship is truly brahmacharya for only by brahmacharya, having worshipped with devotion, does one obtain the Self.

Notes: A sacrifice is celibacy because while performing sacrifices also the sacrificers need to practice celibacy and keep their minds and bodies pure. Same is the case in respect of those who worship Brahman (ishtva) with devotion. They also have to maintain celibacy. Those who seek Brahman should not desire women. They have to sacrifice such desires, so that they can remove the falsehood and uncover their true desires.

2. atha yat sattrayanam ity acaksate brahmacharyam eva tad brahmacaryena hy eva sata atmanas tranam vindate, atha yan maunam ity acaksate brahmacharyam eva tab brahmacaryena hy evatmanam anuvidya manute .

2. Now what people call the sattrayana Soma sacrifice, that really is brahmacharya. Indeed, by brahmacharya, one obtains from the True (sat), the protection of the Self. Now, what people call silence, that is really brahmacharya, for only by finding the Self through brahmacharya does one meditate.

Notes: Sattrayana is said to be a protracted Soma Sacrifice. During this sacrifice also one has to observe celibacy. Silence is also celibacy because silence does not mean mere physical silence, but silencing of all desires, thoughts, attachments and expectations.

3. atha yad anasakayanam ity acaksate brahmacharyam eva tad esa hy atma na nasyati yam brahmacaryenanuvindate, atha yad aranyayanam ity acaksate brahmacharyam eva tat tad arasca ha vai nyas carnavau brahmaloke tritiyasyam ito divi tad airam madiyam sarah tad asvatthah somasavanah tad aparajita pur brahmanah prabhuvimitam hiranmayam.

3. Now what they call fasting, that really is brahmacharya for that Self does not perish which is obtained by brahmacharya. Now what they call the way of the immortal (aranyayana), that really is brahmacharya. Truly, Ara and Nya are the two seas in the world of Brahman, the third heaven from here. Therein is the lake Airanmadiya, there the divine miracle tree (Asvattha) sowering Soma juice, there the invincible city Aparajita and the Golden Hall, Prabhuvimita, built by the Lord.

Notes: Fasting is celibacy because while fasting one has to abstain from sexual pleasure. Besides, both fasting and celibacy involve restraint. Shankara interpreted ansakayanam as indestructible instead of fasting and aranyayana as the ocean path. Some interpret it as the path of hermits. It is actually the immortal path. While going by this path, the souls who have attained liberation, come across two oceans in the immortal region of Brahman, namely Ara and Nya, which are also mentioned in the Kausitaki Brahmana Upanishad.

4. tad ya evaitav aram ca nyam carnavau brahmaloke brahmacaryenanuvindanti tesam evaisa brahmalokah tesam sarvesu lokesu kamacaro bhavati.

4. Now that world of Brahman belongs to those who find the two seas, Ara and Nya in the world of Brahman by brahmacharya. In all the worlds, they have freedom to act.

Section 6
The Experience of Death and the Final Moments

1. atha ya eta hridayasya nadyas tah pingalasyanimnas tisthanti suklasya nilasya pitasya lohitasyety asau va adityah pingalah esa sukla esa nila esa pita esa lohitah.

1. Now these arteries of the heart consists of a subtle matter that is reddish-brown, white, blue, yellow and red. Truly, that sun there is also reddish-brown, white, blue, yellow and red.

2. tad yatha mahapatha atata ubhau gramau gaccatimam camum ca evam evaita adityasya rasmaya ubhau lokau gacchantimam camum ca amusmad adityat pratayante ta asu nadisu sripta abhyo nadibhyah pratayante te amusminnaditye sriptah.

2. Just as a great path goes between two villages, from this (at the beginning) to that (at the end), so do the rays of the sun go to both the worlds, from this to that. They start from that sun and enter into these arteries; and starting from the arteries, they enter into the sun.

Notes: The light that is seen in the sun and in the world during the day also flows in the body in the form of pranic energy along the breath channels. The sun is the provider of both light and energy, which is both gross and subtle. Hence the light and energy in the body is compared to the light and energy radiated by the sun.

3. tad yatraitat suptah samasth samprasannah svapnam na vijanaty asu tada nadisu sripto bhavati tam na kascana papma sprisati tejasa hi tada sampanno bhavati.

3. And when one is thus fully asleep, resting and serene without seeing any dreams, then he happens to enter into these arteries. Then no evil touches him for he has attained the brilliant light.

4. atha yatraitad abalimanam nito bhavati tam abhita asina ahuh janasi mam janasi mam iti sa yavad asmaccarirad anutkranto bhavati tavaj janati.

4. And when one has lost strength and become weak, those who sit around him say, "Do you know me, do you know me?" As long as he has not departed from his body, he knows them.

5. atha yatraitad asmaccarirad utkramaty athaitair eva rasmibhir urdhvam akramate sa aum iti va ha ut va miyate sa yavat ksipyen manah tavad adityam gaccaty etad vai khalu loka dvaram vidusam prapadanam nirodho'vidusam.

5. Now, when he departs from the body, he goes upwards by those very rays, or he goes up meditating upon Aum. While his mind is falling apart, he goes to the Sun for that indeed is the door to that world. Those who know gain entry, those who do not know are shut out.

6. tad esa slokah: satam caika ca hridayasya nadyah tasam murdhanam abhinihsritaika tayordhvam ayann amritatvam eti visvann anya utkramane bhavanty utkramane bhavanti.

6. Of this there is this verse: "Hundred and one are the arteries of the heart; one of them goes to the top of the head. Passing through that one attains immortality; the others serve as the means for going in different directions, yes in different directions.

Notes: The soul leaves the body through an aperture in the head. This is the belief. Before the soul leaves the body, one loses all senses and enters into a semi-conscious state, which is described in the previous verses.

Section 7
Prajapati's Instruction Regarding True Self

1. ya atma apahata papma vijaro vimrityur visoko vijighatso'apipasah satya kamah satya samkalpah so'anvestavyah sa vijijnasitavyah sa sarvams ca lokan apnoti sarvams ca kaman yas tam atmanam anuvidya vijanatiti ha prajapatir uvaca.

1. The self, which is not afflicted with sin, which is free from old age, free from death, free from sorrow, free from hunger and thirst, whose desires are true, whose intentions are true, that should be sought, that should be understood. He who seeks to know the Self and understands it, he attains all the worlds and all desires. Thus, said Prajapati.

2. tadd hobhaye devasura anububudhire te hocuh; hanta tam atmanam anveccama yam atmanam anvisya sarvams ca lokan apnoti sarvams ca kaman iti; indro haiva devanam abhipravavraja virocano'suranam tau ha samvidanav eva samitpani prajapatisakasam ajagmatuh.

2. Then, both the gods and the demons, heard it and said, "Well, let us search for that Self, by searching which one attains all worlds and all desires." Indra from among the gods went forth and Vairocana from among the demons. Without communicating with each other, both approached Prajapati, with fuel in their hands.

3. tau ha dvatrimsatam varsani brahmacaryam usatuh tau ha prajapatir uvaca kim icchantav avastam. iti tau hocatuh, ya atmapahatapapma vijaro vimrityur visoko vijighatso'apipasah satyakamah satyasam kalpah so'anvestavyah sa vijijnasitavyah sa sarvams ca lokan apnoti sarvams ca kaman yas tam atmanam anuvidya vijanatiti bhagavato vaco vedayante tam icchantav avastam iti.

3. They lived there for thirty-two years, practicing celibacy. Then Prajapati asked them, "For what purpose you are staying here?" They said, "The self which is not afflicted by sin, which is free from old age, free from death, free from sorrow, free from hunger and thirst, whose desires are true, whose intentions are true, that should be sought, that should be understood. He who seeks to know the Self and understands it, he attains all the worlds and all desires. Godman, they say these are your words. Desiring (to know) it, we are here.

Notes: Indra and Vairocana did not speak to each other before approaching Prajapati because, beings rivals, they did not want the other person to acquire the knowledge of the immortal Self. It might be why Prajapati made them wait for 32 and years and practice austerities and self-transformation.

4. tau ha prajapatir uvaca, ya eso'ksini puruso drisyata esa atmeti hovaca etad amritam abhayam etad brahmety atha yo'yam bhagavah apsu parikhyayate yascayam adarse katama esa ity esa u evaisu sarvesv antesu parikhyayata iti hovaca.

4. To them, Prajapati said, "That person who is seen in the eye, that is the Self I spoke of. This is the immortal, and the fearless; this is Brahman." "Godman, he who is perceived in the water and in the mirror, who is he?" He replied, "He is the same one, indeed, who is seen in all these."

Section 8

The Demonic View of the Body as the Self

1. udasarava atmanam aveksya yad atmano na vijinithah tan me prabrutam iti tau hodasarave aveksamcakrate tau ha prajapatir uvaca, kim pasyatha iti; tau hocatuh, sarvam evedam avam bhagava, atmanam pasyava a lomabhyah a nakhebhyah pratirupam iti.

1. "Look at yourself in a pan of water and whatever you do not know about the Self, tell me." They both looked at themselves in a pan of water. Prajapati asked them, "What do you see?"

They said, "Godman, we have seen ourselves as we are, a reflection down to the hairs and nails."

2. tau ha prajapatir uvaca, sadhv alamkritau suvasanau pariskritau bhutvoda sarave aveksetham iti tau ha sadhv alamkritau suvasanau pariskritau bhutvoda sarave'veksam cakrate. tau ha prajapatir uvaca kim pasyatha iti.

2. Then Prajapati said to them, "After you have adorned yourselves, worn the best clothes and made yourself clean, look into the water pan. After adorning themselves, wearing the best clothes and cleaning themselves, they looked into the water pan. Prajapati asked, "What do you see?"

3. tau hocatuh yathaivedam avam bhagavah sadhv alamkritau suvasanau pariskritau sva evam evemau, bhagavah, sadhv alamkritau suvasanau pariskritav ity esa atmeti hovaca etad amritam abhayam etad brahmeti. tau ha santa hridayau pravavrajatuh.

3. They said, "We see thus, godman, well adorned, well dressed and clean, just like the way we adorned ourselves, wore the best clothes and cleaned ourselves."

He said, "That is the Self. That is the immortal and the fearless; that is Brahman." They both went away, with their hearts satisfied.

4. tau hanviksya prajapatir uvaca, anupalabhyatmanam ananuvidya vrajatah yatara etad upanisado bhavisyanti deva va asura va te parabhavisyantiti. sa ha santahridaya eva virocano'suran jagama tebhyo haitam upanisadam provaca, atmaiveha mahayya atma paricarya atmanam evaiha mahayann atmanam paricarann ubhau lokav avapnotimam camum ceti.

4. Then Prajapati, watching them (go), said (to himself), "They are going away without having perceived the Self and without having known the Self; and whichever of these two, the god and demons, follow this sacred teaching shall perish." Now, Vairocana, with his heart pacified, went to the demons and preached this teaching to them: the Self alone should be worshipped, the Self alone should be served and he who worships the Self and serves the Self, gains both the worlds, this and the next.

Notes: Vairocana took the teaching of Prajapati literally and believed that the physical form or the body he saw in the water was the real Self. He mistook his self-image as his real Self.

5. tasmad apy adyehadadanam asraddadhanam ayajamanam ahuh asuro batety asuranam hy esopanisat pretasya sariram bhiksaya vasanenalamkareneti samskurvanty, etena hy amum lokam jesyanto manyante.

5. Therefore, even now, if a person does not give (charity), has no faith, and does not perform sacrifices, they say that he is indeed a demon, for this is the philosophy of the demons. They adorn the body of a deceased with the clothes and ornaments, and they beg, thinking that thereby they will win the yonder world.

Section 9

Indra's Quest for the True Knowledge of Self

1. atha hendro'prapyaiva devan etad bhayam dadarsa yathaiva khalv ayam asmin sarire sadhvalamkrite sadhv alamkrito bhavati suvasane suvasanah pariskrite pariskritah evam evayam asminn andhe'andho bhavati, srame sramah parivrikne parivrikno'syaiva sarirasya nasam anv esa nasyati naham atra bhogyam pasyamiti.

1. Now, Indra, before he went back to the gods, saw this fearsome possibility." Just as the Self is well adorned, when the body is well adorned, it is well dressed when the body is well dressed, it is well cleaned when the body is well cleaned, then that Self also should be blind if the body is blind, should be lame if the body is lame, and should be crippled when the body is crippled. It should also perish immediately if the body perishes. Therefore, I see no good in this (teaching)."

2. sa samit, panih punar eyaya, tam ha prajapatir uvaca. maghavan, yac chantahrdya pravrajih sardham virocanena, kim iccan punar agama iti, sa hovaca yathaiva khalv ayam, bhagavah asmin sarire sadhv alankrte, sadhv alankrto bhavati, suvasane suvasanah pariskrte pariskrtah evam evayam asminn andhe'ndho bhavati, sramesramah, parivrkno parivrknah, asayaiva sarirasya nasam anv esa nasyati, naham atra bhogyam pasyamiti.

2. With fuel in his hand, he went back again. Prajapati said to him, "Why did you return, O Maghavan? Did you not go away with Virocana, satisfied in your heart?" He said, "Godman, just as the Self is well adorned when the body is well adorned, well dressed when the body is well dressed, well cleaned when the body is well cleaned, then the Self should also be blind when the body is blind, should be lame when the body is lame, should be crippled when the body is crippled, and it should also perish indeed when the body perishes. Therefore, I see no good in this."

3. evam evaisa maghavann iti hovaca itam tv eva te bhuyo'nuvyakhyasyami vasaparani dvatrimsatam varsaniti sa haparani dvatrimsatam varsany uvasa tasmai hovaca.

3. "Yes, indeed, it is, Maghavan," he said. "I shall explain this to you again. Stay here for another thirty-two years." He lived with him for another thirty-two years; then he said to him.

Section 10
The Self that Wanders in Dreams

1. ya esa svapne mahiyamanah caraty esa atma iti hovaca itad amritam abhayam etad brahmeti sa ha santahridayah pravavraja sa haprapyaiva devan etad bhayam dadarsa tad yady apidam sariram andham bhavaty anandhah sa bhavati, yadi sramam asramah, naivaiso'sya dosena dusyati.

1. "He who wanders happily in dreams, that is the Self." And he said, "this is the immortal, the fearless; this is Brahman." Then he went away, with peaceful heart. But before he went back to the gods, he saw this fearsome possibility. Although, it is true that the Self is not blind, when the body is blind, not lame when the body is lame, although it does not suffer from the faults of the body.

2. na vadhenasya hanyate nasya sramyena sramah ghnanti tv evainam viccadayantivapriyavetteva bhavaty api roditiva naham atra bhogyam pasyamiti.

2. It is not slain when the body is slain, not one-eyed when the body is one-eyed, but (in dreams) it appears as if they kill it and as if they case it. It even becomes conscious of pain (in the dream), as if it were true, and weeps as if it were true. I see no good in this.

3. sa samitpanih punar eyaya tam ha prajapatir uvaca maghavan, yac chanta hridayah pravrajih kim iccan punar agama iti sa hovaca tad yady apidam bhagavah sariram andham bhavaty anandhah sa bhavati yadi sramam asramah naivaiso'sya dosena dusyati.

3. *With fuel in his hands, he went back again. Prajapati said, "Why did you return, O Maghavan? Did you not go away with peace in your heart?" He said, "Godman, although this Self is not blind, when the body is blind, not lame when the body is lame, and although this does not suffer from the faults of the body."*

4. na vadhenasya hanyate nasya sramyena sramo ghnanti tv evainam viccadayantiva apriyavetteva bhavaty api roditiva naham atra bhogyam pasyamity evam evaisa maghavann iti hovaca etam tv eva te bhuyo' nuvyakhyasyami vasaparani dvatrimsatam varsaniti. sa haparani dvatrimsatam varsany uvasa tasmai hovaca.

4. *"Although it is not slain when the body is slain, it is not lame when the body is lame, (in dreams) it appears as if they kill it and as if they case it. It even becomes conscious of pain, as if it were true, and weeps as if it were true. I see no good in this." "Yes, indeed it is, Maghavan," he said. "I shall explain this to you again. Stay here for another thirty-two years." He lived with him for another thirty-two years; then he said to him.*

Section 11

The Self in Sleep

1. tad yatraitat suptah samastah samprasannah svapnam na vijanaty esa atmeti hovaca etad amritam abhayam etad brahmeti sa ha santahridayah pravavraja sa haprapyaiva devan etad bhayam dadarsa naha khalv ayam evam sampraty atmanam janaty ayam aham asmiti no evemani bhutani vinasam evapito bhavati naham atra bhogyam pasyamiti.

1. *"That which is in deep sleep and immersed in itself, knows no dreams, that is the Self," he said. "That is the immortal, the fearless, that is Brahman." He went away, with peaceful heart. But before he went back to the gods, he saw this fearsome possibility. In truth, (in deep sleep) this does not know by itself that 'this is I am' nor any of these things that exist. It is as if it is being utterly dissolved. I see no good in this.*

2. sa samitpanih punareyaya tam ha prajapatiruvaca maghavanyacchantahridayah pravrajih kimiccanpunaragama iti sa hovaca naha khalvayam bhagava evam sampratyatmanam

janatyayamahamasmiti no evemani bhutani vinasamevapito bhavati nahamatra bhogyam pasyamiti.

2. With fuel in his hand, he went back again. Prajapati said, "Why did you return, O Maghavan? Did you not go away with peace in your heart?" He said, "Godman, in truth, (in deep sleep) this does not know by itself that 'this is I am' nor any of these things that exist. It is as if it is being utterly dissolved. I see no good in this."

3. evam evaisa maghavann iti hovaca etam tv eva te bhuyo'nuvyakhyasyami no evanyatraitasmat vasaparani panca varsaniti sa haparani panca varsany uvasa tany ekasatam sampeduh etat tad yad ahuh ekasatam ha vai varsani maghavan prajapatau brahmacaryam uvasa tasmai hovaca.

3. "Yes, indeed it is, Maghavan," he said. "I shall explain this to you further and nothing else other than that. Stay here for another five years." He stayed there for another five years. That makes it one hundred and one years. Thereby, people say that Maghavan spent one hundred and one years with Prajapati, practicing celibacy. He said to him.

Section 12

The Self as the Knower and Enjoyer

1. maghavan martyam va idam sariram attam mrityuna tad asyamritasyasarirasyatmano'dhisthanam atto vai sasarirah priyapriyabhyam na vai sasarirasya satah priyapriyayor apahatir asty asariram va va santam na priyapriye sprisatah.

1. "Maghavan, mortal indeed is this body held by death. It is the support of that immortal, incorporeal Self. The physical self is subject to pleasure and pain. Truly, there is no freedom from pleasure and pain for the physical self; but truly pleasure and pain do not touch the one who is incorporeal."

2. asariro vayuh abhram vidyut stanayitnur asarirany etani tad yathaitany amusmad akasat samutthaya param jyotir upasampadya svena rupenabhinispadyante.

2. "The wind is incorporeal, the cloud, lightning and thunder are incorporeal. Now just as these, arising from that space and upon approaching the highest light, appear in their own form."

3. evam evaisa samprasado'smac carirat samutthaya param jyotir upasampadya svena rupenabhinispadyate sa uttamah purusah sa tatra paryeti jaksat kridan ramamanah stribhir va yanair va jnatibhir va nopajanam smarann idam sariram: sa yatha prayogya acarane yuktah evam evayam asmin sarire prano yuktah.

3. "So does that serene one, arising from this body and upon reacing the highest light appears in its own form. This is the highest person. There that one moves about, laughing, playing, and rejoicing, be it with women, cariots or relatives, not remembering the body in which he was born. Just as an animal is yoked to a cart or a cariot, so is the spirit yoked to a body."

4. atha yatraitad akasam anu visannam caksuh sa caksusah puruso darsanaya caksuh atha yo veda: idam jighraniti sa atma gandhaya ghranam atha yo veda: idam abhivyaharaniti sa atmabhi vyaharaya vac atha yo veda idam srinavaniti sa atma sravanaya srotram.

4. "Now when the eye (of a person) looks into the space, that is the seeing person, the eye is meant for his seeing. Now, he who is aware, 'I smell this,' that is the Self, the nose is meant for his smelling. He who is aware, 'I speak this,' he is the Self, the organ of speech is meant for his speaking. He who is aware, 'I hear this,' he is the Self, the ear is meant for his hearing."

5. atha yo veda idam manvaniti sa atma mano'sya daivam caksuh sa va esa etena daivena caksusa manasaitan kaman pasyan ramate.

5. "He who is aware, 'I think this,' he is the Self, the mind acts his divine eye. Truly, seeing with the divine eye, his mind, the pleasures (hidden in the objects), he rejoices."

Notes: The person in the act of seeing, hearing, speaking etc. is the Self. The Self is able to know beforehand the pleasures hidden in the sense-objects because of his mind, which is endowed with divine powers of reason, intelligence, perception and cognition. Endowed with such awareness and discernment, he grasps the objects with his senses and enjoys them.

6. ya ete brahmaloke tam va etam deva atmanam upasate tasmat tesam sarve ca loka attah sarve ca kamah sa sarvams ca lokan apnoti sarvams ca kaman yas tam atmanam anuvidya vijanat iti ha prjapatir uvaca prajapatir uvaca.

6. *"The gods in the world of Brahman, verily, meditate upon that Self. Hence, they attain all the worlds and all desires. He who finds the Self and understands it, attains all worlds and all desires." Thus said Prajapati, yes, thus said Prajapati.*

Section 13

Reaching the World of Brahman Overcoming the Obstacles

1. syamac cabalam prapadye sabalac cyamam prapadye asva iva romani vidhuya papam candra iva rahor mukhat pramucya dhutva sariram akritam kritatma brahmalokam abhisambhavami ity abhisambhavam iti.

1. From the dark, I proceed to the variegated; from the variegated, to the dark. Shaking off all evil, just as a horse sakes off its hairs, and as the moon frees itself from the mouth of Rahu, shaking off the imperfect body, I, the perfected Self, attain the world of Brahman.

Section 14

A Prayer of the Soul to Prajapati

1. akaso vai nama namarupayor nirvahita te yad antara tad brahma tad amritam sa atma prajapateh sabham vesma prapadye yaso'ham bhavami brahmananam yaso rajnam yaso visam yaso'ham anuprapatsi sa haham yasasam yasah syetam adatkam adatkam syetam lindu mabhigam lindu mabhigam.

1. He whose name is space is the maintainer of names and forms. That in which they exist that is Brahman, that is the immortal and that is the Self. I come to the court of Prajapati, the abode. I am the glory of the priests, the glory of the warriors, the glory of the commoners. I have attained that glory. I am the glory of the glories. May I never go to the white and toothless (state), to the toothless, white and doddering state, yes may I never go to it.

Notes: The white, toothless and doddering state implies old age, signified by white hair, absence of teeth and unsteady gait.

Section 15

Instruction Regarding Instruction

1. tadd haitad brahma prajapatayai uvaca prajapatir manave manuh prajabhyah acaryakulad vedam adhitya yatha vidha-

nam guroh karma atisesena abhisamavritya kutumbe sthitva sucau dese svadhyayam adhiyanah dharmikan vidadhat atmani sarvaindriyani sampratisthapya ahimsan sarva bhutany anyatra tirthebhyah sa khalv evam vartayan yavad ayusam brahmalokam abhisampadyate na ca punar avartate na ca punar avartate.

1. Brahma told this to Prajapati, Prajapati to Manu, Manu to the humankind. He who has learned the Vedas from a family of teachers, according to the established practice, in the remaining time left after performing duties for the teacher, who after securing his discharge and settled in his own house, continues the self-study of the scriptures, has begotten various sons, he who concentrates all his senses upon his Self, who practices non-injury towards all creatures, except in sacred places (where animals are sacrificed), he who acts thus his whole life, reaches the world of Brahman and never returns, yes, he does not return.

A Note on Cover Page Illustration

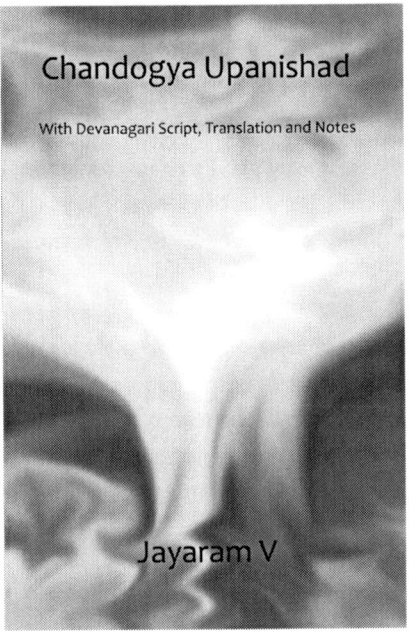

The cover page painting by Jayaram V, shows the flow of the subtle energy of the sun, called prana, flowing down from the sky and the mid-region to the world below. Prana is not the mere air we breathe. It is a misleading interpretation of the word. Air is its outer or grosser form. It is just one aspect of it. The real source of prana is not the air in the mid-region but the sun above. The mid-region is pervaded with the rays of the sun and hence the air that we breath is suffused with that energy, which appears as the effulgence in gods and breath among the mortal beings. That prana flowing down from the sun is the real sustaining power of life upon earth. It is the superior force, impervious to evil and superior to all the organs in the body. The sun symbolizes Brahman, who is described in the Upanishads as the nourisher and provide of food. Notice that the pranic energy which is very bright in the middle upper part of the painting becomes mixed up with dark colors in the lower part, denoting the involvement of the prana with the triple gunas and aspects of Nature. The dark colors in the sky region denote the water bearing clouds (ambhas).

Bibliography

Chandogya Upanishad

Little, Charles Edgar. A grammatical index to the Chāndogya-upanisad. New York, Cincinnati: American Book Co. [c1900].

Lokeswarananda, Swami. Chāndogya Upaniṣad: translated and with notes based on Śaṅkara's commentary. Kolkata, India: Ramakrishna Mission Institute of Culture, 1998.

Pandurangi, K.T. Chandogyopanishad: with English translation and notes according to Sri Madhvacarya's Bhashya. Chirtanur, Tirupathi: Sriman Madhva Siddhantonnahini Sabha ; Mysore : Can be had from Geetha Book House, 1987.

Prasad, Muni Narayana. Chandogya Upaniṣad: with the original text in Sanskrit and roman transliteration / translation with an extensive commentary. New Delhi, India: D.K. Printworld, 2007.

Sadia, oleh W. and Pudja, G. Chandogya Upanisad / [diterjamahkan]. [Jakarta]: Proyek Pengadaan Kitab Suci Hindu, Departemen Agama, RI, 1982.

Sankarananda, Mitra, Raja Rajendra, ed. Chāndogyopaniṣad = The Chāndogya-Upaniṣad : text in Sanskrit; and translation with notes in English from the commentaries of Śaṅkarācārya and the gloss of Ānandagiri. Delhi, India: Bharatiya Kala Prakashan, 2001.

Saraswati, Satya Prakash. The Chāndogya Upaniṣad. New Delhi: International Dayananda Veda-Peetha, [200-?].

Sen, M. Chāndogya Upanisad: Sāmkhya point of view. [Kanpur, M. Sen, 1962]

Subramanian, A.V. Waves from the Chandogya. Madras: S. Viswanathan and Ananda Book Depot, 1985.

Swahananda, Swāmi. The Chandogya Upanisad, containing the original text with word-by-word meaning, running translation and copious notes. Madras, India: R.K. Math, 1956.

Swahānanda, Swāmī. The Chāndogya Upanisad, containing the original text with word-by-word meaning, running translation and copious notes. Chennai, India: Sri Ramakrishna Math [1965].

General Reference

Aiyar, Narayanasvami K. Thirty minor Upaniṣads: revised edition includes Sanskrit texts, English translation. Delhi, India: Parimal Publications, 1997.

Ananthacharya, Chakravarti. Philosophy of Upanishads. Bangalore, India: Ultra Publications, 1999.

Archak, K.B. Upaniṣad and Śaivism. New Delhi, india: Sundeep Prakashan, 2002.

Aurobindo, Sri. The Upanishads, with Sanskrit text, English translation and commentary. Twin Lakes, WI: Lotus Light Publications, 1996.

Barnett, L. D. Brahma-knowledge, an outline of the philosophy of the Vedānta as set forth by the Upanishads and by Sankara.London, J. Murray, 1911.

Basham, A.L. The Origins and Development of Classical Hinduism. New York: Oxford University Press, 1991.

Bhattacharya, A.N. One hundred and twelve Upaniṣads and their philosophy: a critical exposition of Upaniṣadic philosophy with original text in Devanāgarī. Delhi, India: Parimal Publications, 1987.

Brown, George William. The human body in the Upanishads. Jubbulpore, India, The Christian Mission Press, 1921.

Chakravarti, Sures Chandra. The philosophy of the Upanishads. Delhi, India: Nag Publishers, 1979.

Deodikar, Sanjay Govind. Upanisads and early Buddhism. Delhi, India : Eastern Book Linkers, 1992.

Desai, S.G. A critical study of the later Upanishads. Mumbai, India : Bharatiya Vidya Bhavan, 1996.

Deussen, Paul, and Rev. Geden, A. S. The philosophy of the Upanishads. Edinburgh, Clark, 1908.

Deussen, Paul, and Bedekar, V.M., and Palsule, G.B. Sixty Upaniṣads of the Veda. Delhi, India : Motilal Banarsidass, 1980.

Devi, Chitrita. Upanishads for all. New Delhi, India: S. Chand [1973 i.e. 1972].

Diwakar, R.R., and Radhakrishnan, S., Intro. The Upanisads in story and dialogue. Mumbai, India: Hindi Kitabs, 1950.

Easwaran, Eknath. Essence of the Upanishads: A Key to Indian Spirituality. Canada: Nilgiri Press & Blue Mountain Center of Meditation, 2009.

_____. The Upanishads: The Classics of Indian Spirituality. Canada: The Blue Mountain Center of Meditation, 1987, 2007.

_____., Nagler, Michael N., fwd. The Upanishads. Tomales, CA : Nilgiri Press, 2007.

Egnes, Thomas, and Reddy, Kumuda. Eternal Stories from the Upanishads. New Delhi, India: Smriti Books, 2002.

Elenjimittam, Anthony. The Upanishads: Isa, Katha, Mundaka, Mandukya, with an introduction and commentary. Mumbai, India: Aquinas Publications, 1977.

Frawley, David. The creative vision of the early Upanisads. Denver, Colo.: D. Frawley, 1982.

Gambhirananda, Swami. Eight Upanishads: With the Commentary of Sankaracaya, Vol 1 and 2. Kolkata, India: Advaita Ashrama, 2003 and 2004.

Ghose, Aurobindo Sri. The Upanishads. Pondicherry, India: Aurobindo Ashram Trust, 1996.

Giri, Swami Satyeswarananda. The Upanishads. San Diego : Sanskrit Classics, 2006.

Gren-Eklund, Gunilla. A study of nominal sentences in the oldest Upanisads.Uppsala : Univ.; Stockholm : Almqvist & Wiksell international (distr.), 1978.

Grover, Usha. Symbolism in the Āranyakas and their impact on the Upaniṣads: a remarkable cultural upheaval which ever inspires the future thought. New Delhi : Guruvar Publications, 1987.

Hock, Henrich Hans. An early Upaniṣadic reader : with notes, glossary, and an appendix of related Vedic texts. Delhi, India : Motilal Banarsidass Publishers, 2007.

Hume, Robert Ernest. The thirteen principal Upanishads [microform]: translated from the Sanskrit with an outline of the philosophy of the Upanishads and an annotated bibliography. London ; New York : Oxford University Press, 1931.

Johnston, Charles. The great Upanishads. New York: Quarterly Book Department [c1927].

Kadankavil, Kurian T. The quest of the real: a study of the philosophical methodology of Mundakopanishad. Bangalore, India: Dharmaram Publications, 1975.

Keith, Arthur Berriedale. The religion and philosophy of the Veda and Upanishads. Cambridge, Mass. : Harvard University Press, 1925.

Keith, Arthur Berriedale. The religion and philosophy of the Veda and Upanishads. Cambridge, Mass., Harvard university press; London, H. Milford, Oxford university press, 1925.

Krishnamurti, V.G. From J. Krishnamurti to the Upanishads : world order for the 21st century : an Indian vision. Kolkata, India : Writers Workshop, 1990.

Kriyananda, Swami Saraswati. Nine principal Upanishads, with text, translitteration [sic], translation, and notes. Monghyr, India : Bihar School of Yoga, 1975.

Kulkarni, T.R. Upanishads and yoga; an empirical approach to the understanding. Mumbai, India: Bharatiya Vidya Bhavan, 1972.

Madhavananda, Swami. Minor Upanishads. With original text, introd., English rendering, and comments. Kolkata, India: Advaita Ashrama, 1968.

Majumdār, Sridhar. The Vedanta philosophy : in English with original sutras and explanatory quotations from Upanishads, Bhagavad Gītā etc. and their English translations. Varanasi, India: Chowkhamba Sanskrit Series Office, 2000.

Manohar, Mrinalini Vivek. The earlier and later Upaniṣads : a comparative study. Delhi, India: Bharatiya Kala Prakashan, 2011.

Mascaro, Juan. The Upanishads. New York: Penguin Putnam Inc., 1965.

Mead, G.R.S., and Chaṭṭopādhyāya, Jagadīsha Chandra (Roy Choudhuri). The Upanishads / translated into English, with a preamble and arguments. Adyar, Madras, India : Theosophical Publishing House, 1930.

Milburn, R. Gordon. The religious mysticism of the Upanishads. London, Theosophical publishing house, 1924.

Mukherji Anil Kumar, Das, Saroj Kumar, fwd. Upanishad in the eyes of Rabindra Nath Tagore: an anthology of the poet Tagore's writings, interpretative of and related to Upanishadic verse. Kolkata, India: Dasgupta, 1975.

Mukhopadhyaya, Govindagopal. Studies in the Upanisads. Kathmandu, Nepal: Distributed by Pilgrims Book House, 1999.

Muller, Max F. Sacred Books of the East, Vol. 1. Oxford: Clarenden Press, 1900.

_____. The Upanishads. New York : Christian Literature Co., 1897.

Muni, Angirasa. The Upanisads / introduction and translation. Fort Wayne, IN: Sacred Books, 1999.

Narla, V.R. An essay on the Upanishads: a critical study. Hyderabad, India: Narla Institute of New Thought, c1989.

Nikam, N. A. Ten principal Upanishads: some fundamental ideas: a dialectical and analytical study. Mumbai, India: Somaiya Publications, 1974.

Nikhilananda, Swami. Upanishads, Vol.1-4. New York: Ramakrishna Vivekanada Center, 1986, 1990, 1990, 1994.

Olivelle, Patrick. The early Upanisads: annotated text and translation. New Delhi, India: Munshiram Manoharlal Publishers, 1998.

Olivelle, Patrick. The early Upanisads: annotated text and translation. New York: Oxford University Press, 1998.

Olivelle, Patrick. Upanishads: A new Translation. Oxford, New York: Oxford University Press, 1996.

Pandit, M.P. Upanishads: Gateways of Knowledge. Wilmot, WI: Lotus Light Publications, 1988.

Paramananda, Swami. The Upanishads: Translated and commentated. Volume 1. Boston, MA: The Vedanta Center, 1919.

Parrinder, Geoffrey . The wisdom of the forest: selections from the Hindu Upanishads. New York: New Directions Pub. Corp., 1976.

_____. The wisdom of the forest: sages of the Indian Upanishads / translated [from the Sanskrit]. London : Sheldon Press, 1975.

_____. Upanishads, Gita and Bible: a comparative study of Hindu and Christian scriptures. London: Sheldon Press, 1975.

Pathak, Meena P. (Meena Pinakin). study of Taittirīya Upanisad. Delhi: Bharatiya Kala Prakashan, 1999.

Prabhavananda, Swami. The Upanishads: Breath of the Eternal. New York: Penguin Putnam Inc., 2002.

Raja, C. Kunhan, ed., and Pandits of Adayar Library. Daśopanishads, with the commentary of Sri Upanishad-brahmayogin. Chennai, India: Adyar Library (Theosophical Society) 1935-36.

Puligandla, R. "That thou art" : the wisdom of the Upanishads. Fremont, Calif. : Asian Humanities Press, c2002.

Puligandla. R. Reality and mysticism: perspectives in the Upanisads. the University of Michigan, MI: D K Printworld (P) Limited, 1997.

Pundalik, Pandit Madhav. Mystic approach to the Veda and the Upanishads. Chennai, India: Sri Aurobindo Library [1952].

Purohit, Swami. The ten principal Upanishads put into English. New York: Macmillan, 1975, c1937.

Radhakrishnan, S. Indian philosophy. London, Allen & Unwin; New York, Humanities Press [1966].

_____. The philosophy of the Upanisads, with a foreword by Rabindranath Tagore and an Introduction by Edmond Holmes. London, G. Allen & Unwin ltd.; New York, The Macmillan Company [1935].

_____. The Principal Upanishads: Edited With Introduction, Text, Translation and Notes. New Delhi, India: HarperCollins Publishers, India, 1994

Raghavachar, S.S. Sri Ramanuja on the Upanishads. Chennai, India: Prof. M. Rangacharya Memorial Trust; [can be had of M. C. Krishnan, 1972].

Rajagopalachari, C. Upanishads for the lay reader. New Delhi, India: Hindustan Times [1956].

Rajagopalachari, Chakravarti. Upanishads. Mumbai, India: Bharatiya Vidya Bhavan, 1991.

Rama, Swami. Wisdom of the ancient sages: Mundaka Upanishad. Honesdale, Pa.: Himalayan International Institute of Yoga Science and Philosophy of the U.S.A., c1990.

Ranade, R.D. A constructive survey of Upanishadic philosophy; being an introduction to the thought of the Upanishads. Mumbai, India: Bharatiya Vidya Bhavan, 1968.

Reddy, Madhusudan. Yoga of the rishis: the Upanishadic approach to death and immortality. Hyderabad, India: Institute of Human Study ; Delhi: Distributed by Indian Books Centre, 1985.

Rehman, Saif-ur. Indian philosophy: some common concepts in the Vedas, Upanishads & early Buddhism. [Lahore]: [publisher not identified], [2012?].

Rodrigues, Antonio F.X. In search of meaning: a phenomenological reading of the Upanishads. Bangalore, India: Redemptorist Publications India, [198-?].

Roebuck, Valerie. The Upanishads. London, New York: Penguin Books, 2003.

Roer, E., ed. The twelve principal Upaniṣads: text in Devanāgari and translation with notes in English from the commentaries of Śaṅkarācārya, and the gloss of Ānandagiri. Delhi, India: Nag Publishers, 1978-1979.

Sarasvati, Svami Satya Prakash. Parables and dialogues from the Upaniṣads. Delhi, India: S. Chand, 1975.

Saraswati, Swami Sivananda. The essence of principal Upanishads. Rishikesh, India: Yoga-Vedanta Forest Academy, Divine Life Society, 1961.

Scharfstein, Ben-Ami A comparative history of world philosophy: from the Upanishads to Kant. Albany: State University of New York Press, c1998.

Sen, Pritam. God's love in Upanishad philosophies. Mumbai, India: Bharatiya Vidya Bhavan, 1995.

Seru, S.L. The thirteen principal Upanisads: an introduction on Vedanta-sara text with English translation and notes. Delhi, India: Nag Publishers, 1997.

Sharma, Shubhra. Life in the Upanishads. New Delhi, India: Ahinav Publications, 1985.

Shearer, Alistair & Russell, Peter; photos. by Lannoy, Richard. The Upanishads. New York: Harper & Row, c1978.

Shearer, Alistair and Russell, Peter. The Upanishads. Bell Tower, New York: Sacred Teachings, 2003.

Singh, Maan. The Upaniṣadic etymologies. Delhi: Nirmal Publication, 1994.

Singh, Satya Prakash. Upanisadic symbolism. New Delhi, India: Meharchand Lachhmandas, 1981.

Sircar, Mahendranath. Hindu mysticism according to the Upaniṣads. New Delhi: Oriental Books Reprint Corp. : distributed by Munshiram Manoharlal Publishers, 1974.

Sreeram, Lala. The metaphysics of the Upanishads, or Vichar Sagar/ translated with copious notes. New Delhi : Asian Publication Services, 1979.

Sri Upanishad-brahma-yogin. The Yoga Upanishads, with the commentary of. [Madras] Pub. for the Adyar library (Theosophical society) 1920.

Srinivasachari, P.N. The wisdom of the Upanisads. Madras: Sri Krishna Library, 1947.

Subrahmanian, V.K. The Upanishads and the Bible. New Delhi: Abhinav Publications, 2002.

Swāmi, Shree Purohit, and Yeats, W. B. The ten principal Upanishads; put into English. London: Faber, 1970.

Tathagatananda, Swami. Journey of the Upanishads to the West. New York, NY : Vedanta Society, 2002.

Thachil, Jose. The Upaniṣads, a socio-religious appraisal. New Delhi, India : Intercultural Publications, 1993.

Vasus, Srisa Chandra. The Upaniṣads with the commentary of Madhvachârya: part I, Īśa, Kaṭha, Praśna, Muṇḍaka and Māṅḍuka. Allahabad, India: Panini Office, 1909.

V, Jayaram. Brahman. New Albany, OH: Pure Life Vision LLC, 2010.

Vidyaranva, Srisa Chandra. Studies in the first six Upanisads and the Isa and Kena Upanisads, with the commentary of Sankara. Allahabad, India: Panini Office, 1919 [i.e. 1918].

Witz, Klaus G.The supreme wisdom of the Upaniṣads: an introduction. Delhi, India: Motilal Banarsidass Publishers, 1998.

Pure Life Vision Books
Selected Upanishads

This edition forms part of the new translation of the 16 Upanishads by Jayaram V. This is the first major effort to translate the Principal Upanishads in recent times. Jayaram V brings you a fresh look at the knowledge and wisdom of the Upanishads, which contain the essence of Hinduism.

- New translation
- Original Sanskrit verses in transliterated Devanagari
- With Explanatory notes and Bibliography
- ISBN: 978-1-935760-06-1
- Book type: Perfect Bound (paperback)
- Pages: 320.
- Cover Glosse. Dimensions: 6x9
- Includes 14 important Upanishads

Discounts up to 50% are available on bulk orders. **Order your copy** from http://www.PureLifeVision.com

Pure Life Vision Books
Brihadaranyaka Upanishad

The first major translation of the Brihadaranyaka Upanishad in the 21st century. This Upanishad presents many secret doctrines of Hinduism and the significance of certain important Vedic sacrifices. This translation by Jayaram V is useful for both scholars and serious practitioners of Hinduism.

- New translation,
- Original Sanskrit verses in transliterated Devanagari
- With Explanatory notes and Bibliography
- ISBN: 978-1-935760-07-8
- Book type: Perfect Bound (paperback)
- Cover Gloss. Dimensions: 6x9
- No of pages 204

Discounts up to 50% are available on bulk orders. **Order your copy from http://www.PureLifeVision.com**

Pure Life Vision Books
The Bhagavadgita Complete Translation

- Most comprehensive work on the Bhagavadgita in recent times
- Complete text with word to word translation
- Detailed commentary without sectarian bias
- Original and inspiring
- Authoritative and scholarly
- No of pages 874
- Dimensions: 6.14 x 9.21
- ISBN: 978-1-935760-04-7

Discounts up to 50% are available on bulk purchases. **Order your copy from** http://www.PureLifeVision.com

Pure Life Vision Books

The Bhagavadgita
A Simple Translation

- Abridged version
- Complete text with word for word translation
- Ideal for recitation and reference
- Perfect Bound (paperback), Cover Matte
- Page count: 304
- Dimensions: 6.14 x 9.21
- ISBN: 978-1-935760-17-7

Discounts up to 50% are available on bulk orders. For bulk orders, please contact the publishers at the following link http://www.PureLifeVision.com

Pure Life Vision Books

Discounts up to 50% are available on bulk orders. **Order your copies** from http://www.PureLifeVision.com.

Pure Life Vision Books

Think Success – Combined Volume

- Combined volume
- Contains 44 mind-expanding articles
- Comprehensive information on self-help
- Motivational, inspiring and uplifting
- Improves your self-awareness and confidence
- Prepares you for success and achievement
- Guides you to excellence
- No of pages 492
- Dimensions: 6 x 9
- ISBN: 978-1-935760-03-0
- Book type: Bound Blue Cloth w/Jacket on Creme

Discounts up to 50% are available on bulk orders. **Order your copy** from http://www.PureLifeVision.com.

Pure Life Vision Books
Essays on the Bhagavadgita

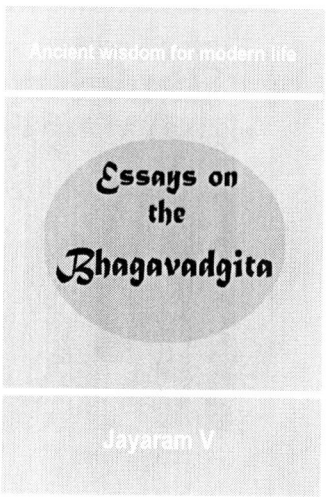

In this collection of essays, you will find a critical analysis of the philosophy, principles and practice of the Bhagavadgita and their relevance to human life. You will understand the true meaning of yoga in the context of the teachings of Lord Krishna and the importance of various yogas. This book will increase your understanding of the Bhagavadgita immensely and help you in the practice of its teachings.

- 35 Informative articles
- With Bibliography
- ISBN: 978-1-935760-09-2
- Book type: Perfect Bound (paperback)
- Cover Matte. Dimensions: 6x9

Discounts up to 50% are available on bulk orders. **Order your copy** from http://www.PureLifeVision.com

Pure Life Vision Books
Introduction to Hinduism

Hinduism is the oldest living religion of the world. It is also the most complex in terms of its philosophy and practices and difficult to understand. This book gives you a thorough and scholarly understanding of the basic and essential aspects of the eternal tradition, useful to both lay practitioners and students alike.

- Covers significant aspects of Hinduism
- Written in easy to understand language
- With Bibliography
- ISBN: 978-1-935760-11-5
- Book type: Perfect Bound (paperback)
- Cover Matte. Dimensions: 6x9

Discounts up to 50% are available on bulk orders. **Order your copy from** http://www.PureLifeVision.com

Lightning Source UK Ltd.
Milton Keynes UK
UKOW02f2322010816

279714UK00001B/158/P